The Brain-Savvy
Therapist's Workbook

The Norton Series on Interpersonal Neurobiology
Allan N. Schore, PhD, Series Editor
Daniel J. Siegel, MD, Founding Editor

The field of mental health is in a tremendously exciting period of growth and conceptual reorganization. Independent findings from a variety of scientific endeavors are converging in an interdisciplinary view of the mind and mental well-being. An interpersonal neurobiology of human development enables us to understand that the structure and function of the mind and brain are shaped by experiences, especially those involving emotional relationships.

The Norton Series on Interpersonal Neurobiology will provide cutting-edge, multidisciplinary views that further our understanding of the complex neurobiology of the human mind. By drawing on a wide range of traditionally independent fields of research—such as neurobiology, genetics, memory, attachment, complex systems, anthropology, and evolutionary psychology—these texts will offer mental health professionals a review and synthesis of scientific findings often inaccessible to clinicians. These books aim to advance our understanding of human experience by finding the unity of knowledge, or consilience, that emerges with the translation of findings from numerous domains of study into a common language and conceptual framework. The series will integrate the best of modern science with the healing art of psychotherapy.

A Norton Professional Book

The Brain-Savvy Therapist's Workbook

Bonnie Badenoch

W. W. Norton & Company
New York • London

David Whyte, "Start Close In," *New & Selected Poems: 1984–2007*, © Many Rivers Press, Langley, Washington. Printed with permission from Many Rivers Press, www.davidwhyte.com.

For information about permission to reproduce selections from this book, write to Permissions, W. W. Norton & Company, Inc., 500 Fifth Avenue, New York, NY 10110

For information about special discounts for bulk purchases, please contact W. W. Norton Special Sales at specialsales@wwnorton.com or 800-233-4830

Manufacturing by Hamilton Printing
Book design by Bytheway Publishing Services
Production manager: Leeann Graham

Library of Congress Cataloging-in-Publication Data

Badenoch, Bonnie.
    The brain-savvy therapist's workbook / Bonnie Badenoch. — 1st ed.
        p. ; cm. — (Norton series on interpersonal neurobiology)
    "A Norton professional book."
    Includes bibliographical references and index.
    ISBN 978-0-393-70639-0 (pbk.)
1. Psychotherapy.   2. Interpersonal relations.   3. Neurobiology.   I.
Title.   II. Series: Norton series on interpersonal neurobiology.
    [DNLM: 1. Psychotherapy—methods.   2. Brain—physiology.   3.
Interpersonal Relations.   4. Memory. WM 420]
    RC480.5.B225   2011
    616.89'14—dc22   2010052113

ISBN: 978-0-393-70639-0 (pbk.)

W. W. Norton & Company, Inc., 500 Fifth Avenue, New York, N.Y. 10110
        www.wwnorton.com
W. W. Norton & Company Ltd., Castle House, 75/76 Wells Street, London W1T 3QT

1   2   3   4   5   6   7   8   9   0

For all who have invited me to accompany them on their journeys toward health

For all who have mentored me in this life

For my family, the bedrock on which I am honored to rest

START CLOSE IN

Start close in,
don't take the second step
or the third,
start with the first
thing
close in,
the step
you don't want to take.

Start with
the ground
you know,
the pale ground
beneath your feet,
your own
way of starting
the conversation.

Start with your own
question,
give up on other
people's questions,
don't let them
smother something
simple.

To find
another's voice,
follow
your own voice,
wait until
that voice
becomes a
private ear
listening
to another.

Start right now
take a small step
you can call your own
don't follow
someone else's
heroics, be humble
and focused,
start close in,
don't mistake
that other
for your own.

Start close in,
don't take
the second step
or the third,
start with the first
thing
close in,
the step
you don't want to take.

—David Whyte, 2007
New & Selected Poems: 1984–2007

"A human being is part of the whole world, called by us 'Universe,' a part limited in time and space. He experiences himself, his thoughts and feelings as something separate from the rest—a kind of optical delusion of his consciousness. The striving to free oneself from this delusion is the one issue of true religion. Not to nourish it but to try to overcome it is the way to reach the attainable measure of peace of mind."

—Albert Einstein's letter to Robert Marcus, February 12, 1950; Einstein Archives 60-424.

"This is the greatest discovery of the scientific enterprise: You take hydrogen gas, and you leave it alone, and it turns into rosebushes, giraffes, and humans."

—Brian Swimme, mathematical cosmologist, spoken at various gatherings

Contents

Acknowledgments

This workbook is very much a group effort. I have learned so much that I now have the privilege of sharing in partnership with my patients and colleagues, resting on the secure foundation provided by my esteemed mentors. The courageous and dedicated people who have been willing to become awake to their suffering in order to heal have my deepest respect. Every person with whom I have had the honor of working is somewhere in these pages. They have taught me about myself, about the way the brain and mind work, about the depth and breadth of human resilience, about the survival of laughter and play in the midst of heartrending adversity. While great care has been taken to protect privacy, the substance of their journeys anchors every page. Each of you has my profound gratitude.

My colleagues continue to sharpen my mind and delight my heart through the dialogues that unfold in consultation groups, study sessions, daily conversations, and writing together. The many hours spent over the years with long-time partners-in-healing Lisa Schenitzki, Judy Chamberlin, Rachel Lee, and Nola Casserly have encouraged all of us to dig deep into the heart of relationally fostered neuroplasticity. Kate Cook and Theresa Kestly have taken me into their lives to explore how interpersonal neurobiology forms a living partnership with psychodrama (Kate) and sand tray work (Theresa). In our mutually enriching consultations, Susan Gantt and Rich Armington have given me a deep introduction to systems centered psychotherapy for groups and the synergies that abound with interpersonal neurobiology (IPNB). The many fellow travelers with whom I have the privilege of conversing regularly and occasionally add new flavors with every encounter. Coease Scott, body worker extraordinaire, instigated an interdisciplinary IPNB community in Portland, Oregon, where we wade in deep with application of the core principles. Marion Sharp and Debra Pearce-McCall, inaugurators of the Portland State University IPNB program in which I am privileged to teach, add new dimensions and flavors in their broad view of IPNB application in many disciplines. The GAINS community (Global Association for Interpersonal Neurobiology Studies) provides ongoing support for the development of these ideas about applying the science to practice. The group of us that publishes the quarterly journal *Connections and Reflections* continually inspire one another to think more deeply, broadly, and accurately about translating the science into practice. Our editorial staff, Carol Landsberg, Debra Pearce-McCall, and Robin Cohen; our regular contributors, Richard Hill, Kirke Olson, Lauren Culp, Jeff Anderson, Diane Ackerman, and Sarah Peyton; and those who write for us from time to time always stimulate new integration. As I am writing, I hear these voices and feel the encouraging presence of these colleagues with every word.

I am particularly grateful to my colleagues Oren Raz and Rose Jade, who with wise eyes, both professional and human, read the manuscript, offering many useful suggestions that made this a more user-friendly book. From single words to broad ideas, these two people have added a great deal. This kind of honesty, support, and encouragement make the writing process a truly interpersonal effort.

As I was digging into the writing process, coherence psychologists Robin Ticic and Bruce Ecker contacted me to talk about the possible convergence between IPNB and their work. Bruce Ekcer and Laurel Hulley, the originators of coherence psychology methodology, had uncovered the principles of changing implicit memories in the course of their practice and written about them for over a decade. Now, new scientific evidence is revealing the foundation for this process. Robin, Bruce, and Laurel were generous with their time and wisdom in our long conversations, refining my understanding of the process and contributing a great deal to the clarity of this endeavor. Much gratitude to you for giving so much.

I am fortunate to have had numerous mentors on this IPNB journey. Three stand at the foundation. Dan Siegel was my first teacher of brain, mind, and relationships, and he remains a continual inspiration, particularly in regard to the importance of this work for fostering a more awake and compassionate world. The core principles of neural integration and how relationships shape the mind are always at the center of my thoughts, along with his kind face. Allan Schore's continual advocacy of long-term therapy for longstanding wounds and his passionate insistence on the importance of right-mode to right-mode interactions between patient and therapist give me the courage to take similar stands. Conversations with him have refined and clarified my thought. Lou Cozolino's broad view of the foundations of IPNB and impeccably clean style inspire me to write about these dense and sometimes difficult ideas with as much accuracy and clarity as I can muster. The work of two other scientists undergirds much of my understanding. Stephen Porges, investigator of the autonomic nervous system, and Marco Iacoboni, discoverer of mirror neurons in humans, have been generous with their time in helping me gain a clearer understanding of their groundbreaking work. Beyond these five stands a cadre of brain researchers and theoreticians who are revolutionizing our ideas about healing. To each one, much appreciation and gratitude.

Three makers of images grace these pages and my life. Ron Estrine's pictures of the brain and hand model are elegant and accurate. We worked side by side during the writing of *Being a Brain-Wise Therapist*, and his images appear again here. As my patients do their sand tray work, they often gravitate toward the richly painted figures of Georgia Mann and the warm clay images of Debbie Berrow. The art these two women create captures the essence of the inner world in ways that have provided healing pathways for so many people. I am glad to call them my friends as well.

It is a joy to be working with the people at Norton again. Special appreciation to my editor, Deborah Malmud, to Vani Kannan, Libby Burton, Kevin Olsen, copy editor Margaret Ryan, and illustrator John McAusland. Their encouragement to make the application of interpersonal neurobiology even more tangible has added a layer of delight to this enterprise. This has felt very much like a family affair because of their support. Which brings me to the nest in which this book has been written—my dear family close in. Cindy, Tom, Andy, Kate, Jocelyn, Parker, Patti, and Riley give me every reason to write about ways to foster attachment and healing. They are all heartening influences in my life, creating an internal and external space in which I absorb, integrate, and then write. Sheltering in their love, care, and gentle sense of humor provides me with the living experience of the kinds of brain-healing connections that I'm seeking to capture in words.

One of the themes in this book is how empathic inner communities support a healthy and joyous life. All of those acknowledged here are "my people"; they live within me, sharing their wisdom from moment to moment as I live and write. I cherish each one. It goes without saying that in the process of integrating all this wealth, any interesting mistakes are entirely of my own crafting.

Preface

As people begin to learn about interpersonal neurobiology, the urge to apply it
well and often in therapy and in life can become compelling. This workbook
extends an invitation to immerse ourselves in the wonders of the embodied
and relational brain and mind (Siegel, 2007, 2010a, 2010b) until we are "dyed"
with a new way of perceiving that will permanently alter our relationship with
ourselves and others. I believe it took me at least 50 such immersions to be
able to walk the talk in daily life somewhat reliably—and to talk the walk within the empathic flow of therapy. And still my own immersion and integration
remain a daily developing process. With dedication and focus, this embodied
knowledge can enrich our perception and then find its integrative way into the
flow of our therapeutic work.

Neuroscience is undeniably becoming part of our daily experience as the
media regularly offers bits and pieces of the science, with speculation about
what the new discoveries mean. However, much as these partial glimpses are
fascinating, they do not provide the life-changing big picture of how brains,
minds, and relationships shape one another from conception until death.
When we cultivate a broad understanding of the principles, particularly as integrated and developed in the concepts of interpersonal neurobiology (IPNB)
(Cozolino, 2006, 2010; Schore, 2003a, 2003b, 2009a, 2009b; Siegel, 1999, 2006,
2007, 2010a, 2010b), a door can open, a shift in awareness can occur, that supports more clarity about the human condition, coupled with greater kindness
in thought, word, and action. In that opening, we discover a greater capacity
to nurture the heart with the brain in mind. This combination of clarity with
compassion can ground therapy and life in a new foundation that potentially
brings benefit for the larger world. Our work builds on that done by innovators

and integrators such as Daniel Siegel, Allan Schore, and Lou Cozolino, who have each taken the raw materials of scientific discovery and created a paradigm-shifting, society-changing vision. Now, we have a rich opportunity to weave these principles into practice. I can't imagine more valuable work.

During these past 2 years, I have had the opportunity to join in conversations with groups of therapists, teachers, social workers, and others about my book *Being a Brain-Wise Therapist* (Badenoch, 2008). The comment I hear most frequently is that readers come away with a different sense of how to serve as a healing presence with their patients, their families, their students, and themselves, in addition to gaining practical ideas about how to include the brain and mind in the therapeutic conversation. As we bring brain-informed seeing into our relationships, the processes from which behaviors arise become more visible, until it becomes difficult to *not* understand why people do what they do. This is such an important threshold to cross because research tells us that attuned relationship is the single most important variable in the healing endeavor, and that nonjudgmental acceptance is the most efficacious component of attunement (Bohart, 2003; Bohart, Elliott, Greenberg, & Watson, 2002; Bozarth, Zimring, & Tausch, 2002). Because our brains continually judge as part of our basic survival wiring, strong connections between our emotionally vivid limbic circuits and our integrative middle prefrontal region are needed to slow the judging process so that we can be receptively present to all our patients bring to us. Every page of this workbook is devoted to fostering that process in us.

A number of us who have been practicing IPNB for some time have found that the pathway to a more completely embodied awareness falls naturally into three parts:

1. Becoming personally acquainted with our own brains and minds;
2. Gaining sufficient confidence in our knowledge of neural processes to bring the brain into the counseling room; and
3. Reflecting on and writing down our therapeutic narrative—our inner implicit and explicit story of how IPNB-informed therapy supports emerging mental and relational health.

For the first step, as poet David Whyte (2007) says, we must "*start close in*" (p. 362; see complete poem in frontispiece), *bringing to light unacknowledged, often implicit, aspects of our inner world* that may stand in the way of fully receiving whatever our patients need to experience and integrate. As we devote conscious attention to this process, we are also developing our inner caring observer, the part of our psyche that can remain in a state of kind observation while deeply resonating with our patients' emerging experience. Said neurobiologically, this internal process promotes *integrative neuroplasticity*, knitting circuits of the brain together so that we have an increasingly coherent mind and greater capacity for empathy and kindness (Siegel, 2007). At the same time, we become a living laboratory for solidifying our knowledge of the workings of brain and mind, as our growing left-mode knowledge expands into right-mode experience. In short, *the first part of the workbook is devoted to cultivation of our personal inner roots of clarity and compassion.*

Although part of this work emerges through reflection, IPNB also encourages us to recognize the brain as *relational*, meaning that our neural circuitry is in continual conversation with the firings in other brains (Iacoboni, 2007, 2009). Getting the feel of this is not always the easiest shift in perspective, given that our eyes reinforce the illusion of separateness. However, as we become more tangibly aware of the pervasive influence we have on one another's brains, we can see the wisdom of amplifying our movement toward self-discovery by sharing our process with another person. For this reason, I strongly recommend that you find a listening partner right at the outset, someone who will work his or her way through this workbook with you, so that both of you will be able to share your emerging experience at each stage. Having insights and even difficulties received by an attuned listener is one of the most powerful ways to foster integrative neuroplasticity (Siegel, 2010b; Siegel & Hartzell, 2003). At a conscious level, this warm, receptive space often allows us to sink more deeply into our inner world through progressive levels of awareness, making the implicit, explicit. Below conscious awareness, this synchronous dance of attunement weaves together the body, limbic, and cortex of both speaker and listener (Marci, Ham, Moran, & Orr, 2007; Marci & Reiss, 2005; Schore, 2009a, 2009b; Siegel, 2010b; Siegel & Hartzell, 2003). It is difficult for me to imagine practicing *interpersonal* neurobiology without such a partner. If at first you feel shy about this undertaking, it may be helpful to inquire internally about the reason for that response. Take your time with this decision until it feels right, and know that joining with another at any stage in the process will provide additional support for developing both clarity and compassion.

The practices in Part I can usefully become lifelong companions because daily experience will continue to challenge us and there is no end to integration. Meanwhile, the second part of the book encourages a focus on *firming up our understanding of some key IPNB concepts and merging this left-mode understanding with our growing felt sense of the principles.* This process is supported by abundant examples of how this embodied wisdom can be used in a variety of therapeutic situations. Because our goal is to internalize the flow of the healing process, rather than to flesh out work with specific kinds of patients, I chose examples with that focus in mind. We are seeking a paradigm shift so that *the way we think about therapy, the way we practice, and the way we talk with our patients* are all infused with our felt sense of the brain's movement toward integration. This adds a substantial bundle of fibers to the tapestry of our therapeutic process, and the more seamlessly it is woven into the cloth of therapy, the better it will support and enrich the empathic flow. Having the knowledge internalized sufficiently to create this permanent shift in viewpoint suggests a four-step process that is discussed in Part II:

1. Gaining a solid enough grasp of the concepts so that we don't have to struggle to find the ideas or the words (largely a left-mode process);
2. Integrating our already-cultivated personal immersion in the concepts with our growing knowledge, so that we can viscerally as well as cognitively recognize what is happening within our patients (grounded in right-mode experiencing, linking now with left-mode knowing);
3. Transitioning from learning to speaking (an integrative process); and
4. Integrating these three aspects into a whole-brained, easily flowing awareness that naturally provides the foundation for all we *are* and all we *do* in therapy.

To this end, the second part has sections that deepen our knowledge of some of the core principles, accompanied by some reflection on and writing about the meaning of these concepts for practice. Engaging with our listening partners, we will then practice speaking about the brain, playing with the concepts, and finding our unique voice for sharing this new world with our clients. This shift from taking in new learning to speaking about it involves different brain circuits and possibly heightened autonomic arousal because we are going public with our knowledge—all of which makes practicing out loud essential. We will also spend time with specific examples drawn from work with patients, and then have space to reflect on, write about, and discuss applying this deepening understanding with particular patients of our own. Each principle may suggest additional ways of *being with* as well as clarifying opportunities to *speak about* the brain with our patients. Taking the time to alternate between studying, reflecting, speaking, and writing gives our brains the opportunity to weave sturdy neural nets carrying this new information. Because repetition can then further strengthen this new awareness, spiraling through these chapters a few times, until we feel solid enough to live and speak from this perspective, will be a good investment of time and resources.

Because our brains are complex systems, constantly seeking to move toward greater integration and coherence through a process of differentiation, followed by linkage of these differentiated parts (Siegel, 1999), the fourth step— experiencing an easy flow of brain wisdom within the therapeutic moment— may occur without much effort. The increasingly differentiated strands of right-mode and left-mode learning will naturally coalesce into a sturdy web of IPNB wisdom. Experiencing the emergence of this integrated picture as it gradually becomes an ever-present part of our understanding is a clear sign that brain awareness is becoming an embodied, ingrained trait of being rather than a temporary state of mind.

The final step offered in Part III—becoming aware of and writing about our *implicit and explicit narrative of the therapeutic endeavor*—further supports the integrative process by drawing the themes of our working assumptions about therapy into a conscious story. By now, we will have significantly developed our caring observer capacity and filled ourselves with a good deal of wisdom about brain, mind, and relationships. So we will be in a solid position to begin reflecting on both the *conscious parameters* and largely *out-of-awareness patterns* that are constantly present in therapy. In a real sense, the picture we hold, consciously and unconsciously, about how we humans are wounded and how we heal creates a room into which we invite our patients, and prepares a particular kind of meal for their nourishment. A couple of examples may help. Because I consciously understand that we are not a single self, but instead a collection of states of mind, I invite my patients to meet and heal the many aspects of their inner world. Were I to believe that we are all single selves, I would be sending out a different invitation. At a more foundational—and often unseen and unconsidered—level, if my deep implicit memory carries a lot of uncomforted despair, then I may invite my patients into a right-mode environment with a black hole in the center into which we may all fall if their emerging despair touches my implicit wound.

As part of our increasing neural integration, we can begin to tease out the personal story that forms the blueprint for our practice, allowing it to reveal ways in which we are ample containers for our patients' unfolding inner experience, as well as illuminating areas where we unconsciously limit our patients' inner forays to avoid touching our own pain and fear. The act of holding this larger picture in consciousness can provide us with an inner sense of security that gives our patients a solid, if unspoken, foundation for their healing explorations.

Although the separation we often experience is an "optical delusion of consciousness" (Einstein, 1950), it may nudge our minds toward the belief that what lies within us is private. What we know of mirror neurons and resonance circuits (Iacoboni, 2009; Siegel, 2007) suggests that our internal world—our intentions, our emotions, and perhaps much more—radiates to our patients, shaping their neural circuitry as they dance with our inner assumptions. Over time, these states of mind become neurally ingrained as we are internalized as part of their inner community. This process uses similar circuitry as our earliest attachment experiences. A young patient recently told me that he could feel how his father's wordless instruction to stop raging and give up the struggle poured into him. He was a 3-year-old child at the time, simply being held and soaking up the inner world of this all-important person. He began to trace his lifelessness to these moments when, quite unconsciously, he partook of his father's deepest implicit convictions about how the world works. As we worked together, he experienced me as the caring witness of his painful prison and as a human being with a deep well of enthusiasm, optimism, and confidence in life's possibilities (thanks to having received many years of wonderful therapy myself). Over time, he internalized me as one who supports and encourages the expression of the full range of his emotional aliveness and as a tangible inner presence embodying these qualities.

As we absorb the meaning of the research that suggests that interpersonal oneness is a reality, we may be struck by the importance of therapists' mental health. Taking the next logical step, we can see significant implications for how we train counselors, psychotherapists, psychologists, and psychiatrists—all of us whose very presence can aid or hinder the neural changes that underlie our patients' capacity for mental balance, resilience, fulfillment, and compassionate living. Although many training programs encourage or insist on a certain number of hours of therapy, this time in treatment does not necessarily foster awareness of the student's own brain and mind, attachment patterns, implicit memories, internalized states of mind, and other crucial elements of the inner landscape that affect the way we relate with our patients. One heartening development is that some programs are offering mindfulness practices as the foundation for nonjudgmental acceptance of our patients. The hope is that programs will also begin including, at the heart of the curriculum, the kind of work we are undertaking in this book as part of each class rather than segregated in a separate class or moved to the periphery. In this way, we might be able to balance the necessary didactic learning with experiences that develop solid internal ground before seeing that first patient.

What do I hope for with this book? That it will offer a path of personal transformation leading to professional efficacy and fulfillment that arises from a deep vision of and respect for the inner workings of ourselves and others. Such awareness fosters compassion and kind actions in all of us, surely the primary basis for sustaining this planet. The book is truly a WORKbook, and so it is saturated with practices to progressively broaden and strengthen neural integration. Feel free to creatively adapt the practices to the needs of each individual.

In terms of process, we can't rush the emergence of integration. In fact, inner coercion and pressure to quickly move toward being a certain way as a therapist or human being is likely a replication of something our families or society have taught us. In any case, it is counterproductive. Instead, being present to each part of the process will provide fertile ground for the integration that wishes to take root naturally within each of us. Agricultural and botanical images like those sprinkled throughout this introduction arise from my felt sense that we are fortunate participants in a rich and natural growth process. Sliding into a different metaphor, I hope this workbook will be a companion for you, becoming dog-eared and marked up until it gains a life of its own within you—a little like the stuffed toy made real by his young owner's continual loving play in *The Velveteen Rabbit* (Williams, 1922/1983).

The Brain-Savvy
Therapist's Workbook

Part I

Preparing Our Brains and Minds for Relationship

The Personal Practice of Interpersonal Neurobiology

Introduction

Following some of the agricultural images in the last chapter, we might say that we are about to *dig in* to the work of self-transformation. However, that may conjure up images of the logical left poking around in the experiential right for answers. Instead, we are going to practice the art of creating an atmosphere in which our right-mode processes can speak for themselves, while we listen to our bodies and minds as they gather up the strands of our history into a coherent narrative—a whole-brain process. Given that between 5 and 30% of us carry our emotionally vivid history in the left hemisphere and logical language in the right (Holder, 2005), we are going to use the terms *right-mode processing* and *left-mode processing*—rather than right and left hemispheres—to talk about the distinct ways in which our brains process information. These terms may also helps us sense two distinct flows of energy and information, each with their essential part to play.

To deepen our awareness of our right-mode processing, the first part of the workbook offers six sets of experiences, to be shared with our listening partner, to help strengthen four capacities:

- Observing ourselves with kind, nonjudgmental acceptance;
- Expanding our ability to listen to the whisperings of our right mode;
- Developing explicit clarity about the patterns and inhabitants of our inner world; and
- Building an emotionally resolved narrative that rests on the compassionate release of all those who have injured our development.

Because these are not discrete processes, development of one opens the door to the others. For example, witnessing ourselves with kindness and acceptance brings the inner quiet that makes us available to the often wordless voices from the right mode, and focusing our attention to uncover states of mind that usually lie hidden fosters our capacity for observation. Taken together, these four encourage neural integration of the very circuits that make it possible for us to live as attuned human beings (Siegel & Hartzell, 2003).

You will find that Part I is relatively short on research and long on experience. When we revisit these topics from our patients' perspective in Part II, the ample research cited there will help bolster our knowledge so that we feel secure when we speak with those we see about their brains, minds, and relationships. However, this part is personal, so focus on our inner processes takes the stage.

I want to encourage all of us to take up gentleness toward ourselves as our primary support as we move into this deeply personal process. It is a rare person who does not have an overt or covert critical observer. As I am writing right now, struggling sometimes to find just the right word or idea, I can hear a voice that says, "Come on, you can do it. Don't get up and eat ice cream. Stay with it." No doubt intended as encouragement, the voice actually engenders pressure and anxiety with its covert message that I will be failing in some way if I jump ship right now. I feel the impact of these conflicting flows of energy on my body (tension in my chest and legs), nervous system (slightly elevated heartbeat), mind (less clear thinking, feeling of being at odds with myself), and on my overall well-being (definitely less than when I started writing). Now, if I allow myself to change my angle of vision and gaze with kindness on the critical voice, my mind widens to gently hold both that voice and my writing self. My chest experiences a feeling of expansion, my heart rate slows, I feel a smile inside, and both words and well-being come much more easily.

This simple shift of perspective reorganizes our neural firings by increasing the number and kinds of circuits available to us. Attending in this way is also an act of differentiation that allows us to distinctly hear the various active states of mind as they speak to us—"I want to stop writing now" and "Keep going." At the same time, the breadth of our gaze alleviates the conflict by allowing the neural activations of the two voices to be seen without judgment, preparing the way for integration. As the two voices move out of contention, our integrating brain usually offers a sure sense of our next best step. In this case, more writing flowed easily, but I might also have heard a different message—"It's time to stop for now." Either one would have been imbued with the feeling of calm certainty, accompanied by ease of execution. This coherence of mind and behavior is one of the signs of an integrating brain.

With each experience offered in these next few chapters, there is an opportunity to begin by listening to your inner responses to the task. As best you can, attend to your body, nervous system, and mind, discriminating the voices/states of mind activated by anticipation of the work ahead. There is some writing space offered for these reflections in each chapter. Every time we move from a pushy, critical, fearful, or tense stance to an open, relaxed, ac-

The Brain-Savvy Therapist's Workbook

cepting state of mind, we are building the brain structure of regulation and kindness. If we enter this state with regularity, it can gradually become a trait of mind—just the way we are, without effort.

So now you are being offered your first task—persistent gentleness toward self. Take a few moments to kindly sense and then write about your response to that invitation in your body, nervous system, and mind, noticing also its effect on your overall well-being. As best you can, use descriptive words rather than explaining *why* you respond that way. Description flows from and supports kind observation, whereas explanation supports further entanglement with the internal state and engages left-mode processing to figure things out.

_____

_____

_____

_____

_____

_____

_____

_____

_____

_____

Taking one further step, notice your response to doing the writing (or possibly not doing the writing). Does some part of you feel critical, frustrated, angry, congratulatory, or proud of what you wrote—or upset and ashamed because you didn't write? If there is noticeable tension about the process, with great gentleness return to kind acceptance of what you wrote and how you wrote it—both product and process—or the simple truth that you chose not to write. As you relax again into nonjudgment, you may begin to get the sense of how slippery and relentless the team of inner critics can be.

We often encounter a big fork in the road right here as the judgers make their regular and unbidden appearance right in the midst of practicing acceptance. One path leads to upset born of not being able to do it right AGAIN, whereas the second path offers kind acceptance of the ongoing process. Because our society, generally speaking, places such a high value on achievement over process, the sense that we continually fall back into a judgmental space can stimulate neural nets that contain feelings of failure and shame. Most of us have an unconscious implicit roadmap of learning that looks like this:

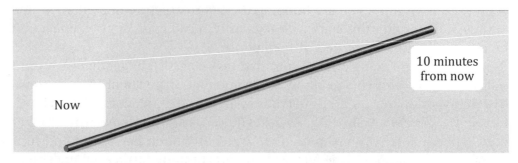

Now

10 minutes
from now

In actuality, when we are dealing with deeply ingrained neural nets, especially when they are anchored by long-established mental models that date back to childhood, the process more often looks like this:

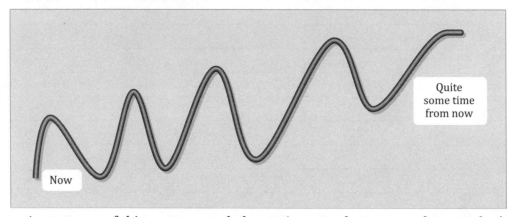

Now

Quite
some time
from now

Acceptance of this pattern can help us give ourselves grace when we don't change our self-critical voice all at once. Although sudden rewiring of old patterns is neurobiologically possible, in general, ingrained neural nets have the strength of strong ropes woven of many strands through repetition. Because of this neural strength, they have a greater probability of being reactivated in the presence of familiar conditions. The roots of these patterns lie within our limbic circuits, which act so quickly that the momentum of self-criticism likely overwhelms our minds before the integrative circuits can intervene. So if our minds snap back to judgment easily, we may be able to understand that this makes sense, given the amount of neural strength created by repeated encounters with criticism—first from external sources and then repeated internally for decades. As we relax into understanding, we may begin to see this experience as another opportunity to bring kind acceptance to bear on the situation. Gentle persistence in this process will gradually create a life-altering rewiring of our brains.

This is an excellent time to connect with your listening partner for the first time. If you haven't selected anyone yet, you may want to pause here to consider whom to invite—as well as reflecting with gentleness on any hesitation in finding your right person. Given the rewiring power of interpersonal con-

The Brain-Savvy Therapist's Workbook

nection, it is difficult to overestimate the value of joining two minds in the endeavor to create a nonjudgmental space. While you two will certainly develop many styles of connection within your unique relationship, I am going to suggest you begin with a particular way of relating. Let the listener do only that for a while: listen—but listen fully, being present with as little judgment and as much standing-in-the-other's-shoes as possible. The speaker can begin to share what he or she is noticing about body sensations, emotions, and perceptions in regard to critical voices and the state of nonjudgment. From there, the speaker can range freely into his or her inner world, following the trail of the visceral experience. If a silence arises, listener and speaker may find it useful to respectfully be with it until the next layer of inner experience emerges. At some point, the speaker will sense that he or she is complete for now—and you two will change roles.

For some, this may be an easy and natural process, whereas for others, the act of speaking into silence or the state of receptive listening may bring upwelling sorrow, anxiety, anger, or a whole host of other bodily sensations, emotions, and resistance. As you explore the experience of sharing with one another, it is most helpful to make room for all that has arisen from the process, treating it with the same gentleness, curiosity, and respect as the original topic. Far from being a detour, this ability to notice and flexibly move in the direction of what is *present in the moment* will further strengthen the circuits of awareness and regulation. To round out this speaking–listening time, take a few minutes to reflect on your experience here, in writing.

Reflection, *being heard*, and *writing* form the core of the process that we will now undertake. Let's also take a quick look at the content of the chapters in Part I. We begin with "Opening a Nonjudgmental Space." Abundant research suggests that we can exercise the circuits that give our minds the capacity for focus and acceptance just like we exercise our bodies to improve strength and flexibility. Two styles of meditation, undertaken in sequence, can support this increase in receptivity as we expand our caring observer state of mind. Throughout the first part of the workbook (and possibly also throughout life), this developing capacity becomes the foundation for the rest of our inner expedition.

The second and third chapters, "Exploring Our Implicit Seas" and "Gathering the Filaments of Memory," invite us into awareness of two kinds of implicit experience. As we attend to our right-mode processing, we will find that we ride on a constant flow of unrecognized assumptions about how the world works, what are called *mental models* or *implicit patterns*. Even though these are called *memories*, they don't resemble our everyday experience of recalling an event that happened in the past. Instead, they appear more in the body as behavioral impulses, bodily sensations, and emotional surges, also revealing themselves as perceptions about the meaning of various experiences in the present moment. In other words, they shape every thought, feeling, and action of our lives as the usually undetectable lens through which we see the world.

This is the first kind of implicit memory. We can picture the second kind as encapsulated/dissociated pockets of neural nets, usually resulting from uncomforted trauma or relational struggles, cut off from the integrating flow of the brain. When touched by current experience, they open into activity and radiate their emotional impact throughout our being, often disrupting our daily functioning. In the case of either kind of memory, we are captured by what we might call the *eternally present past*. One hallmark of these memories is that they bear no time stamp, so we have no sensation of remembering when they flow into our experience. They are literally not integrated in time, so they are always experienced as present, whether or not our minds know cognitively that they happened in the past.

One way we can approach catching glimpses of the implicit world is to engage in art as a medium for direct expression of these mostly wordless realms; I will suggest some helpful projects here. Another means is reflecting on the patterns we see repeatedly emerging in body and perception, especially within our closest relationships. Using these two processes, we can foster our capacity to be aware, in general, of our right-mode voice, as well as begin to touch the patterns and pockets in our deeper mind. As these eternally present blueprints for our anticipated future and dissociated memories emerge into explicit/conscious awareness and are met with vivid perceptions that disconfirm their current truth, they become available for transformation (Ecker, 2008, 2010; Ecker & Hulley, 1996, 2000a, 2000b, 2008; Ecker & Toomey, 2008). It is also possible that simply the act of focusing on our inner world with kindness, particularly in the company of our listening partner, works to modify these implicit patterns below the level of conscious awareness (Schore, 2003a, 2003b; Siegel, 2007, 2010b).

Another perspective on the inner world opens to us when we become acquainted with the different states of mind within us; this is our work in Chapter 4—"Fostering an Empathic Inner Community." We can think of memory as centered on events in time—single occurrences or repeated experiences—or view our encoded experiences as multiple states of mind that develop as we internalize those with whom we have had emotionally significant relationships. An angry father may be paired internally with a frightened child, or a playful mother with a spontaneous child. As we look reflectively within, we will be able to sense which of these pairs supports our healthy development and which contains patterns that lead to painful, unempathic relationships with ourselves and others. As a means of making this inner world more concrete and as a tool of integration, we turn to art and kind awareness again to portray and heal this unfolding community. Dissolving the tensions between the members of these pairs will create greater inner harmony and pave the way for us to guide our patients toward their own increasing resolution of these inner struggles.

As we work our way through these four chapters, we will no doubt enlarge our awareness of the inhabitants and stories of the frequently unseen world that guides our daily life. Because we have done it mindfully, with gentleness, and accompanied by our listening partner, our window of tolerance—the degree of affective experience we can tolerate without becoming dysregulated—will likely also increase. This expanding window becomes the foundation for our work with patients because we have developed our capacity to listen to the embodied voices of our right mode and compassionately contain and regulate emotionally vivid experiences.

Now that we have worked toward drawing the circuits of our body and right-mode processing into greater integration and embraced them with kind awareness, the way is now open for "Joining the Strands of Narrative" and "Practicing the Art of Compassionate Release," Chapters 5 and 6. While narratives ultimately find expression in the stories we tell ourselves about the meaning of our lives, they first show themselves in the shifting patterns of our daily experience. In terms of process, our left mode depends on information flowing from the right to create our story. When we do not attend to the right mode, we often simply make something up to satisfy our need for making sense. When the right-mode information is fragmented or partial, the story forms around logical conclusions drawn from these bits and pieces. This is a cohesive narrative (Siegel, 1999), with fragments glued together first by lived experience and then by words. As more of our right-mode circuits move out of fragmentation and dissociation, they add depth of understanding to the story, creating an increasingly coherent narrative that makes comprehensive meaning of our history.

Let me give you an example. Coming from an abusive past, my patient's cohesive narrative included self-hatred, a strong sense that she ruined everything she touched, and the conviction that her life was a waste. As she became viscerally familiar with her inner community and could sense the river of intergenerational pain that had been passed to her, the meaning of her history changed. She saw herself as one daughter in a tragic line of victimized women extending back to at least her great-grandmother. While she felt kinship with these women, she also knew she was participating in stopping the flow of pain through the generations and so was distinct from them, too. This was not cognitive storytelling, but meaning-making from deep contact with her right mode's store of experience. As she progressed through layers and layers of narrative expansion, compassionately releasing all those who had been harmed and subsequently harmed her, the change in the quality of her presence from agitated and tight to peaceful and joyous was palpable.

Each of us may find that at this stage of our integrative work, it is as though the curtain opens on the inner world, and we are able to sink into the depths of our family's history. I am reminded of images of soldiers coming home from Vietnam, the war of my youth. They often showed a close-up of one wounded young person, followed by a widening panorama of all the injured being treated. While the content of our story may not be as purely painful, we may have that same sensation of expanding awareness of our family's multigenerational narrative. This broad embrace of the history we have internalized and are now transforming sets the stage for compassionate understanding and release of all those who have impacted our lives.

As we walk through these aspects of self-awareness, we are paralleling the expedition we ask our patients to undertake. I have found great value in walking ahead down the forest path, sometimes with help from a trusted therapist, sometimes with a colleague skilled at listening, and sometimes on my own. Although research suggests that some of the same integrative circuits come into play in the processes of attuning with ourselves and another attuning with us (Siegel, 2007), it is also true that our neurobiology is profoundly interpersonal because we are hardwired to shape one another's brains from birth until our last breath. Some of you may already be discovering the benefit in forming a listening partnership with someone who is also engaged in the pursuit of increased personal coherence through this process. For those who haven't turned that corner, I am returning to this idea again because research

The Brain-Savvy Therapist's Workbook

tells us that the third repetition of an idea may be the point where thought becomes action.

This is not the only process that can support neural integration, increased personal coherence, and relational richness. However, it is one path that honors our neurobiology, our psychology, and our persistent search for meaning and enriching relationships.

In Preparation

To make the most of the upcoming experience . . .

Find a blank journal that appeals to your aesthetic sense, with or without lines.

Then locate a drawing tablet of a size that pleases you and intuitively feels like it would meet your needs. Be sure your fingers resonate with the texture of the paper. Now, select some drawing implements that feel right in your hand. Do you need many colors? Do you like the look and feel of crayons? Markers? Chalk? Pen and pencil? All of them? Be sure to try them in your nondominant hand, too. Test the weight and aroma of each one. Listen inside to what you *need* more than what you want.

Now, set them aside.

Then, it will be helpful to have a conversation with your listening partner about the process ahead. How often might you meet? What location would feel conducive to deep listening? Do you need some guidance about how to listen? What resources might you employ? Reflecting together on any concerns and anticipations you have about this partnership is a good first step to settling into ease with one another. Even in this first conversation, see if you can find a rhythm of giving and receiving in a leisurely and thorough way.

Now, taking up gentleness as our primary ally, we set sail.

Chapter 1

Opening a Nonjudgmental Space

Let's begin by taking a moment to notice, with kindness, our response to the invitation to approach our inner world. Our bodies might give us signals that we are experiencing relief, caution, anxiety, excitement, and many other possibilities. Attending to these messages, words for them may enter our consciousness—*tight gut, expanding chest*—culminating in an awareness of the feeling—*worry, joy*. Accurately describing the feeling, rather than explaining the reason for it, calms our amygdalae (Hariri, Bookheimer, & Mazziotta, 2000). The research can't tell us whether the calming happens because the application of words to feeling links the two hemispheres together in a way that promotes regulation or because one state of mind feels understood by another internally—or both. In any case, we can help our brains build the circuits of regulation by kind noticing of our state in the moment and writing a few descriptive words right here.

_____

_____

_____

_____

_____

_____

_____

_____

We can also notice if we feel impatient at being asked to pause. The pace of life has accelerated to such an extent that many of us have become deaf to the inner whisperings of our moment-to-moment experience. Our ingrained nervous system patterns and the accumulated neural strength of years of rushing may lead to discomfort with and resistance to a change of speed. Small shifts in much-reinforced habits require focus, commitment, and patience while the new neural pattern gains strength. I moved my vitamins from one place to another and could feel the tug of resistance to/unfamiliarity with going to the new location. If we find ourselves chomping at the bit with the leisurely start of this chapter, it likely reflects the way we are wired in terms of pace—and we can also notice the push toward speed with kindness, identifying the body sensation, letting that sensation find words for the body's response as well as the feeling, and writing them here.

_____

_____

_____

_____

_____

We slow down because the price of speed is steep. As we lose contact with our own depths, we may find ourselves in an interpersonal desert as well, cut off from the continual subtle messages resonating between all human beings. At a stoplight, a situation that forced me to pause, I glanced at a young woman waiting for the "walk" sign. She returned my gaze and we held eyes for a moment of human recognition that warmed me. The encounter lingered for a while as a sensation of warmth and connection, a strong reminder of how we feed one another's brains and minds on a continuing basis, especially when we make paying attention a priority. Taking many small breaks throughout these beginning chapters will help us develop the habit of listening to the continual flow of messages from our right mode until such awareness becomes a trait that emerges effortlessly both in regard to ourselves and others. This single capacity to slow down and be "with" may well be the largest contributor to our personal coherence, our capacity to provide secure attachment for our children, and our ability to foster a healing milieu for our patients.

Observing with Kindness

As we do these practices, our emphasis is on kind observation, rather than observation alone, because we are seeking to cooperate with our brain's natural flow toward coherence, leading to the subjective experience of well-being and the capacity for attuned relationships. This integrative process has two steps: *differentiation* followed by *linkage*. Developing our ability to observe our minds is an act of differentiation that allows us to experience ourselves as separate from the moment-to-moment events arising in our brains and minds. Kindness links our observing mind to these flows of energy and information through the gentle touch of comfort and understanding. Taken together, they complete an integrative circuit in the brain that likely uses similar pathways as attachment.

Take a moment to sense this for yourself. First, step back to a neutral place and observe the flow of your bodily experience, your emotions, and your thoughts, sensing that none of them is you. How does your body feel when you observe in this way? Then add kindness to the observation, embracing all of your experience, and attend to the shift in your body. Go back and forth a few times and then write some descriptive words about your body's response to both ways of observing.

_____

_____

_____

_____

_____

_____

_____

_____

_____

_____

_____

The Road to Receptivity

How might we begin to create space within our being for a profoundly receptive state of mind? Another way to ask this is how do we expand our capacity to stay engaged with our caring observer in the presence of intense experience? Taking guidance from the ancient traditions of meditation and mental culture, one place to start is *to develop the capacity for focusing our minds on a single experience (the breath, our footfalls) as the foundation for being able to relax into receptivity while maintaining attentiveness to the present moment.* If we don't first develop the capacity for a singular focus, as we try to settle into receptivity, our normally unexercised and therefore undisciplined mind is likely to wander off into sensory experience or memory, losing our caring observer self along the way. Daniel Siegel (2007) offers the metaphor of the mind as a wheel with a hub of awareness, a rim of individual experiences, and spokes that tie them together. When we exercise our attentional capacity sufficiently to reside in the hub at will, that state of mind of focused attention has moved in the direction of becoming a trait, and can then support our ability to direct our awareness to any point on the rim. With further development, we can also choose to sit in the hub as a caring observer, noticing with kindness whatever arises internally (memories in the form of sensations, thoughts, feelings, behavioral urges, and more) or comes to us from the outside (sensory and relational experience). However, if our ability to stay in the hub is intermittent and tenuous, then any activated neural firings with sufficient strength can pull us off center and into the thicket of experience (see Figure 1.1).

I am sitting here writing, with my caring observer keeping me company for the most part. Focusing mainly on the flow of ideas in my mind, I am also witnessing that focus, holding my process in kindness. Although I am aware of other sounds in the house, they stay mostly on the periphery, not demanding too much attention from my writing mind or my caring observer. Then Riley the beagle barks with gusto right next to me as a squirrel runs across the win-

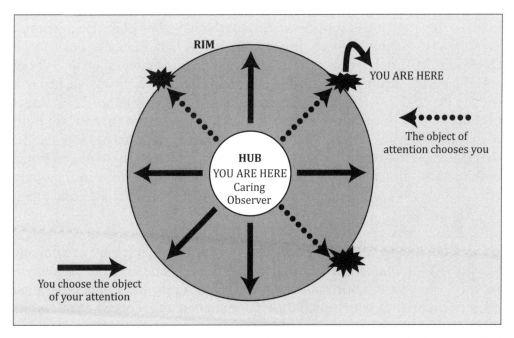

Figure 1.1. The Wheel of Awareness, based on Daniel Siegel (2007). Throughout the day, we may find our sense of self located either on the rim, where we have been pulled by external or internal events, or settled in the hub and directing our awareness to points on the rim as we choose. Our ability to do this depends on strengthening our attentional capacity just as we strengthen our muscles—through focus and repetition.

dowsill. In retrospect, I see that my nervous system jumped, yanking me to the rim to attend to the perceived danger. My caring observer and focused writing mind were left in the dust as all of my awareness shifted from hub to rim. As my sympathetic nervous system calms, my mind sinks back into the hub, then supports me reaching out for more ideas and words to put on this page. After a bit, I notice that at some point writing went to the periphery and my caring observer disappeared, as my mind became preoccupied with worry—about deadlines, the illness of a friend, whether there would be enough dog food tonight, and the thousand other nagging uncertainties that are part of daily life. Concern for the past and its influence on the future carried me away from consciously attending to the present moment. It is as though I experienced some rapid time travel without holding the trips in the larger focus of my kindly observing mind. Instead, I flitted around on the rim, tossed from one spot to another in response to the tide of inner events. So goes our mind on the way to increasing the strength of our attentional capacity and caring observer, until these states of mind gradually become more stable traits of being.

As we sit with the flow of events, we may begin to notice that the hub experience has two components—one that allows us to direct our attention as we choose, not pulled away by every internal and external stimulus that comes our way, and the other that gives us a more spacious viewpoint from which to embrace our inner life. It is likely that these two layers reflect a progressive increase in neural integration, with the anterior cingulate playing a major role in our growing ability to focus (Brefczynski-Lewis, Lutz, Schaefer, Levinson, & Davidson, 2007; Holzel et al., 2007) and the burgeoning integration of the body and the limbic region, with middle prefrontal circuits via the insula, expanding the depth and strength of our caring observer (Lazar et al., 2005). As we become settled in the latter state, we may become aware that we are more than the comings and goings of our embodied and relational experience, and that this expansive state of mind is the space in which all these neural firings unfold. As this inner angle of vision matures and becomes neurally ingrained, we can more easily sit in nonjudgmental receptivity with ourselves and others (see Figure 1.2).

Let's take a few minutes to sense the difference between hub and rim experiences. Settling as best we are able into our caring observer, we can encourage the last few minutes of our lived experience to come to mind. From there, we might be able to notice moments when our focus was strong on a single object we had chosen for attention, as compared to moments when our minds wandered from topic to topic, led by the automatic neural firings arising in response to internal and external promptings. In addition, we may be able to sense an additional quality of experience in which a part of our mind looks out over both experiences of focus and wandering, observing with kindness the comings and goings of our mental activity—as we are doing now through re-

The Brain-Savvy Therapist's Workbook

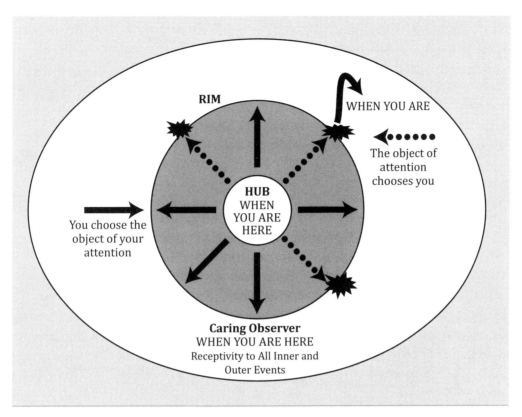

Figure 1.2. A New Dimension of the Hub Experience Emerges. With additional practice, it is as though the hub has enlarged sufficiently to hold both the experience of the wandering mind and the focused mind.

flecting on our last few moments. Giving words to these experiences often increases clarity, and questions often open the door to awareness. So here are some questions that can provide a focus for further defining our inner experience.

- How do your *body* and *nervous system* feel in a *state of wandering*?
- How do your *body* and *nervous system* feel in a *state of focus*?
- How do your *body* and *nervous system* feel in a *state of caring observation*?
- What is the *feeling quality* of each experience?

Make some descriptive notes about the differences you discover.

_____

_____

_____

_____

_____

_____

_____

_____

_____

_____

_____

_____

_____

_____

_____

    If you dog-ear this page and return to this practice of kind observation of your just-completed experience many times over the days and weeks ahead, you will help your mind develop the capacity to track these shifts with greater ease and accuracy, not only in retrospect but in the moment they are emerging.

Increasing Our Attentional Capacity

To further develop this capacity, we can engage in a mindfulness practice borrowed from the Buddhist tradition. Variations of this method of focus are used currently in secular settings as a means to reduce stress, foster mental and physical healing, manage chronic pain, as well as increase well-being even in the face of ongoing difficulties (Kabat-Zinn, 2003, 2005; Kabat-Zinn, Lipworth, Burney, & Sellers, 1986; Miller, Fletcher, & Kabat-Zinn, 1995). This daily exercise will strengthen our attentional capacity, changing brain function and gradually building brain structure that also supports development of our caring observer (Lazar et al., 2005). It is technically simple but challenging in execution, particularly in the beginning.

Cultivating Focus

Preparing your body, find a quiet, comfortable place to sit in a chair with your feet flat on the ground, or cross-legged in a chair or on the floor. A straight spine will also help, as will allowing your hands and arms to be in their most natural and relaxed position.

If it is comfortable, close your eyes, and then pay attention to the *sensation* of the breath coming and going in your nostrils. This is different than thinking about breathing. Let your mind rest in the physical sensation of inhalation followed by exhalation—the changing temperature of the breath in your nostrils, or the rise and fall of your chest or belly. You can place a hand on either chest or belly if that increases your ability to attend to the movement of your breath. Each day, take a moment to sense where your focus falls most naturally—nostrils, chest, or belly. There is no need to change the depth or length of the breath. Just be present with the sensation.

When the mind wanders, notice with nonjudgmental kindness that your mind is engaging in its normal activity, and gently redirect it to the sensation of the breath.

Doing this each day for at least 20 minutes will give you a good start on creating a greater capacity to focus.

In the spirit of slowing the process down again, it would be helpful to pause and practice right now, followed by writing a bit in the Mindful Awareness Journal on the next few pages.

As you begin practicing, finding time to share your experience with your listening partner will help develop the pattern of internal focus followed by interpersonal connection. Taken together, mindful awareness and attuned relationship (what Daniel Siegel, 2007, calls integration of consciousness and interpersonal integration) form the foundation for the healing experience we want to offer our patients, so it will be most helpful to practice them together in our own process.

We are offering the beginning practice of one common style of meditation here. Because you may find that using sound or an image while sitting, or attending to your footfalls while walking, is of greater assistance in developing focus than following the breath, experimentation is encouraged. However, eventually settling into one consistent practice will yield the best results because the new neural net is then regularly strengthened. If you find that you want to move more deeply into meditation on the breath, you can continue to focus on the sensation, feeling the inhalation extending throughout your body, then throughout the room, and eventually throughout the cosmos. There is no rush in moving from stage to stage of this practice; in fact, allowing ourselves to mature and become settled before starting the next level is a good idea.

It is customary to have "good" days and "bad" days with this practice, labeled with these judgments if we listen to our preconceptions about success as filtered through our judging minds. When we are able to observe through the lens of kindness, our caring observer will simply notice that our minds have greater momentum toward wandering one day than another. If we center ourselves in the value of persistently doing the practice rather than our tendency to want to see steady progress (as we define it), we will settle more easily into the pattern of attentional exercise.

Over an extended period of time, this practice is intended to create a state

Mindful Awareness Journal

Please use these pages to gently describe (not explain) both your *experiences* of and your *judgments* about the meditative practice. Track your bodily sensations, nervous system activation, and emotional surges as they relate to both your experiences and your judgments. It will be helpful to do this writing practice for several weeks, even if you are a seasoned practitioner of these methods of focus and receptivity. If images come up in your mind, it can be helpful to draw them in your journal as well. If you find writing and drawing helpful, continue in the journal you purchased for this inner expedition after these pages are filled.

_____

_____

_____

_____

_____

_____

_____

_____

_____

_____

_____

_____

_____

_____

_____

_____

_____

_____

_____

_____

_____

Mindful Awareness Journal

_____
_____
_____
_____
_____
_____
_____
_____
_____
_____
_____
_____
_____
_____
_____
_____
_____
_____
_____
_____
_____
_____
_____
_____
_____
_____
_____
_____
_____
_____
_____

Mindful Awareness Journal

of mental activity called *samatha* in Pali, best known as the language of the earliest extant Buddhist scriptures. The etymological roots of *samatha* suggest pacification of mental agitation, leading to calm abiding and sustained voluntary attention that can last for hours (Ray, 2004; Wallace, 2006). For each practitioner and for the same practitioner on different days, the resulting state of mind may bring a different flavor—expansiveness, joy, equanimity, and compassion are some possibilities. However, for our purposes, the emergence of this strong attentional capacity undergirds the next step in becoming nonjudgmental witnesses of ourselves and our patients.

Sitting in Receptivity

Now we are ready to loosen our grip on focused attention to practice receiving everything that arises in our consciousness. Sitting here a moment ago with closed eyes, I was aware of my seat on the chair and my feet on the floor, the rain splashing against the window, the soft snore of my sleeping beagle, the rhythm of my heart, my thoughts playing with words about mindful awareness, the flow of energy coursing through my body as if being rocked in a cradle, the small smile curving my lips and crinkling my eyes, the angle of my head, and on and on, welcoming all inner and outer experiences as they crested and ebbed in awareness. Some of the experiences had hooks that sought to pull me fully to their location on the rim—will the snoring beagle have enough food for dinner and what should I do about that? However, for the most part in those few minutes, I was able to stay in my caring observer, enjoying the subjective experience that all this activity was taking place within a larger, more enduring self. For me, in this state of mind this time, there was a sense of receptivity, a hint of humor, and a feeling of warmth and fullness in the chest. I noticed an undercurrent of criticism about the dog food worry, and held that in as much kindness as I could muster as well, being aware that I also had a judgment about my judging. Humor is essential in moments like this.

If we have come some distance in developing our ability to focus our attention, we may notice that as we sink into receptivity, an underlying quality of centered alertness undergirds and supports our awareness of moment-to-moment experience. We are anchored internally so that newly arising events don't pull us as easily to the rim.

Now, try sitting in receptivity for a moment or two—eyes open or closed, spine straight, hands and arms comfortable—and record your description on the Mindful Awareness Journal pages. It will be helpful to notice with kindness not only the experience itself, but any judgments—positive or negative—that you have about it. You might also make note of the subjective difference between focusing on the breath and sitting in receptivity. If you find that writing and drawing enrich your experience, then continue your daily reflections and drawings on the journal pages included here and then on into your personal journal. During your next visit with your listening partner, sharing your experience with receptivity will help deepen and anchor this practice.

Meditation as a Foundation for Therapeutic Presence

One approach that seems especially suited to developing those aspects of our mind that make us particularly effective as relational human beings and therapists is to combine these two practices each time we meditate. After focusing on our breath for 10 or 15 minutes, we can move into expansive receptivity for a similar period. This movement from one to the other facilitates the carryover of focused attention into the practice of receptivity, grounding it in stability beneath the moment-to-moment emergence of a kaleidoscope of internal and external events. I sometimes experience the overall process as beginning with attention like an arrow, and moving to relaxing into the sensation of becoming a cradling basket, *without losing the underlying sense of full and focused attentiveness.*

Over time, we will likely notice that our ability to direct and sustain focus begins to show up as a trait in daily life, and we sense that our minds sometimes automatically step back to witness with care all inner and outer events. When this latter experience emerges, unbidden, in stressful situations, we know that our brain integration is developing to the point that our amygdalar response to threat no longer dis-integrates the connections between the limbic and prefrontal regions. As we invest more time and attention, what was first an effortful practice becomes a reliable neural net, and is eventually experienced as an enduring aspect of our personality. This process of neural strengthening is just like weaving a nautical rope. The initial strand is not very strong and can be easily broken, but with the addition of more well-woven fibers, it can hold a large ship in place.

At the beginning of practice, it may seem that the only way to maintain focused receptivity is to sit still, with attending to the ebb and flow of experience the only task at hand. However, the outcome of consistent effort is to add a layer of ongoing processing to all our activities. As our practice matures, we may notice the feeling of looking through "deep eyes" as we both watch and participate in whatever is going on. *The state of mind engaging in the rim and the state attending to the ongoing flow of all that is coming from the rim are gathered into the state of mind that watches nonjudgmentally, with kind attention.* Eventually, these states of mind work together seamlessly.

This kind of broad integration leads not only to the experience of empathy and compassion, but also to actions that naturally arise from this more coherent state of neural activation. When the circuits of our danger-sensing amygdala are well-woven with our prefrontal circuits, our actions flow from states of mind that are less influenced by our wounded history and more guided by empathic, morally grounded considerations that turn out to foster health for ourselves and others. All this is to say that the commonly expressed fear that meditation can lead to passivity turns out not to be grounded in neurobiology—although it is also true that people can use these internal experiences as hiding places in response to unhealed wounds. Buddhist psychologist Jack Kornfield (2007) says that his therapist calls this "the monk's defense."

With that single warning about hiding out in mind, I encourage you to commit to doing these practices every day, at least while you are making your way through this workbook. I suspect if you do, they will become your lifelong supports. It is as though we are preparing a warm, safe room into which all unhealed aspects of our minds can come to find compassionate acceptance on their way to integration into the unfolding narrative of our lives. Then, from this spacious interior, we can warmly contain all that our patients bring us as well. In the next chapter, we begin to make deep acquaintance with our implicit world, a process that will rest easily on the foundation we are building with these practices.

Chapter 2

Exploring Our Implicit Seas

As we seek to engage with ourselves in an attitude of calm, kind curiosity, we're going to start by getting acquainted with the roots of the memories that shape our ongoing experience. At the earliest stages of our lives, especially during the first 12–18 months, we all form an ocean of memories encoded as bodily sensations, emotional surges, behavioral impulses, perceptions, and sometimes fragments of images, largely in right-mode processing. With repetition, these neural firings accumulate into mental models comprised of foundational flows of energy and information that literally become the sea of expectation in which we swim (Schore, 2003a, 2003b; Siegel, 1999). These implicit memories, as modified by later experience to a greater or lesser degree, are of particular importance because they encode our attachment experiences (Cozolino, 2006; Schore, 2003b; Siegel & Hartzell, 2003). As such, these neural nets inform our anticipation/expectation of how relationships will transpire; they guide our behavior within relationships that have emotional meaning for us; and, through resonance circuits, they even nudge us in the direction of people who will relate to us according to these established patterns. Familiarity of pattern breeds connection before it sometimes breeds contempt.

Because the therapeutic relationship most often has elements of an attachment experience, these implicit memories come into play from the first encounter in the emotional intimacy of therapy. Our patients come to us, having made an inner decision to share vulnerable aspects of their lives with a stranger. At the deepest level, their genetically rooted search for connection means that they have an embodied need for attunement and nonjudgmental acceptance. This unspoken bid for connection will touch the attachment circuits in us as well as in them (Schore, in press). In fact, it might be possible that the style of therapy we choose to practice and the way we implement that style are at least partly guided by our own attachment experiences. We reflect more fully on this point in Part III. Without a doubt, these patterns form an inner implicit paradigm of how we viscerally expect relationships, including those in therapy, to unfold. If we have implicit patterns created by dismissive parents who had a marked inability to attune, our patients' wordless bid for attachment may be met with our unwitting blindness to their signals. Those of us who grew up in stormy households may feel anxiety as we meet our patients, braced for the burst of chaos that our implicit world anticipates. If we have been fortunate to have parents with solid attunement leading to secure attachment for us, or if we have repaired earlier wounds so we have earned such security, we are more likely to greet our patients with warmth, have confidence in their resilience, and possess ample internal space in which their emotionally vivid journey can unfold. The impact of these inner assumptions, located dominantly in right-mode processes, is profound, and often unnoticed, because our perceptions are so continuously colored by the whisperings of our implicit world.

Let's pause for a moment to notice with kindness any implicit experiences arising from the previous paragraph. Directing our attention inward, in an act of what Daniel Siegel calls *mindsight* (2010a, 2010b), let's invite awareness of any bodily sensations and flows of emotion that may have been stirred by the three sentences about different patterns of attachment—distant, chaotic, and warm and stable. Then write a bit about what you discovered, *describing* your inner experience of each pattern rather than *explaining* it. Descriptions allow us to stay present with these flows of energy and information, whereas explanations pull us toward left-mode functioning. The time will come when we connect these experiences together into a narrative, but for now, we are just seeking to expand our capacity to listen with inner ears to our right-mode processes.

_____

_____

_____

_____

_____

_____

_____

_____

_____

_____

_____

_____

_____

_____

Then, take a moment to also notice if you have a critical or congratulatory response about how you did the practice of sitting with your sensations and emotions nonjudgmentally. Interestingly, congratulations are the flip side of criticism—a judgment in their own right. Both pull us away from kind observation and a calm nervous system. See if you can experience the shift between a judgmental to an observing state, and write a few descriptive words about both.

_____

_____

_____

_____

_____

As we move through these early chapters, we will deepen our awareness of the kinds of early attachment that shaped our deepest expectations. By the time we are working with narrative in Chapters 5 and 6, we will be able to give words to these foundational experiences. For now, we are going to attend to whatever our implicit world wishes to share as a first step.

Recognizing Implicit Memories

It goes without saying that cognitive acknowledgment that we do indeed have implicit memories within us doesn't do us much good unless we can become conscious of them and attend with healing care to those that aren't serving us well. However, moving into visceral awareness of the waves in our sea of implicit memories presents us with some sticky challenges. We are used to having our memories show up like this: "Remember when we walked on the beach with the neighbor kids and you found your first sea star?" The explicit memory that is called up by such a question is experienced as having *happened in the past*; having a *beginning, middle*, and *end*; being associated with *pictures*; and being fairly *easy to call into conscious awareness*. Implicit memories are very different. They reside out of the usual flow of time that gives us the sense of memories slipping into the past. Instead, they are with us as continual *bodily sensations, surges of feeling,* and *automatic behavioral impulses,* as well as *perceptual biases,* influencing every current experience. In other words, they are not integrated with our usual sense of time, but instead are the *eternally present, embodied past* within which our lives unfold. As we begin to pay attention, we may notice that we are being carried on an ocean whose waves rise and fall in response to internal and external nudges.

Often these are wordless experiences, usually below the level of conscious awareness (meaning that they can be noticed but mostly aren't), and without pictures to tie them to the events out of which they were formed. They show up mostly in the way we continually relate to ourselves and others, and in the broad patterns of how we expect our lives to unfold. As we begin to develop the capacity to spot these patterns, we will see that they play a powerful formative role in molding each relational encounter. We may also notice that the more intimate the connection, the greater the shaping power of the implicit. With our mates and our children, the attachment ties are so strong that these patterns are deeply stirred. Long-term therapeutic relationships make their way to this same rich depth—in both therapist and patient.

Let me share a story. Beginning in one of our early meetings, I noticed that every time I moved even a little bit forward in my chair, my young patient would recoil slightly as though his body remembered being struck. Tears stung my eyes as though I had injured him, but I didn't pay as much attention to that. That was as far as my conscious mind took me. However, over time, without my choice, permission, or awareness, my body gradually adopted an awkward rigidity as my implicitly entangled state of mind sought not to trigger his implicit fear of impending violence. In retrospect, I can feel how the usual flow of my body's response to my experience of connection was arrested. My first conscious awareness of the problem came when I noticed that I had developed a pattern of dreading the hour I spent with this patient. This didn't make sense to me, particularly since I had begun with, and still felt, such liking for him. As I sat with the dread, my body began to reveal its rigidity, taking me ultimately to my deeply ingrained need to keep my father from breaking down. As the implicit became explicit, I was more able to differentiate between this young man's need for me to allow him to make living contact with his inner pain and my urgent need to keep my father psychologically intact when I was a very young child. With some work in my own therapy, I was able to resolve the rigid response to the implicit prompting as well. But the real point of the story is how subterranean and powerful implicit communication between two people can be (Ginot, 2009; Schore, in press).

With this experience in mind, it seems likely that most ethical violations spring from implicit entanglements in which dis-integrated aspects of the therapist's inner world are touched by and resonate with patients' deep patterns. If this process stays out of awareness, eventually the therapist is revolving around the patient in a dance that replicates early attachment wounds for both of them. I have worked with therapists who have crossed boundaries in ways that are difficult to understand unless we can clearly see their unique inner world to become aware of the implicit hooks that caught on their patients' vulnerable spots. Each one has said almost the identical words: "I watched myself doing this, knew it was wrong, and couldn't stop." As we become better listeners to our own inner processes, the likelihood of us being similarly caught will greatly decrease. At the same time, such deep resonance can also be a source of profound empathy (Ginot, 2009)—which we explore in Part II.

Not all implicit memories remain wordless. At times, these surges of energy and information do find expression as our left-mode processing seeks to make sense of what is flowing in from the right. Midway through our first session, a patient said to me, "I will be dangerous to your spiritual health. You'd better watch yourself with me." His eyes were wide with fear as he thrust his hands into the cracks between the couch cushions as though to stop himself from hurting me. He had no sensations of remembering some long-ago experience of being seen as a ruinous person by both of his elderly parents. Instead, he was simply stating an obvious truth—anyone getting involved with him is at risk of losing his or her grip on life as meaningful. Even after we uncovered the reason for this expectation, his dread of wrecking relationships, his pervasive anticipation of rupture and disaster as his inevitable fate, remained very powerful well into our therapeutic experience.

Implicit memories don't change because we now understand them. They change in response to their juxtaposition with a disconfirming perception when both the implicit memories and the current perception are emotionally vivid (Ecker, 2008, 2010; Ecker & Hulley, 1996, 2000a, 2000b, 2008). These juxtapositions often take the form of repeated interpersonal experiences that relationships can be different from the patterns of our ingrained mental model. My young client and I found that the new implicit seed took root best when the ground was tilled by the ingrained pattern awakening within him to be met by my genuine welcome. He watched me for signs that my sense of life as positive and meaningful was being destroyed by his presence, and gradually, through resonance with my real delight in him and my ongoing optimism, his implicit pattern began to shift to an expectation that he could be worthy of care and that there might be mutual benefit, even in close relationships.

All our memories in at least the first year of life are solely implicit, and all our subsequent memories, even when they are explicit, have an implicit dimension, meaning that bodily sensations, behavioral impulses, emotional surges, and perceptions are part of every encoded experience. However, after the first 12–18 months, these implicit fragments are more often integrated, via the hippocampus, into explicit memories, with that capacity becoming more stable and reliable by our fourth or fifth year. If we think of anything recent and pleasant, it is likely that we will immediately experience visual, auditory, tactile, emotional, bodily, and perceptual components of the experience, while being aware that it also happened in the past. This is the implicit plus explicit form of memory that pervades our everyday life. I love Christmas lights, so as I think of driving about the neighborhood in these last few weeks of December, I see lights/hear carols/taste cinnamon tea/feel my shoulders relax and my chest warm/enjoy the smile of delight/perceive that the world is a good place in this moment—all in the twinkling of an eye, thanks to the intricate neural net created by that repeated experience, with implicit and explicit aspects of memory rolled into one.

Experiencing Our Implicit World

So far, we have mostly considered concrete examples as a means to feel our way into implicit memory because simply understanding it as a concept doesn't get us much closer to the real thing. Now we are going to spend time dipping our toes into our own implicit sea. Because implicit memory is rooted in right-mode processing, it will be helpful to initially listen to its messages through the body and then to use art as a way to shape and contain that experience. This would be a good time to round up the art supplies you selected at the beginning of this process and invite your listening partner to join with you in this exploration. Two attuned minds amplify the benefit of the practices.

First, let's prepare by entering a kind, nonjudgmental state of mind in regard to ourselves, as best we can. You may notice how this intention activates your caring observer and allows you to receive more easily whatever is arising in the moment. To begin, notice how your body feels as you contemplate allowing your implicit world to speak to you. In a few words, describe your bodily sensations here.

_____

_____

_____

_____

_____

Now, call to mind a particularly pleasant or meaningful experience you've had in the last few days or weeks. Allow it to fill your mind and body—a kind of time travel that can take you to a rich inner experience that is closely based on the original. In a leisurely way, sit in openness to your body's sensations, noticing, noticing, noticing, not directing or judging, as best you can. Then use this space to write a few descriptive words—*hands and feet warm, chest relaxed, eyes crinkled*, for example.

_____

_____

_____

_____

_____

To further encourage awareness of the implicit aspect of this experience, turn your attention to your drawing materials. Sense which colors feel particularly energized right this moment. Using your nondominant hand, let a drawing emerge naturally from the remembered experience—not necessarily a drawing of the content of the experience, but giving form to the flow of energy and information moving though your body. Sit with your drawing for a bit to sense if it is complete. Then sit a little longer, noticing your response to the drawing itself and to the act of drawing by becoming aware of the movements your body wants to make; the feelings welling up first as bodily sensations, then taking form as specific emotions; and the thoughts in your mind. Write a bit.

_____

_____

_____

_____

_____

_____

_____

_____

_____

Returning to the memory that prompted this drawing, notice how contact with that experience influences your perception of yourself and the world, and then how the experience of drawing may amplify or change those perceptions. Write a few descriptive words about that here. As you write, as best you can, remain in your compassionate observing state of mind, noticing the shift-

The Brain-Savvy Therapist's Workbook

ing flows of energy and information as they move through your body in response to your inner experience of your outer activity.

_____

_____

_____

_____

_____

   Repeating this practice many times, with the focus on positive experiences, will help develop the neural nets for listening to your right-mode processing. It is like developing an ear for the many strands of music that make up a symphony. Daily practice is most effective because it regularly fortifies the new pattern, increasing its synaptic strength. When that is coupled with sharing what both of you are discovering in conversations with your listening partner, more neural change occurs through interpersonal joining. As best you can, stay centered on the bodily aspect of the implicit until you can easily sense the flow of energy and information as it rises and falls in your muscles, heart, lungs, stomach, throat, colon, skin. You may experience these as small or large changes in tension, depth of respiration, heart rate, stomach agitation or calming, skin sensitivity, lump in the throat, or an impulse to move. From there, awareness of the flow of feelings will follow naturally, accompanied by the perceptions that arise from these.
   Let's try it again now. Enter your caring observer state of mind, think of a pleasant or meaningful recent experience, notice the bodily sensations and movements that arise with the memory, and write a few descriptive words here.

_____

_____

_____

_____

_____

   Now let a drawing emerge from the flow of energy and information. After the drawing is complete and you have rested with it, sense what you can about your perception of yourself and the world in this moment. Do you notice warm acceptance or tense criticism of yourself right now? Do you feel pleased, accepting, or critical of your world in general? Do you have a sense that your life experience is meaningful or empty and random? Do you anticipate that you will be able to manage your life well, no matter where events take you, or that life may possibly overwhelm you with its challenges? The answers to these seemingly enormous and possibly abstract questions actually arise out of our implicit flow in any given moment. The possibilities offered here are the far ends of a continuum of potential responses, and you are invited to listen to the subtleties of your actual experience rather than choose an option from those offered. Taken together, these questions invite us to experience ourselves, our current world, our past experiences, and our imagined future—all of which are profoundly impacted by our implicit "underlife." Taking some leisurely time again with your drawing, write some descriptive words about your bodily experience, the flow of emotion, and the perceptions that arise from it.

_____

_____

_____

_____

_____

_____

_____

_____

_____

_____

In these exercises we are seeking to become sensitive to the various ways that our implicit sea can make itself known to our listening mind and to our mind's eye. The content is far less important right now than the process of paying attention in this way. As we come into deeper contact with ourselves, we will naturally be able to do the same with and for others—family, friends, coworkers, patients. The attuned mind develops a broad bandwidth for listening to flows of energy and information. Over time, the state of mind in which we listen to right-mode processing is strengthened into a trait of being, making it possible for us to be aware of the flow of relational and motivational information continually connecting people, even in the midst of our daily activities.

Before we go on to more practices, a word about drawing with the nondominant hand may be helpful. In theory, our nondominant hand connects us with the hemisphere of our brains that holds implicit memory. This is generally the right hemisphere, but for a small percentage of people, regardless of handedness, right-mode processing may occur in the left hemisphere (Holder,

2005). As a result, it is helpful to try drawing with both hands to see which one most powerfully connects us to the felt reality of our experience. Drawing in this unaccustomed way also sometimes alleviates fears that our art won't be good enough because we generally don't expect ourselves to do very well with this less practiced hand. This lowered expectation may allow for a freer flow of experience onto the paper. In any case, art offers a way to directly contact and express the mostly wordless right-mode processing that reveals implicit patterns. It is at least worth several tries to see if the flow of image and color gives meaningful and relieving form to your inner world.

Sometimes our personal history may have caused us to distrust the messages of our bodies as they seek to make our feelings known to us. If our parents were able to attune and accurately reflect our state of mind to us—"You look sad right now"—it is likely that we learned to trust our own inner knowing. If they could not offer this mirroring to us, we may have difficulty hearing or believing these messages. This is especially true if we were mirrored inaccurately or told to change what we were experiencing. I vividly remember bursting in the back door at the age of 6, declaring, "I hate Johnny!" My mother said, "No, you don't," as she continued to wash the dishes. Right this moment, I can feel my whole body tighten as my outgoing energy yanks itself inside. This is quickly followed by my chest collapsing, my body turning away, and tears stinging the corners of my eyes—embodied shame. She no doubt didn't want me to grow up to be a person filled with hate, but in the moment, I learned that my sense of my feelings was wrong, so I could not trust myself to know them. If these experiences are repeated regularly, usually enacted by well-meaning parents trying to protect us from the relational difficulties that caused them hurt, we often simply stop listening to ourselves. If this was our experience, we may initially find some difficulty with these implicit listening practices. Persistence, especially when coupled with the kind listening of another, will gradually open the neural connections that allow us to hear our inner voice and restore our faith in the truth and value of our embodied feelings.

Implicit Memories of Early Attachment Experiences

Having spent some time developing the ability to listen to our right-mode processes, we are going to shift our focus to implicit memories that may directly touch our early attachment experiences—whether they were warm, cold, or chaotic. Situations that have the potential for perceived or real rejection, as well as for warm connection, can touch these deep places. Again, we are more concerned here with developing the capacity to listen with our caring observer than to make sense of the information we are receiving, so we will be monitoring bodily sensations, action impulses, and feelings for the most part.

One situation that can bring up concern about potential rejection is walking into a group of strangers for a social occasion. If we show up to teach or otherwise engage in professional activities, we are often protected from the purely social aspects of the situation, but when we enter that cocktail party alone, we are internally exposed to our implicit models about how we will be received.

If possible, do this practice with your listening partner. Settling into your caring observer, travel in your body and mind to a time when you went alone into a social gathering of strangers. What do you notice in your body just before you cross the threshold? Stay there for a little while, compassionately noticing everything that arises as sensations, feelings, and behavioral impulses. Let the bodily sensations and feelings flow into a drawing, and then write a few descriptive words below if they naturally arise.

_____

_____

_____

_____

_____

Now spend a few moments kindly noticing any judgments (critical/congratulatory) you had about yourself as a social person or your process of listening, drawing, and describing. Notice and describe how judgment affects your body and your feelings. Then notice the shift in your state of being when you are able to release judgment and embrace the experience with your caring observer.

_____

_____

_____

_____

_____

Exposing ourselves to the possibility of rejection can touch our attachment circuits, and so can coming face to face with a genuine offer of warm connection. We might feel drawn toward the warmth and genuineness of that person or sent into frightened withdrawal because attachment was painful and terrifying for us as infants—or have a response somewhere in between. Settling once again into your caring observer, call to mind and body a time when someone offered you warm connection. This might be someone close to you or a new person. Attend to your bodily sensations and impulses to move, and to your feelings—with compassion and tenderness. Then draw and describe a bit about your experience and your judgment of that experience.

_____

_____

_____

_____

_____

_____

_____

_____

_____

_____

As we continue to approach our implicit world slowly, respectfully, and gently, we may have the sensation of spiraling down into our deeper mind, bringing a change of perspective that allows us to sense how _our implicit roots underlie and make sense of our fixed beliefs and behavioral strategies._ From this viewpoint, there is a deep coherence between these aspects of our being and functioning that isn't apparent if we approach from the cognitive and behavioral surface.

Moving through these practices, our brains may also begin to make connections between these experiences and patterns in past relationships, including perhaps our earliest childhood interactions. Because our brains are always seeking greater integration, these linkages are natural occurrences as we draw various strands of experience into awareness. Even our intention to attend with kindness creates a fertile milieu for neural integration.

Let's pause here for a moment to check in with how the pace and pattern of this process is feeling. For those of us accustomed to reading, reading, reading without a break, the continual requests to pause and move into an interior experience, scare up drawing materials, write only descriptive words, and take time to reflect at leisure may feel disruptive, irritating, stupid, or any number of other ways that all have an impact on the body, and maybe especially, the nervous system. You may also be reading only, without practice—and that will carry certain feelings with it as well. One of them might be that there is a lot of repetition in this chapter as we move from experiential moment to experiential moment. Doing the practices will likely bring a feeling of freshness with each one, while only reading about them may feel boring. Allow yourself to feel, with curiosity and openness, your bodily and emotional response to the process and how you are engaging with it. Then describe that. Comparing notes with your listening partner may be a worthwhile experience at this particular juncture.

_____

_____

_____

_____

_____

It isn't surprising that our effort to engage with our right-mode processes might meet with some resistance, especially because the path comes in the form of a book with lots of words and lots of stimulation for the neural nets of academic study. Rewiring ourselves into a state of mind that always allows for elements of leisurely reflection amidst the words takes a lot of dedicated work. Kindness and persistence are the keys—and impatience may be just another familiar companion along the way for some time. Gentleness and humor in the face of that resistance or impatience is a real gift to us.

As we have been working through these practices, we may notice that we are already developing an inner pattern for this process—first, moving toward or into our caring observer, then noticing and describing the experience, then kindly attending to our judgment about the experience. With each pass, we are adding neural strength to the circuits that foster our ability to make this kind of relationship to self and others a mainstay of our daily life. Regular repetition is the key, as I have said several times already. New neural nets need as much consistent care as a young sprout. It may be a good idea to dog-ear the pages containing the practices you want to repeat regularly and make them part of your day's routine until state becomes trait. Then the practices will gain the momentum to carry on without conscious support.

To conclude our reflections before moving on to other aspects of memory in the next chapter, let's sum up and do one final bit of writing. Implicit memory offers us several clues about its presence: bodily sensations, behavioral impulses, surges of emotion, and shifts in perception—sometimes accompanied by fragments of images. The other day, I saw a mostly bald man, with a big warm smile, whom I thought was in his 60s, holding the hand of a small child. I had been deep in thought and a little grumpy about all the year-end accounting I needed to do for our nonprofit. As I caught sight of them, my heart literally warmed, my chest expanded, my face grinned, my hand felt small in my grandfather's grip, and I was suffused with the perception of being loved in a world set right on its axis. The shift in body, feelings, and perception was so sudden and thorough that it startled me.

Now, invite your deeper mind to share moments when you have experienced such a shift, and then write descriptively about each aspect—bodily sensations, behavioral impulses, surges of emotion, and changes in perception. See if you can feel at ease with this flow of energy and information coming to you as you hold it in your compassionate embrace. Sense any judgments you have about what you receive and about your ability to receive it. Do this several times if your mind offers you a few rich experiences. Then spend some time with your listening partner, sharing both the experiences and the process that has developed in this chapter.

_____

_____

_____

_____

_____

_____

_____

_____

_____

_____

_____

_____

_____

_____

_____

_____

_____

_____

_____

_____

_____

_____

_____

_____

_____

_____

_____

_____

_____

While the primary goal of this chapter has been to develop our capacity for right-mode listening, the kind attention we've offered our inner world and the compassion we've received from our listening partner have also silently woven together the circuits that increase regulation and integration. We have been changing brain function and building brain structure. Using our growing listening skill, we are now going to move on to deeper acquaintance with specific aspects of our inner world in the next two chapters.

Chapter 3

Gathering the Filaments of Memory

We all dance, from moment to moment, within the music of our memories. Sometimes we might say, "Oh, that's just a memory," as though the neural reawakening of the past ought to have no impact. Yet, if we adopt a scientific viewpoint, we see that memory defines much of our experience. When we are in utero, our nervous systems form memories of how safe or unsafe our world is. We come into birth with some levels of neurotransmitter activation, some neural firing patterns, and even attaching and soothing behaviors already shaped by these experiences (Field, Diego, & Hernandez-Reif, 2006). Our infant brains are genetically prepared to seek the eyes, breasts, and hands of our mothering person, whose care will build the very structure of our limbic and cortical circuitry (Cozolino, 2006; Schore, 2003a, 2003b; Siegel, 1999). Even at the level of our genes, there is memory of attachment as certain genes are silenced and others expressed in response to maternal care (Hill, 2010; Morgan & Whitelaw, 2008; Whitelaw & Whitelaw, 2006). On we go through life, accumulating new memories, ingraining existing patterns through repetition, and modifying old patterns as well. We continually experience these flows of energy and information within our embodied and relational brains.

Before we focus on our own symphony of recollections, we are going to spend some time gaining a visceral sense of the pervasiveness of memory and the ways that our remembrances can become fragmented instead of coherent. By teasing apart the various aspects of memory playing within us, we can become discriminating observers of the neural patterns shaping our current experience. I encourage you to read all of this slowly to begin to taste the way memory plays within you. We will pause in a few places for reflection and writing. In addition, encouraging ourselves to be continually aware of our responses to reading these words will further develop the neural nets of caring observation.

Memory's Influence on our Past, Present, and Future

What we are learning about our brains has made it clear that as we walk through the moments of our lives, we ride on these memory patterns, even when we aren't consciously thinking about the past. Memory is held in a number of different brain systems operating in parallel, without direct neural connections with one another (Milner, Squire, & Kandel, 1998). For example, there are no direct connections between the limbic region of the right mode and the modules of consciousness and language in the left mode. Only those right-mode neural firings that are gathered into the integrative circuits connecting the two hemispheres gain a pathway to the left. This means that much of our inner life remains permanently out of awareness while continuing to influence our next moves. As we saw in the last chapter, implicit memory flows continually within us, shaping our perceptual slant, the tone of our feelings, and the sensations and behaviors of our bodies. Most of this happens without our consciously attending to it, as the IS of our lives.

At the same time, both within and outside our conscious awareness, our brains—whose firing patterns change at least four times per second—are largely following wired-in paths whose probability of being activated is influenced by the neural strength of the particular pattern (Siegel, 1999). Although we don't know the full story about why particular neural nets come most frequently into consciousness, we suspect that some neural circuits are strong, like magnets, and so are drawn into consciousness regularly (Siegel, 1999). This gives us the sensation of continuity, despite the dance of discrete firings in our brains—similar to our perception of the flow of images on the screen in spite of the breaks between frames on predigital filmstrips.

Let's begin with the influence of memory on our perception of the past, present, and future. When we direct our attention to the *past*, we initiate neural firings that enliven old experience within us. Under certain circumstances, we add some energy and information of this moment to the memory, which will be re-stored when we are no longer attending to that particular flow of energy and information. At the very least, we will have a memory of remembering. In another process, this one occurring outside conscious awareness, a dedicated set of circuits weaves together the discrete flows of memory within our brains into patterns of personal relevance (Buckner, Andrews-Hanna, & Schacter, 2008; Fox, 2008; Greicius et al., 2008; Horovitz et al., 2008). Originally believed to be active dominantly when our conscious minds are in a less focused state, we now know that these integrative circuits fire most of the time (Raichle, 2010). Thus, in ways that are mostly imperceptible to conscious awareness, our brains are constantly modifying the ever-emerging past that shapes our present and future.

Let's sit with the idea of a constantly changing past for a moment. We may be able to taste the conscious part of this memory-modifying process a bit by inviting a recent memory of an upsetting time into conscious awareness. Notice its impact on your body and nervous system. Then add the energy and information of kind observation to the memory and notice how it shifts your visceral experience of the recalled past. Write a brief description of your bodily and emotional response to the memory alone and to the memory with caring observation added.

_____

_____

_____

_____

_____

_____

_____

_____

_____

By doing this practice frequently, we may be able to sense that we do not have to be bound by one particular version of the past. The kind focus of our minds can increase our neural integration so that we hold the events of our history in a larger context, both objectively and subjectively. This shift in perspective reshapes the meaning of past experiences and thereby changes their impact on our daily lives.

Now let's shift our attention to the *present*. Much of our current experience rides on memory of the past. Via both the influence of implicit mental models and the patterns of anticipation ingrained by experience in our neocortex as invariant representations, we experience new events through the lens of knowing what comes next (Hawkins & Blakeslee, 2004; Siegel, 1999). Without the inner guidance of these invariant representations that arise with repeated experience, we would face each situation as though it were brand new and move like babies through a continuously unknown world. Instead, as our brains differentiate, they form neural nets that function as shortcuts to our next steps and allow us to enact many behaviors without conscious thought. The nature of these thoughts, feelings, and actions may support healthy living or tie our bodily sensations, emotions, perceptions, and relational choices to the patterns of a traumatic, painful, or lifeless past.

The present does offer us another opportunity. When we focus mindfully, we can participate in the creation of vivid new memories by attending to the full range of the novel experience coming to us in that moment—the shape, fragrance, hue, and texture of a leaf; the joy radiating from a child's face as she swings high in the sky. By activating the cortex in a different way, through attending to the senses, we are less tied to invariant representations formed by past events and more available to fresh encounters.

Let's take an attentive moment to taste this experience. Choosing any object in your vicinity, cradle it in your hands and allow it to fill your senses as it rests in the center of your attention for a moment or two. What sights, sounds, tastes, textures, aromas does it evoke? When your mind drifts away, bring it back to the object with great gentleness, settling again into the experience of your senses. Notice the influence on your body's sensations, your feelings, and your perception of the world at large when you focus your attention in this way, for even a short while. Also be aware of any judgments that might arise about how you are doing this practice. Then write three short notes: Describe your object; describe your body sensations, feelings, and perceptions now; describe your judgments and their impact on your body and perceptions.

_____

_____

_____

_____

_____

_____

_____

_____

_____

When we wish to be able to keep an experience with us forever, literally alive in the neural firing patterns of our brains, we can support this deep ingraining through sustained focus coupled with regular visits to the memory. Through mindful attention in the moment, we are able to take in the experience in a more present-centered way so that it is less influenced by the accumulated top-down neural firings that tell us the present and future are just like the past. Instead of the memory being completely overlaid with past melodies, we can more clearly hear the lilt of this experience as unique (Hawkins & Blakeslee, 2004; Siegel, 2007).

When we sold our home of so many years, I felt sadness at leaving our well-loved garden, but having recently delved into neurobiology, I thought that perhaps I could take the spongy grass and flowerbeds with me. So I spent quite some time both sitting in my favorite place and gazing upon the garden, and then more hours wandering about, touching, breathing deeply, and sensing the meaning of having worked the earth here. I thought less about losing it, and more about being in it. The day we left, I felt the wrench of my final visit to the deep backyard, but as we arrived at our new home—a temporary residence with no real garden space—I found that I could still walk in my former garden if I focused my attention on being present there rather than on the loss. Over time, I trusted that my old garden could be a living, present, loamy sanctuary for me.

Mindful focus in the moment can also create an internal space for us to add new themes and melodies to even our most ancient memories, sometimes changing the implicit flows completely (Ecker, 2008, 2010; Ecker & Hulley, 1996, 2000a, 2000b, 2008; Ecker & Toomey, 2008). This work of consciously drawing the past into the present is especially powerful when we are gathering the circuitry containing the emotionally vivid experience into the caring observer's kind embrace of the event (Siegel, 2007, 2010b). This will be our primary personal work in this chapter, so I will save the details for later.

When we reflect on the *future*, we may feel as though we are deliberately separating ourselves from memory to create something new. Yet we experience the future from within the neural firing patterns of our brains, which are actually flows of anticipation based on past experience. Because of that, memory influences how we are able to implicitly (mostly) and explicitly (somewhat) frame the future.

Some of my patients are so dominated by painful or frightening implicit memories that they can't imagine a future that is different from the past. "I *will always* be alone." "I *will always* be the garbage that should be thrown out." "I *will never* feel settled and satisfied with one person." Even at the explicit conscious level, they cannot create an image of a different possibility because the implicit past is really the eternal present, and, by extension, the only future until these memories are integrated with a sense of time. After much work to transform and temporally integrate the implicit, these people are able to say something different. "I *was* alone in the past, and I see now that I am not alone because at least you and I are together." "My parents *saw* me as garbage, so that is what I believed. Now, I know that I am as valuable as the next person." "I *felt* tossed from one person to the next because my mother had a constant string of lovers. Now, I can imagine the fulfillment of being with one person for a long time." The change of tense and the absence of *always* and *never* are as indicative as the content, showing that these implicit knowings are being integrated into explicit memories that can then be experienced as truly past. At the same time, the juxtaposition of vivid disconfirming perception from the present moment has changed the content of the implicit as well (Ecker & Toomey, 2008).

These implicit whisperings can carry messages of strength, resilience, and connection as well as the trapping patterns generated by painful and frightening experiences—"I will never feel truly alone"; "I can always find help to figure things out"; "I have enough strength to make it through anything." This supportive implicit comes from attuned relationships at the beginning of life and is amplified by the empathic companions we attract along the way. These flows of energy and information exist side by side with those that keep us locked out of the rich possibilities within us.

Let's spend a little time being open to awareness of any *always* and *never* places in our memories. Settling into your caring observer, say internally, "I will always . . ." and then stay in a state of relaxed attention to hear what your deeper mind may bring to you. With kindness, hear the words and also notice the impact on your body, feelings, and perceptions. Then take a moment to write the words you heard and describe (rather than explain) what you experienced with the words.

_____

_____

_____

_____

_____

_____

_____

_____

_____

_____

Staying again in your caring observer, try it with "I will never . . ." and then write as you did with *always*.

_____

_____

_____

_____

_____

_____

_____

_____

_____

_____

Now take a moment to notice any judgments about your *always* and *never* places, as well as about how you did this process, treating yourself with great tenderness. If you found some judgments, write a few words about the impact of judging on your body, feelings, and perceptions.

_____

_____

_____

_____

_____

Even when we aren't so completely dominated by implicit expectations that we can't form an explicit expectation different from the past, sometimes the future is split for us. We may be able to consciously imagine a different set of circumstances and relationships, but find that the manifestation falls short. In those cases, our implicit knowing about what is possible for us, coupled with the power of other well-established neural nets, overrides our conscious desire for change. "Some day my prince/princess will come" is followed by attraction to the same unavailable person who echoes the losses of childhood. Tenderness, openness, and curiosity about these constraints can put us in a state of mind to receive the part of us that holds such rigid certainty about how our life will unfold. When we follow that part to the root of the compelling implicit mental model and add experiences that disconfirm it, our core guiding perceptions can and do change.

Fragmented or Dissociated Memory

In addition to the way memories influence our experience of the past, present, and future, our minds can become fragmented along different kinds of fault lines when painful and frightening experiences are not met with repairing attunement and care. These shards of experience remain separate from the flow of integrating energy and information in the brain, and because they are so disconnected from possibly mediating input, they are easily triggered by an internal or external reminder. Then they often burst into full activity, taking over our minds, bodies, and relationships. Because this pattern is so autonomous, we are all subject to a takeover. That is why our quality of life and our capacity to be steady agents of healing for our patients depends directly on how much integration our brains have achieved (Siegel, 2010b).

Let's taste some possible memory patterns of incomplete integration. To begin, we may notice *flows of implicit memory that are distinct from the messages of our conscious minds.* For example, in spite of her overt longing and active search for intimate connection, my patient's implicit conviction that no one would stay connected with her exerted a compelling pull toward ongoing isolation. As an infant, she had reached out for her mother, only to feel her turn inward and away in the midst of a prolonged depression that lasted throughout her infant and toddler years. Now, in the grip of this compelling flow of energy and information, my patient creates seemingly valid reasons to stay separate—too busy, too tired—and finds numerous undesirable characteristics in anyone who might choose her. All of this behavior makes logical sense to her left-mode processing, leaving her feeling abandoned by God and humankind because no one suitable comes her way. Underneath, her behavior is driven by the ongoing irrefutable and futility-instilling message: "You will always be abandoned."

Take a moment to invite your deeper mind to show you any places where your conscious intention about what you want and its actual unfolding diverge. Sitting in receptivity for a few moments, see what comes to mind and body. Then, notice any judgments your mind is offering about the content or the process, and write a bit about the divergence, its impact on your body and emotions, and any judgments that arise. Take a moment to hold all of this in kindness as well.

_____

_____

_____

_____

_____

_____

_____

_____

_____

_____

_____

_____

_____

_____

Dis-integrated implicit memory can also take another form of *lying dormant in dissociated pockets and springing into action only when touched by internal or external experience*. One new patient came in reporting that he thought he was "going crazy." A few weeks prior, he began having severe heart palpitations every time the traffic light turned green. I asked him if anything else had happened at that time. After considerable reflection, he remembered that he had been playing basketball and had a powerful collision with another player, hitting his head against the upright that holds the basket. He was shaken up, but kept playing. His first green-light/heart-palpitation experience occurred on his way home from that game. Knowing that what fires together, wires together and survives together (Hebb, 1949; Post et al., 1998), I was curious about the synchronicity of the two experiences, but said nothing to him. After working with the body sensations for several sessions, he had the compelling physical sense of having been badly shaken (a feeling that his neck was contorted and his head injured), but had no explicit memory of any time that had happened. He decided to ask his mother. She told him that when they were driving together when he was about 9 months old, the light had turned green, she had accelerated, and another person had run the light, crashing into the side of the car right behind her seat and spinning them around violently. This was in the days before it was mandatory to strap kids into the backseat, so his carrier was on the front passenger seat. The old-fashioned seatbelt holding it came loose, and his head banged into the side window. His mom said, "That was too bad. We were having fun. I was showing you how the traffic lights changed and you seemed so interested." Neither of them was badly injured, and the story was lost in the labyrinth of family history. However, the blow to the right side of his head in the basketball game had activated the long-buried neural net, pulling up the vision of the light changing to green, coupled with the panic he had felt at the time of the accident.

It is likely that most of us have some of these implicit pockets, and we can invite them into conscious awareness later in the chapter. At the same time, almost all of us entertain *another kind of memory splitting in which we see and hear the internal video of an experience, while remaining cut off from the bodily and feeling aspects*. Sometimes we're unaware because we're not making an effort to attend to the whole experience, and when we do, the pieces of the memory fall together into a coherent whole. However, sometimes the memory division is more profound, reflecting the way we initially encoded the experience, and possibly its relationship to other similar memories. For many years, I could clearly visualize rolling down a mountainside in an aged Volkswagen when I was 18, coming to rest about 500 feet below the roadway. I knew I had survived the accident well, needing only some stitches and chiropractic help. However, no matter how hard I tried, I couldn't connect with what it felt like to be helpless and out of control like that. It was as if that part of the experience was on the other side of a door that was held shut by unseen hands. My inability to remember wasn't harming my life, but my lack of a visceral sense of the accident was curious to me. Many years later, in therapy, working to recover from significant childhood trauma, I experienced a memory whose major felt components were helplessness and lack of control. As I emerged from the work, the memory of the roll down the mountain came back spontaneously and with full force. In my therapist's office, I had the experience of tumbling and screaming and coming to rest at the bottom, out of breath and instantly searching for injuries. I also immediately understood that the split in the Volkswagen memory was riding on the back of the separation between thought and feeling that had occurred when I was much younger.

On rarer occasions, usually marked by sudden, violent trauma, *whole memories can be sheared away from conscious awareness, even though as adults we have the neural maturity to encode these experiences as explicit memories.* The impact is so strong that the stress chemicals block movement from the amygdala (implicit memory) to the hippocampus (explicit memory), leaving us with intense bodily sensations, behavioral impulses, emotions, and perceptions that are not attached to any memory of an incident. Often, signs that the body is experiencing the visceral memory of something that can't be immediately explained is the first indication that the experience is coming into explicit, conscious awareness. My colleagues and I have worked with several veterans who had gaps in their memory around traumas that others had witnessed. One young man began to have the behavioral impulse to shield the right side of his face whenever he relaxed. As he and his therapist followed this implicit fragment, other parts of the tragic attack began to gather around this one strand of the neural net. Eventually, in the embrace of the warmth and clarity of his therapist, he became regulated enough to tolerate the whole memory in consciousness, gradually integrating it into the ongoing flow of his brain.

At the far reaches of trauma, *memory is held in discrete packets belonging to separate selves—what we currently label dissociative identity disorder.* From the neurobiological perspective, this disorder is a natural extension of the principle that the greater the trauma, the greater the neural and neurochemical constraints to integration. It is difficult for me to use the term "disorder" because this kind of splitting is actually a highly adaptive strategy in the face of intolerable trauma. From the subjective perspective, we can see that what goes unseen and uncomforted remains isolated within our brains and minds.

Entering the Realm of Our Memories

The way in which memories integrate and fail to integrate within us follows these basic patterns, but the specifics of how we each encode our experiences are as unique as our fingerprints. In the remainder of this chapter, we are going to slowly and gently enter the realm of our memories, touching them with kind attention, beginning to weave what is separate into the flow that is unfolding within. It will be helpful to keep your journal and drawing materials nearby so you can express and contain what comes to you. This would also be an excellent time to work with your listening partner. We do know that shared mindful attention exponentially increases the integrative possibilities (Siegel, 2010b) and also helps maintain a sense of safety that can allow us to go more deeply into our minds (Porges, 2007). In addition, the attuned presence of another person begins to silently rewire our flow of implicit memories into patterns of greater security, through the moment-to-moment, out-of-conscious-awareness synchronicity that we experience as healing empathy (Marci, Ham, Moran, & Orr, 2007; Marci & Reiss, 2005; Schore, in press). If what you uncover proves to be too powerful for the two of you to contain, I encourage you to find a therapist who is at ease working with the emotional vividness of the deeper mind and understands the importance of attunement and empathic presence in supporting neuroplastic change.

As we begin, rather than immediately digging around for memories that may need healing—a primarily left-mode processing approach that is rarely effective—we can rely on our deeper minds to offer abundant possibilities. *The primary principle of this work is to allow it to unfold according to its natural pattern, slowly or swiftly, in small bites or larger doses, always without coercion or judgment about how it is supposed to happen.* Our brains are hardwired to move toward integration, so offering our flow of implicit memory and dissociated neural nets safe haven will, by itself, lift one of the constraints that keeps certain circuits in our brains separate from the flow of the larger system.

No need to worry about where to begin because daily events will often bring some aspect of memory close to the surface as a starting point. In your journal, you may want to accumulate a list of experiences in which you feel like *your visceral response is out of proportion to the event—either in the direction of increased agitation or sudden emotional deadness.* This change in magnitude is often the signal that you are reacting to the release of old flows of energy and information, touched by what is happening in the moment. As a means of defense, sometimes our systems escalate, and sometimes they shut down . If you jot down the situation and the bodily feelings that came up, you will have a good chance of being able to activate the same neural pattern when you are ready to focus on memory work.

Ideally, your listening partner will be present when you begin to explore this process, so he or she can provide support as your compassionate witness—perhaps offering a few words of guidance as you go through the steps below, as well as the comfort of presence, as memories emerge. It will help to read through these steps a couple of times before beginning to practice. There is also a summary of the steps in the box after this more detailed version.

1. In preparation for this more advanced practice, spend a few moments settling into your caring observer state of mind, cultivating the intention to be both awake to the inner world and kind toward whatever your mind offers.

2. Then, either open yourself to experiences in the last day or two, or focus on one of the experiences from your journal, asking your mind to bring to conscious awareness the unsettling event that most needs help.

3. Sit in receptive attention, not seeking to move your mind in any particular direction. This part is particularly important because we need to give our deeper mind's right-mode processing an opportunity to speak without being directed by the left-mode need to know. With a little patience and practice, you will notice that most of the time, a recent memory will arise as a picture, words in your mind, a surge of emotion, or a wave of bodily sensation; or the journal experience will become more vivid in those ways.

4. Once that memory is present, focus your mind on the bodily sensation associated with the memory as best you can. Focusing on the body takes us to the root of vertical integration that draws on predominantly right-mode processes and gives us a means to tug on earlier-formed neural nets that contain the same sensations.

5. Ask your deeper mind to show you an earlier time when your body felt just like this. Again, sit in receptivity and openness as best you can, keeping your focus on your body. If you feel resistance to doing this, also notice and nonjudgmentally accept that. When we have needed to keep painful and frightening experiences out of awareness for a long time, there can be understandable internal concern about such exposure. Put in neurobiological terms, the neural nets of protective dissociation have been reinforced, sometimes for decades, to provide for our survival. There is good reason to be grateful for the service provided by these internal blockages. They have both protected us from being overwhelmed by disruptive memories coming up from our deeper mind, and formed a barrier so that incoming experiences will not cause additional pain to our wounded inner world. At first, encountering these protectors may be as far as you can go with the process, and it can be extremely

helpful to just sit in gratitude with "them." In time, they will respond to kindness and patience, opening the door to your deeper mind.

6. Frequently, our minds will carry us to the next step inward, to an implicit or explicit memory, or to a symbolic image that captures a felt experience. Implicit memories will often manifest as an increase in bodily sensation and emotion, sometimes accompanied by a sense of wanting to move the body in a certain way, but without a story in pictures or words. Our earliest attachment experiences are encoded in this way. Explicit memories often make their appearance as scenes from the distant past, sometimes in the form of still photos, sometimes as moving pictures, sometimes as conversations in the mind. Our capacity for explicit memory begins in the second year of life, but isn't solid until we are 4 or 5 years old. When a symbolic image arises, it is often our mind's summary of a repeated felt experience—a tiny roly-poly bug in the corner of a huge carton, a child with a transparent body, a balloon disappearing into the sky. Whatever arises, our most important task is to receive it with gentle curiosity and ample care. When we can, we stay in our caring observer, creating a safe, contained space for our limbic world. Our listening partner's presence adds a second caring observer, strengthening the neural circuits of regulation and comfort.

7. For most people, when memories arise, they feel as though they are observing the scene or experiencing the sensations from a distance. When that is the case, we want to bring our caring observer into living contact with the energy and information in the memory. Just as you can walk into each room in your house, you can move toward any experience in your mind. For example, if my deeper mind brings me to a memory of my child self, alone in my bedroom, I can walk toward her, look into her eyes, or place my hand on her shoulder. Then I can let down the boundaries between my caring observer and my limbic child a bit to let her feelings and sensations flow into me. We might call this *empathy through identification*—with one part of our mind feeling felt and understood by another, with the neural circuits of our middle prefrontal cortex sending regulating, soothing fibers to the amygdala as part of the dance of integration. We can approach any symbolic representation of our experience with the same care and attention. If you arrive in the memory from the viewpoint of your child self or completely swathed in the sensations and feelings, simply abide there, while encouraging your caring observer and your listening partner to hold the experience.

8. As the memory unfolds, either through awareness of the events or through a pattern of sensations and feelings, our task is to track, track, track. We want to allow as much of the memory to come into our awareness as we can, while remaining within our window of tolerance—that space within which our caring observer or our listening partner's caring observer can remain connected to the limbic experience without being overwhelmed by it. If you feel you are

moving beyond your capacity to stay in connection, by opening your eyes, breathing deeply, slowly pressing your feet into the floor, and focusing on the room and your listening partner you can help shift the energy more into the present moment, reducing your activation.

Neuroscience teaches us that when we make the implicit, explicit and provide an experience that disconfirms the one in the original memory, we alter the energy and information in the neural nets holding the remembered experience. For example, if we call into emotionally vivid awareness a time when we felt humiliated, and at the same time, we feel valued, received, and understood by our caring observer and our listening partner, this new experience begins to modify the old, forever changing the way that memory is experienced. The more accurately the new living experience provides an emotionally vivid disconfirmation of the original implicit mental model formed in earlier experience, the greater its efficacy (Ecker, 2008, 2010; Ecker & Hulley, 1996, 2000a, 2000b, 2008; Ecker & Toomey, 2008). Because the conscious mind seeks coherence, it can't accommodate two opposite conscious knowings, so seeks to dissolve one. Sometimes a single experience of disconfirmation is sufficient to shift our old implicit knowing into a new pattern. Often, as enough of these experiences accumulate over time, we change the way we perceive ourselves in general—in this case, as a worthy person—not only in a particular memory.

9. We are beginning to have evidence that these tender, revised neural nets may remain open and available for strengthening for a number of days before they are re-stored in their altered form (Ecker & Toomey, 2008; Suzuki et al., 2004). In the days following memory work, we can assist this change by visiting the new state of comfort and resolution often. Both aspects are important. Comforting presence weaves the circuits of regulation between the amygdala and orbitofrontal cortex, and focusing on the resolution itself strengthens the change in implicit knowing. Calling the visceral experience to consciousness several times a day and sitting with it for a few moments will do a great deal to add neural strength to this new, more integrated state of mind. For you and your listening partner to hold the new experience steadily through the week will add the power of interpersonal integration to the experience.

10. When the memory naturally rounds itself out—sometimes simply shutting off when your mind determines enough has been processed, sometimes following the memory to its conclusion—it can be helpful to consciously bring the part you encountered in the memory into the present. Your caring observer can extend that invitation by encouraging the younger part to notice that he or she now lives with the adult self and that he or she is in *this* room rather than the old family home or wherever the memory took place. This movement in time is important because even explicit memories have an implicit layer, and that part has existed outside time in the eternally present past. Now, it is

becoming part of the actual past where it will exert less disruptive influence on the lived present. Consciously assisting this process can deepen and hasten this kind of temporal integration.

11. Drawing and journaling can be powerful aids in moving toward the integration of memories. As you may already have discovered, drawing with the nondominant hand can give expression to right-mode processing that isn't accessible to words, and journaling may give containing form and shape to what emerges as the implicit becomes explicit. As you experiment with creating pictures and stories, you will find your own unique best way to use these resources. Even though the busyness of our lives may pull us away from these more time-intensive endeavors, it will be valuable to try these modalities as a way of illuminating additional implicit strands and consolidating explicit gains.

12. This is demanding and tiring work, so it is important to rest deeply during periods of time when you are in the trenches of memory with yourself. Rest also enhances the neural conditions for the new energy and information of the altered memory to be integrated through the activity of the medial prefrontal cortex and associated circuits, the so-called "default network" (Fox, 2008; Greicuis et al., 2008; Horovitz et al., 2008; Raichle, 2010).

During this period of intensive reflection and openness to the shards of memory, we will work our way through this cycle many times until the process becomes a well-worn and trustworthy path within our brains. As mentioned above, one way to identify an opportunity is to notice any out-of-proportion responses we have to current circumstances—rage at a child's toys lying about, deep shame welling up because of a small mistake we've made, sobbing when we say a temporary goodbye to a loved one at the airport. At the other end of the spectrum, we may feel dead when we know it would be appropriate to feel sorrow or anger. Our caring observer will gain skill in spotting these hallmarks of memory dis-integration as opportunities for healing work. After a few experiences with the process, you will find your own rhythm and pattern, only needing a brief outline to keep you on course. In the box below, is a summary of the steps that can act as that guide.

Reviewing the Process for Integrating Memories

1. Settle into your caring observer.
2. Open your mind to any troubling experiences you have had in the last few days.
3. Wait with kind attention and curiosity for your mind to bring you the recent memory.
4. When it arrives, focus on the bodily sensations associated with it.

5. Ask your deeper mind to take you to an earlier time when your body felt just like this.

6. Wait with kind attention for your right-mode processing to bring the earlier memory to you, whatever form it takes. When it arrives, receive it with your caring observer's gentle and curious attention.

7. If you are observing the memory, slowly move toward it with warmth and respect, allowing yourself to merge with the feelings and sensations. If you are within the memory when it arrives, stay with that, inviting your caring observer to hold the experience.

8. Mindfully track, track, track as the memory unfolds as far as it is able. Call to mind and body the perception and experience in the present that disconfirms the implicit knowing in the memory. *Note: If the memory feels like it is going to overwhelm you, open your eyes, breathe more deeply, press your feet into the floor, and focus on the room and your listening partner.*

9. Strengthen the neural net of the new state of comfort and safety as well as the disconfirming experience throughout the week by returning to the end point of the memory work frequently.

10. As the memory naturally rounds itself out, consciously bring the part you encountered in the memory into the present.

11. As you feel inclined, draw to give expression to the implicit and journal to assist the movement from implicit to explicit.

12. Get some rest so your mind can integrate the new experience.

We will all be involved in this process of memory integration throughout our lives, attending to parts of our unfolding experience that don't naturally fall into their coherent place. Comfort and understanding aren't always available in difficult or traumatic times, but we can always return to the neural pathways that hold these dis-integrated experiences and draw them into the compassionate embrace provided by our integrating brains. Extensive work in this area is the best preparation for helping our patients integrate their own memories. When our minds hold well-worn paths for this process, we are able to walk with confidence into their inner worlds with them. Not only will the practice of memory integration flow effortlessly, but our personal experience of increased coherence and the well-being that results from gathering up the shards of memory will support our patients' willingness to undertake this journey as well. In the next chapter, we explore the inner world from a different but complementary perspective: that of states of mind. Taken together, our awareness and personal integrative healing in these two realms can become powerful allies in our commitment to fostering mental health and kind relationships everywhere we go.

Chapter 4

Fostering an Empathic
Inner Community

Our deeper mind, and its influence on our daily experience, can be viewed through the lens of time as a series of accumulating memories. As they become more integrated, these memories unroll like a magic time-traveling carpet whenever we look back along the history of our lives. We can also encounter our inner world as a community of internalized relationships that continually makes itself known in the patterns of our external relating. A playful father is seen internally side by side with his laughing daughter in memories of times past, and today's adult woman often has a preference for joyous living. A lonely, mournful mother gently swings on the porch with her young silent son at her side in memory, while the current-day man unfailingly falls for melancholy women who cannot absorb the comfort he offers. Internalized pairs like these form the substance of the multiple states of mind living within each of us. Rather than a single self, we are a community responding to inner and outer events with all the relational resources shaped by our past.

Let's pause for a moment to sense our reaction to the idea of a community inside—which might be anything from "Of course" to "That's weird" or "That's baloney." Adopting the stance of your caring observer, sample your body's response to the idea as well. Then write a few descriptive words about both your emotional and bodily states. At any point in these preliminary practices, it would be helpful to engage with your listening partner.

_____

_____

_____

_____

_____

_____

As we begin this investigation, I want to acknowledge the wonderful work of Richard Schwartz (1997) in developing internal family systems therapy. Our slightly differing approaches to this work rest on the same foundation of experientially discovering the multiplicity and malleability of the inner world at about the same time. This single reference is to acknowledge that commonality and also recognize that my work here does not derive from his.

Neurobiological Basis of Inner Communities

Neurobiological research suggests to us that we begin absorbing the *intentions and emotions* of others at least from birth (Dobbs, 2006). These are encoded together with the firings of our *sensory system*—sights, sounds, textures, tastes, smells—as well as with our *response* to our experience of the other person—including the activation in our body, nervous system, limbic region, and cortex. Because what fires together, wires together (Hebb, 1949) and then survives together (Post et al., 1998), we subjectively experience these neural nets as an internalized relational pair (or group, if the interaction involves more than one other person), filled with the flow of energy and information that permeated the original interaction as we received and perceived it. This is an important sentence: These states of mind (1) continue to interact as a *pair/ group*; (2) their ongoing interaction is infused with the *relational quality* of the initial interaction; and (3) what we encode is influenced by our *neuroception* and *perception* of the encounter. I am borrowing the word *neuroception* from Stephen Porges (2007) to talk about the way we begin to respond to and internalize others even before we are consciously aware of the process. Once we become aware, we can talk about our *perception* of the encounter. Both are influenced by the encoding from previous experiences. As we discussed in the last two chapters, our earliest relationships form a lens of implicit memory that becomes the expectation through which we see other relationships, so we don't come to any new encounter with a clean slate.

Let's walk through a fairly detailed example. Matt's mom brought him to therapy when he was a little less than 4 years old because he was jumpy and afraid of new people. After she shared some family history, I began to form a picture of Matt's internal world. His father was frequently angry with everyone in the household, creating an internal pair of scared child–loud, scowling dad. The father sometimes looked at his son when he glowered and yelled, and sometimes looked at someone else, but either way, Matt was always drenched in towering waves of anger. As a result, his amygdala became hypersensitive, telling his nervous system to be on guard for the next onslaught, unless he was with someone who was both calm and familiar. At those times, the waves could subside, although they never completely went away. In addition, since everyone was afraid of his father, Matt had no refuge and no comfort, so the neural nets holding this internalized pair remained mostly dissociated from the rest of his developing and integrating brain. Attunement integrates; lack of attunement maintains dissociation. As a result of both these implicit and explicit memories, when meeting new people, Matt's relational brain would energize his nervous system as he prepared to defend against the next disruption. We can perhaps feel these two flows of energy and information happening simultaneously. At the implicit level, this youngster was always prepared to be scared, and at the level of states of mind, this internalized father–son pair was not able to integrate with the child's developing brain. This meant that when an internal or external event touched these neural nets, Matt would experience an overwhelming sense of fear, whether or not something truly frightening was happening. We might picture these aspects of Matt's brain as shown in Figure 4.1.

When Matt was 4 years old, his maternal grandfather came from Israel for his first visit. In one of our parenting sessions, his mother told me the story of their first meeting. Matt didn't sleep well for a few days before Grandpa arrived. When it was time to go to the airport, he had a stomachache and felt like throwing up, then hid behind his mother as Grandpa came out of the security area to meet them. As her father embraced Matt's mom, he reached his hand down toward his grandson, who shrank onto the floor. In an inspired gesture, Grandpa sat down on the floor, too, right in the middle of the airport, and was gradually able to penetrate the thick haze of fear that was shrouding his grandson's vision.

It was a long visit, and over the weeks, Matt and his grandpa became fast friends, overcoming the language barrier through play and creating the beginning of a laughing grandpa–joyous grandson internalized pair. Then, one day, something irritated the older man, and he turned his scowling face toward his grandson—who had no part in the irritation. The expression on his grandfather's beloved face awakened the rageful father–terrified child pair, flooding Matt's body and mind with the familiar signals of danger. He threw himself on the ground, hiding his face and screaming. Considered from the present-day viewpoint of a small expression crossing Grandpa's face, this seemed like an enormous overreaction, so Matt was sent to his room to get calm—something he was not able to do on his own. Sobbing in terror (coupled now with abandonment), he eventually fell into an exhausted sleep—and an opportunity to

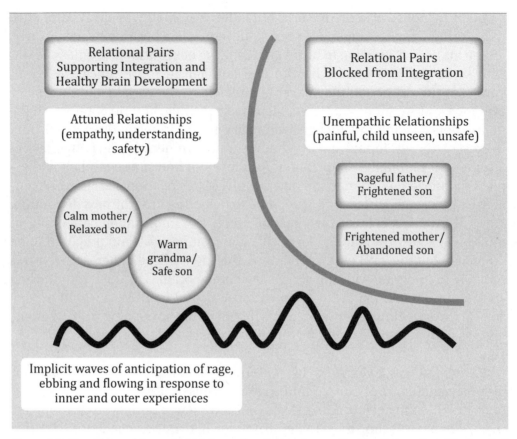

Figure 4.1. Two Flows of Energy and Information Supporting or Blocking Integration. The implicit continual activation of the child's nervous system in preparation for defending against the father, and the split-off pair that is unable to integrate because no empathic other comforted and understood the boy in regard to these particular experiences.

comfort the frightened child was missed. We can see that both the implicit strand of wariness and the dissociated internal pair are already playing a role in how new relationships unfold even in a boy of 4.

If Matt didn't have help with resolving the tension between the members of this inner pair, in adulthood we might find a man who continually has to cope with an agitated sympathetic nervous system, and who may respond to perceived threat with either fight (angry father) or flight (frightened child). *Either member of any pair can come to the surface when present-day experience activates the neural nets holding that duo.* Often, we think much more about the native half of the pair—our inner child, for example. In reality, the imported person has an equally active life within.

Experiencing Your Inner Community

Let's see if you can locate one of your pairs internally. Engaging first with your caring observer, call to mind and body someone with whom you have had a longstanding relationship that has been mostly positive. Allow one or more scenes from that relationship to come into your mind, bringing the accompanying bodily sensations, emotions, and possibly behavioral impulses. Notice how the inner encounter colors your experience in the present moment. Write a few descriptive (rather than explanatory) words about your encounter with this internal pair, being open to the state of mind and body of the other person as well as your own. Looking into the other's eyes can provide a gateway into the experience of that person's internal world.

_____

_____

_____

_____

_____

_____

_____

_____

_____

_____

_____

_____

As your mind moves about in the sea of memories associated with this person, you may notice that more than one pair developed within this relationship. With friends, for example, perhaps the dominant experience is one of companionable goodness, with many memories belonging to an empathic friend–empathic friend pair. However, there might also be a second, smaller cluster of memories in which you experienced a lack of attunement with this friend, creating a pair of clueless friend–disappointed friend. With a sense of curiosity and kindness, go back to your inner pair and see if there are further aspects that come to mind. Then write a bit about that experience from the viscerally felt viewpoints of both people in the pair. As we become attuned with these states of mind, we participate in, rather than guess at, the inner world of the pair.

_____

_____

_____

_____

_____

_____

_____

_____

Engaging your caring observer once more, invite your deeper mind to bring forth examples of times when both people in this pair became active in your relational life. You may become aware of pronounced or subtle shifts in your body as you move from one person in the pair to the other. Notice changes in perception, behavioral impulses, and emotions as well. You may become aware that your mind wants to judge those experiences as good or bad. See if you can create space in your mind to regard that judgment with kindness also. Then take some time to write about the events that called up this pair and how each person made his or her presence known. If you run out of room here, you may want to continue in your journal, and you may want to compare notes with your listening partner at this point.

_____

_____

_____

_____

_____

_____

_____

_____

_____

_____

_____

_____

Differentiating our Inner Community Members

When we do this kind of exploration, we are engaging in a process of *differentiation*, looking and listening for the discrete inner voices that make up the larger flow of our relational experience. One patient said, "Before I began to look at *who* gets active inside, my mind felt like a huge ball of confusion, a three-ring circus—only without the rings, just everything milling around." In that tangle of energies, he was not able to find a single focal point to begin the process of coaxing order out of chaos. However, as we adopted the viewpoint of states of mind, he began to distinguish the visceral experience of his "absent father's presence" from that of his clinging mother. An absent father can indeed have a presence—in this case, one that constantly whispered, "Detach! Hide!" in his inner ear, costing him three marriages by the time he sought help.

As we have discussed, our brains are complex self-organizing systems that operate by certain rules. The part of the pattern relevant for this process is that, in complex systems, *differentiation precedes linkage*—and that these two processes together constitute the creation of a new, more integrated state (Siegel, 1999). As we are able to engage our curious and compassionately observing mind in the process of distinguishing our inner pairs, we may find that we can approach the states of mind carrying the wound with a greater degree of regulation. This increased regulation then allows pairs that have had an independent/dissociated existence to become part of a linked community that fosters well-being and opportunities for relational goodness for the whole person. By working with each member of the pair, we gain even greater differentiation. Then, as the tension between the two resolves, this pair becomes available for integration with the ongoing flow of brain processes. Initially, the inner imported other may feel like a foreign intrusion in our mind, but, in reality, this person is shaped from the same neural sea as those parts we experience as native. By the time we are internally aware of our community members, they are all an integral part of us. If we are in a healing process, this means that they partake of an impetus toward wholeness that the outer prototype may not share. This is hopeful, indeed.

Practicing Inner Community Integration

In the rest of the chapter, we are going to follow this integrative path, first meeting our inner community members in a process of differentiation, then engaging with them in a way that promotes their empathic integration. Although each of our inner communities is unique, the mind's propensity toward integrating empathic states of mind and isolating those that carry uncomforted pain means that there is a certain overall *layered structure* that seems to apply to most of us. Figure 4.2 offers one way of visualizing this inner world.

As you spend some time digesting this diagram, notice with kindness whether your body wants to move toward or away from this information. Where on the continuum from wariness and hesitation to curiosity andopenness do you find yourself? It may be helpful to write a few descriptive words about your inner world's response to being seen and understood in this way.

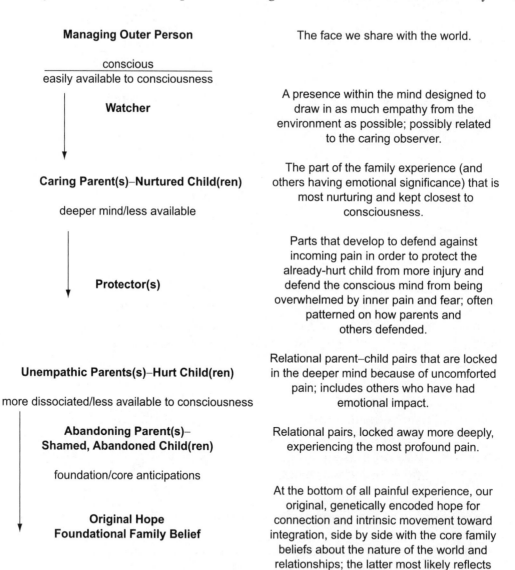

Managing Outer Person — The face we share with the world.

conscious
easily available to consciousness

Watcher — A presence within the mind designed to draw in as much empathy from the environment as possible; possibly related to the caring observer.

Caring Parent(s)–Nurtured Child(ren) — The part of the family experience (and others having emotional significance) that is most nurturing and kept closest to consciousness.

deeper mind/less available

Protector(s) — Parts that develop to defend against incoming pain in order to protect the already-hurt child from more injury and defend the conscious mind from being overwhelmed by inner pain and fear; often patterned on how parents and others defended.

Unempathic Parents(s)–Hurt Child(ren) — Relational parent–child pairs that are locked in the deeper mind because of uncomforted pain; includes others who have had emotional impact.

more dissociated/less available to consciousness

Abandoning Parent(s)– Shamed, Abandoned Child(ren) — Relational pairs, locked away more deeply, experiencing the most profound pain.

foundation/core anticipations

Original Hope Foundational Family Belief — At the bottom of all painful experience, our original, genetically encoded hope for connection and intrinsic movement toward integration, side by side with the core family beliefs about the nature of the world and relationships; the latter most likely reflects implicit mental models.

Figure 4.2. Inner Community Prototype. While every inner community is unique, the way our brains process empathic moments in contrast to painful or frightening experiences creates a layered structure that we can picture like this. The content of the layers will develop according to the particular circumstances of our lives.

The Brain-Savvy Therapist's Workbook

_____

_____

_____

_____

_____

_____

Within us and with our clients, some members of the inner community may feel hesitant to be discovered. Sometimes inner children are wary of all adults, and internalized parents who have been abusive are often resistant at first. However, the resistance will usually soften as we remind ourselves that these inner others are us. As we said above, this distinction is crucial, bringing hope for internal resolution even if external parents never change.

Identifying Inner Community Layers

Now we're going to begin to make this general framework of internal layers personal. Settling into your caring observer and using the diagram in Figure 4.3, we are going to start to identify which parts of ourselves and which parts of those we have internalized might inhabit the various layers. Consider this a preliminary estimate, more aimed at getting a feel for the layering process than accurately identifying all the states of mind having various degrees of integration or dissociation. Approaching this task with curiosity, openness, and acceptance can give you inner ease that will encourage these states of mind to make themselves known. More will become available if we approach this as a listening project rather than digging around in our minds with the shovel of our left-mode processing. Receptivity is the key.

• Our *managing self* is generally our social face as exhibited by our familiar roles: mother, father, therapist, child advocate, artist, gardener. Acquaintances frequently identify us via these roles. Allow your mind to run through your week to see which states of mind most frequently interact with the world.
• The *watching self* stands at the gateway between your conscious life and your inner world. The neurobiology of this particular state of mind is not clear at this point. Many patients have memories of a watching self, at a very early age, well before their brains had sufficient maturity and integration for a caring observer to emerge. However, when we experience this aspect of ourselves, there can be strong similarities with that kindly observing state of mind. At other times, it seems as though this watching self goes through a similar learning and developmental process as the rest of our mind; some watchers feel broken and overwhelmed by events, and then are able to gain strength and

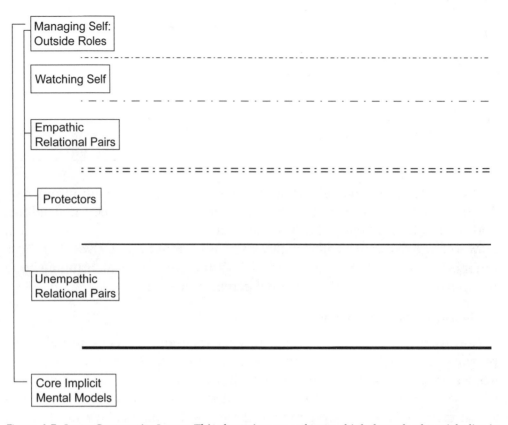

Figure 4.3. Inner Community Layers. This chart gives us a place to think through who might live in each of the layers, in preparation for allowing our right-mode to create a picture that captures the inner experience. The lines go from broken to bold and solid, indicating, in a general way, the degree of separation from our conscious awareness.

perspective with support. People have sensed their watching self as a fox perpetually sitting on the edge of every sand tray, a pair of kind eyes, a bodily sense of alertness and wider vision—yours will be equally unique. Settling into your caring observer, be available to anything your deeper mind might want to share with you about this part of your inner world. If nothing comes up for now, it will likely become clearer as we deepen the process of inner community awareness.

• *Empathic relational pairs* usually remain below the level of conscious awareness, but are often easily accessible if we direct our attention toward meaningful moments in the past. With just a glance at my early years, I can experience the presence of my fifth-grade teacher and my schoolgirl self, for example, getting a visceral sense of warmth, containment, and connection. These empathic pairs are integrated into the flow of our brains and support our resilience, belief in connection with others, solid sense of self, creativity, and the many specific and unique positive qualities of life shared by those whom we internalize. Most of the significant people in our lives have offered us several relational flavors, so it is the usual case to have part of someone in this layer and part in another. I'm aware of a sliver of my father in this empathic zone as my body feels him toss me playfully in the air when I was very young, even though much of him resided in the dissociated depths until therapy released him. Opening yourself to whatever information may come from your deeper mind, jot some notes about your possible empathic pairs on your chart.

• Our *protectors* may surface when either an internal or external event causes our sympathetic nervous system to activate in the presence of a perceived threat, and we leave an integrative state to focus on how to defend ourselves against the pain or fear we anticipate. The tactics of our defensive strategy—or in subjective terms, the tools our protectors use—stem either from capacities we have developed based on our genetic predisposition, temperament, and relational learning, or from the protective styles of those we have internalized. If school was our safe place, we may jump into left-mode processes to avoid an onslaught of feelings. If we have or had an angry parent, we may push back aggressively when threats come our way. If our parents ate lots of sweets to quell uncomfortable feelings, we may feel pulled toward Baskin-Robbins at moments of intensity. It is interesting to note that these protectors are bidirectional, defending our outer functioning self from too much disruptive contact with the pain-filled and frightened parts of our inner world, as well as building walls against outside experiences that may touch places inside that are already wounded. While we learned many of our strategies in relational settings, this is one layer that is sometimes without obvious pairs. Again settling down inside, let your deeper mind bring you a preliminary look at your protectors and take a few notes on the chart.

• Now we are going to begin to gently explore those states of mind generated by painful or frightening encounters that have remained uncomforted—the *unempathic relational pairs*. This seems an appropriate name since they were generated in situations that lacked empathy and continue now to be out of empathy with one another. If we were to think about how this layer might have looked when we were children, teens, or young adults, it might be significantly different than now. Over time, some painful states get reinforced, or, if we are fortunate, later empathic relational experiences release some of these states of mind from their timeless prison so that they can join the ongoing flow of the integrating brain. We may find several aspects of a particular parent—one that shamed us, one that ignored us, one that struggled to be in sync—together with the corresponding child, teen, or adult. Others outside the family who have had a significant hurtful or frightening impact may also come to mind as we reflect. One athlete I worked with found that his lifelong swimming coach was not only the largest presence internally, but that the patterns generated in that relationship were also the most consistently destructive in his current life. For now, identify any pairs/groups that come easily to awareness, and see if you can sense how each person in the couple or group continues to express him- or herself in your daily life. Make a few notes about who is present on your chart.

• *Core implicit mental models* lie at the foundation of our ongoing experience. But preceding these models we find two originally optimistic, genetically driven forces: a *push toward neural integration*, and a *yearning for attachment* with nurturing others. Unless we have organic constraints, these two genetically grounded surges may grow dim, but they never go out completely. So, side by side with this hopeful energy and information, our *core implicit anticipations* about how life will unfold, generated in our earliest relationships and perhaps modified in later relationships, continually whisper to us about our value, what we can expect in relationships, how hopeful or despairing the world is, and more. Those implicit knowings that were generated via empathic encounters will support growth and join with the wired-in movement toward integration and attachment. Those resulting from unempathic relationships will continue to be at odds with our inborn movement toward healthy development. They are laden with our earliest (and sometimes ongoing) painful and frightening experiences, encoded as implicit memories in our body, nervous system, and limbic region, and often finding expression through our cortically based beliefs about life. Although these implicit experiences were generated in relationship, they often show up more as flows of energy and information that run like thematic rivers through our daily lives. They may make their appearance as pairs, but often they do not. Settling once again into receptivity, see what you can sense about the strength of your hope for connectedness, implicit flows that support this hope, and the specifics of implicit mental models that whisper of despair and separation from self and others. When you feel ready, make a few notes on you chart.

As you complete this preliminary exploration, sit with your chart a bit, allowing any additional input from your deeper mind to come into your awareness. Spend a moment to sense any judgments you may have about how you did this process, making a brief note in the space below about how these judgments influence your body and feelings. Then hold the entire process in the kindness of your caring observer for a bit.

_____

_____

_____

_____

We have begun an integrative process with which our minds will now want to cooperate. In this state of heightened awareness and curiosity, vivid dreams, flashes of awareness through the day, intuitive insights, increases in bodily sensations or flows of feeling, and shifts in perception may signal our deeper mind's efforts at integration. It will be helpful to give words to these experiences in your journal as they arise.

Creating an Inner Community Drawing

Having gotten a feel for the layers inside, we're now going to give our right-mode processing an opportunity to enrich and deepen this experience. Our relational lives are encoded originally in right-mode processing for the most part, and our visceral knowing about our inner community arises first in that largely wordless part of our brain. This makes drawing a supportive medium for moving more deeply into our felt awareness of the inner community. You will likely need the room provided by a large sheet of paper—a 2 x 3-foot piece of newsprint may be just right. Now select whatever pencils, crayons, or markers offer you a range of colors and textures—and aromas, in the case of crayons—that feels right to your body. Taking a few minutes to attend to your deeper mind's preferences about materials will help you settle into a listening state of mind.

Keeping Figures 4.2 and 4.3 nearby, create your unique inner community drawing, replete with colors, textures, images, photographs, or anything else, as your intuition guides you. Your drawing may have both words and pictures; feel free to use your nondominant hand to create the flow of color and form, and your dominant hand to write legible words, as your inner wisdom suggests. Some drawings are quite simple, whereas others expand into murals. There are two examples at the end of this chapter (Figures 4.4 and 4.5) if you feel you would like a little visual prompting. Although they appear in black and white, they were originally in color, so some of their aliveness is lost in translation. Your inner community picture may look nothing like either of these. I have seen drawings that emerged as circles, landscapes, abstracts, and rows of boxes—some mostly words, some with no language at all. The most helpful start is perhaps being able to visualize the layers, and then let that information flow organically onto the paper in whatever form it chooses to take.

Those in the empathic layers and those whose pain and fear keep them locked in the timeless depths will likely have a very different visceral impact on your body and feelings. Those pairs whose warmth and support have fueled the goodness in your life from behind the scenes often leave a feeling of integration and ease, whereas those whose ongoing conflict and misery you have had to keep at a distance bring changes in nervous system activation, bodily sensations, surges of feeling, behavioral impulses, and perceptions about self and others—all in the direction of dis-integration. As best you can, allow all of these to arise within your receptive mind. It is helpful to set aside an extended period of time for this initial drawing experience—perhaps an hour or two.

Before setting out, notice how your body, emotions, and perceptions are responding to the task ahead. What is your anticipatory mind telling you will happen? Write a few words so you can compare your expectation with the actual experience.

_____

_____

_____

_____

_____

_____

After completing your project, spend some time with it. As part of this reflection, you may be able to deepen your awareness of the influence of these pairs by selecting one of the empathic duos and placing one hand on each member of the couple. Sense the flow of energy and information from first one, then the other. Notice any difference arising in your body, feelings, and perceptions as you alternate between the two, and describe it here.

_____

_____

_____

_____

_____

_____

_____

_____

_____

_____

Now do the same with one of the unempathic pairs, cycling back and forth between receptivity to your native state of mind and the imported state of mind of the other person. You may find that your mind spontaneously shows you times when each of these has been active in your daily life. Spend a few moments describing this experience as well.

_____

_____

_____

_____

_____

_____

_____

_____

_____

If you have any pairs that don't include a native state of mind (e.g., your parents relating to one another), try the same practice with them, alternating between the energy and information of each one, then describing the experience.

_____

_____

_____

_____

_____

_____

_____

_____

_____

Now, set aside your drawing for a day or two. When you have another leisurely period of time, return to see if there is anything you would like to add or change. At any point in this process, you may have included your listening partner, or you may choose to share your drawings with each other now—an experience that is sure to deepen your awareness and may even provide a platform for beginning to integrate some of the isolated community members. For this particular meeting, it may be especially helpful to listen without feedback for an extended period so that each of you has the chance to sink deeply into what the drawing can bring to the surface.

Working with Each Member of the Inner Community

This project is leading us through a profound experience of *differentiation*, allowing us to hear and experience the discrete flows of energy and information that guide our lives—sometimes outside our awareness, sometimes well within consciousness. This lays the groundwork for the next part of the process: working internally with each member of the inner community who is not linked with the ongoing flow of the developing brain. In general, the empathic pairs are well woven into our healthy experience, whereas some protectors, unempathic pairs/groups, and the core implicit paradigms of family pain and fear usually remain outside of integration. For many of us, it probably makes immediate sense that we would be able to make living contact with our native states of mind—our inner children. However, because of the way we internalize others' deep intentions and layers of emotion via mirror neurons and resonance circuits, we seem to often be able to access the intention and emotion beneath the obvious surface expression of our non-native pairs as well.

Experimenting with this, as we will later in the chapter, will make it more tangible, but let me share a brief experience. Seeing a raging father inside, my patient, from her caring observer state of mind, asked him what was hurting or scaring him. With gentle persistence, she kept asking, looking into the angry eyes inside. Then she saw the intensity fade into fear, accompanied by a sick feeling in his/her stomach. At that point, we were able to bring safety (the disconfirming experience), comfort, and regulation to this father state of mind, resulting in compassion rather than animosity between this inner father and daughter.

How is this possible? We are just beginning to understand how much we internalize from others (Iacoboni & Badenoch, 2010; Mukamel, Ekstrom, Kaplan, Iacoboni, & Fried, 2010), but we might imagine that the deeper layers of emotion that are present beneath the defensive display of anger may also leave lingering signs in facial expression, posture, gestures, eye gaze, and prosody, a trail of clues that can be apprehended by our calm, receptive minds. Or could it be that we internalize much more of another's inner world than the nascent research regarding resonance can confirm for us at this point?

Based on decades of experience, almost everyone I have worked with has been able to approach the internalized others and move through these layers of experience, gradually and permanently dissolving the outer emotion into the more tender inner experience that is driving the hurtful thoughts, words, and deeds. By resolving the pain and fear in both members of the couple, the disruption between them is ameliorated, and the misery in the individuals as well as the relational tension between them dissolves. Many of the messages we carry about relationship are encoded in the interactions between these interwoven states of mind. They are often locked in the timeless implicit realm, leaving their mark on our most vulnerable relationships in surprising ways.

Let me share an example. Cerise came to me because all of her close relationships ended in her pulling away when emotional intimacy became intense. We worked our way through a number of childhood memories in which she had felt overwhelmed by her mother, but this work did not produce much change in her relational apprehensions. We began to ask her deeper mind to guide us toward the source of her unchanging fear. Almost immediately, she felt the behavioral impulse of backing away while she saw an image of her parents in their ballet of mutual avoidance. We began to focus our attention on these two internalized dancers. Much as we did in working with her child states of mind, we asked both inner parents, in turn, what was hurting or scaring them. Requesting inner guidance again, she got the sense that we could begin most easily with her father. Waiting in receptivity after her question about what was happening inside him, Cerise began to sense in her body the same behavioral impulse to pull away that she felt when a lover wanted increasing connection. Staying with this movement and letting her father know that we would remain with him, she began to have an intuitive sense of his frightening loss of connection with his depressed mother, experiencing it not in a cognitive but in a visceral way. We offered understanding, comfort, and continuous connection—key elements of what had been missing for him throughout his childhood, and thus a disconfirming experience. In her body, she could feel his emotional tension release as the brain circuitry holding this locked-away pain opened to the new relational experience we were offering.

We then moved on to do the same work with her mother. However, Cerise experienced these wounds as so much more complex and variegated that many inner experiences were required before her inner mother began feeling a relaxation similar to what she had experienced with her father. We can trust this inner process to unfold in its best way, even when it takes a long time. Sometimes the tangled implicit memories that hold a particular inner state in place require us to simply be present over and over again as we make our way through the layers. In the presence of safety and care, through the kind and gentle holding that creates a cradle in which painful experience can emerge, the healing will happen as quickly as it can, even when that is slowly.

As we worked with Cerise's mother, we noticed that her inner father watched the process between us and his wife. Instead of backing away, he seemed curious and open to understanding the nature of the wounds underlying her behavior. As soon as her mother came to peace, she and her husband were able to form a more connected relationship internally. Their implicit dance of avoidance was over.

If we think about this process in neurobiological terms, we can imagine that Cerise's mirror neurons and resonance circuits encoded her father and mother's dance within their daughter, wordlessly embedding the dynamics of their relational pattern in her developing brain. Intertwined with the neural net holding the experience of the child who had absorbed this lesson, we would find the representation of her parents continually whispering their message of caution and avoidance. In the absence of comfort and attunement, such neural nets remained dissociated from the ongoing flow of her developing brain, with a strong probability of activating within Cerise when someone approached her with the offer of close connection.

As Cerise became receptive to her inner parents, she created a safe space to encourage neural integration. In this state of mind, her middle prefrontal region was engaged and open to attune with (and therefore integrate with) this formerly isolated circuit. Because we consciously approached the states of mind that brought the experiences her parents needed—safety, continuous presence, and comfort—the disconfirming experiences needed to change the implicit patterns they carried were available. Subjectively, her parents' fear and pain were soothed and regulated. These circuits were no longer operating alone, but instead connected by care and understanding to the integrative regions of her brain. After completing this round of resolving experiences, Cerise's encounters with her parents in other memories that had originally contained this same emotional valence of avoidance now showed them softened and more available to one another. It was as though working with them around their pains and fears had soothed similar pangs throughout the system. The resolution of her inner parents' avoidance turned out to be the key to change in Cerise's outer life. Once the two inner parents gained empathy for and connection with one anther, her fear of closeness became a distant memory that she experienced as a brief behavioral impulse to back away that she no longer needed to follow.

It is most important to know that these experiences are not guided visualizations, imaginary creations, or cognitive guesswork. Instead, we are paying attention to the body to follow the neural trail back to experiences encoded at earlier times in our lives. We are entering the limbic sanctum where old wounds lie entombed—not too dramatic a word, given the degree of dissociation and the fact that these memories are literally frozen in implicit timelessness. Because we used our sensory and nervous systems, as well as our mirror neurons and resonance circuits to create this inner community, we subjectively experience these states of mind as living beings within us. They whisper of hope and despair, tell us how close or distant we should be with others, whether we are worthy or worthless. Because we are a bundle of genetic influences, temperament, and experiences beyond the family, their inner presence doesn't always determine what happens next. However, when they carry significant dissociated pockets of relational pain, their influence is powerful, often arising at the moments we are most vulnerable.

In truth, we are these states of mind. Once we have internalized someone, he or she is part of our neural real estate, not really a foreigner anymore. However, when the caring observer part of our brain (or the brain of another attuned person) is allowed to create the right (i.e., sufficiently nurturing) conditions, we can differentiate these flows of energy and information so that they become part of the larger stream of our developing and integrating brain. Patience and gentleness are the keys to making our way back through the inner generations. Our states of mind not only seek to be rescued from their prison, but they also need be heard, felt, and seen, sometimes repeatedly, before the aspects of their experience are sufficiently gathered and known to be able to integrate them.

Recognizing that working with our inner community is a lifelong endeavor, let's begin our practice. Working at such a deep level can touch some powerful bodily sensations and emotions. Doing this process with your listening partner can, as always, broaden the field of empathy and expand the window of tolerance for both.

You might begin with an upsetting current-day experience, as we did with memory resolution, or simply ask who inside needs help.

- From there, you can engage the now-familiar process of attending with kindness to the bodily sensations and behavioral impulses that arise as you sit in receptivity.
- When you feel settled in this experience, ask your deeper mind to take you to a time when your body felt like this before.
- As a memory comes to mind, sense the pair (or group) that had this experience. This may be a native part of you and an imported state, or two imported people—or more.
- You may immediately have a right-mode sense of which person is most available for relationship in the moment. If not, asking internally almost always yields a felt answer.
- Approaching the person you are going to help, allow your internal boundaries to come down sufficiently so that you have a visceral sense of the other's experience. As we felt in memory work, this kind of empathy through identification provides rich attunement that directly allows your caring observer to link with the experience of the formerly isolated part—an act that creates neural connec-

tions between the limbic and middle prefrontal regions in preparation for integration with the ongoing flow of the brain.

- Receptively listening to whatever emerges and providing a disconfirming experience will gradually lead to resolution, which many feel as a release of tension and calming throughout the body. This may happen in a single internal visit or unfold over many.
- As this state of mind feels settled, you can then turn to the other member of the pair and offer the same kind of empathy through identification, receptive listening, and well-crafted disconfirmation.
- As these transformed states of mind take root, holding them consistently over the next week or so can help to strengthen the tender new neural nets.

As with memory work, internal pairs sometimes come up from implicit-only memory, perhaps a mother–infant pair. At times, we will still be able to distinguish one flow of energy and information from the other; at other times, we may be completely taken over by first one and then the other, feeling the bodily sensations and emotions of a frightened child, followed by the visceral experience of an insecure mother. If each of us can trust that our mind will bring us the next pair that needs to be healed in order for neural integration to continue, then we can sit in receptivity with all of this, sensing the kind of disconfirmation that our intuition suggests.

You will have many distinctive experiences as you pursue this work, and no words here can begin to capture the unique surprises in store. After your first passage through this process, talk with your listening partner about how both of you experienced it. Was this an entirely unique experience? What was most meaningful for you in the process? What was most difficult? How was it to do this with another person? Then write a bit about this initial experience, so you can look back on it after you have done this process a few more times.

_____

_____

_____

_____

_____

_____

_____

_____

_____

_____

_____

_____

_____

_____

_____

_____

_____

_____

_____

_____

_____

For many people, this kind of work brings linkages that were thought to be impossible. The father of one of my young patients died without speaking to his son about the disruption caused by the father's mental illness. This left a residue of anger and hatred in this young man, along with fear of getting close to anyone. We worked for many months with the internal pairs that held the chaos, shame, and terror of his father's bipolar rampages. At the end, inner father and inner son were at peace, filled with understanding of what each had endured and assured of the love they felt for one another beneath the illness. Had we worked only with the child part of him, the disruptive father would have remained inside, a constant source of fear. Perhaps even more significant is the loss this young man would have endured by never having an inner father who could provide nurturance. These living bridges can change the quality of life in unforeseeably healing ways.

As you make your way through several iterations of this process, notice your mind's response to the pace of the work. Sometimes the length and depth of holding required to change deep pockets of disruption can be tiring or disheartening. Take a few minutes here to be gentle with any impatience, discouragement, or sense of hopelessness that you are experiencing in your body, feelings, or thoughts. Sharing these with your listening partner can ameliorate any strain and reinvigorate hope. Write whatever comes to body and mind about the quality of your process with your inner community here.

_____

_____

_____

_____

_____

_____

_____

_____

_____

_____

_____

_____

_____

_____

_____

_____

_____

_____

_____

_____

You may also find it helpful to write some notes in your journal and to revisit the inner community drawing to sense changes in integration that may have developed as we brought connection and attunement to those inside.

This process of self-discovery that includes both those who have hurt us and aspects of ourselves that may have been hurtful is built on the certainty that people cause harm because they have been hurt, not because they are inherently evil. Neurobiological research supports that idea, recognizing that some genetic conditions as well as relational learning lie at the heart of the difficulty for those whose dysregulation leads them in the direction of doing small or grievous harm.

The notion that people are doing the best they can, even when what they do is harmful, often pushes strongly on old learnings and on fears that if we develop compassion toward those who have hurt us, we will become vulnerable to them again. In Chapter 6 we will take a long look at the art of compassionate release. For now, take a moment to notice with kindness your body's response to the idea that we are all doing our best; then write some descriptive words. You may also find that various inner community members have different views on this subject. Note that, too.

_____

_____

_____

The Brain-Savvy Therapist's Workbook

_____

_____

_____

_____

_____

_____

_____

_____

_____

One reason we may find it difficult to acknowledge that we are doing the best we can is that we are left with this question: Can we forgive ourselves and still find the will to heal the implicit roots of our harmful actions? Sometimes when the pressure of guilt is removed, we may relax and turn away from the work. Finding the balance and integrity to commit ourselves to being attentive to our inner world takes a good deal of dedication and an ongoing awareness that we can either work to heal the deeper layers of our inner community or we can live by the pain- and fear-filled rules that keep them trapped within us. I don't believe there is a third option. However, when we are able to find that dedicated intention, the outcome of approaching our inner community in this fashion is neural integration accompanied by profoundly expanded compassion and well-being.

In these last three chapters, we have focused primarily on gaining conscious, whole-brained awareness of right-mode processing that often exerts its influence from below our conscious awareness. As therapists, we are constantly immersed in some level of implicit activation because relational experience has its roots in the right. Any healing that we do in these deep places will benefit not only ourselves, but our patients—and everyone else with whom we interact. We have paid particular attention to areas of dissociated neural nets, in the form of memories and states of mind, as well as the eternally present past of the implicit sea in which we swim all the time. As we integrate more of these formerly isolated parts of our inner world and shape the implicit sea in the direction of optimism, healthy attachment, and well-being, our compassionate embrace will expand. We will also find that the life story we tell ourselves will begin to develop in the direction of greater coherence, aliveness, and meaning. In the next chapter, we explore the nature of narrative and then do some writing.

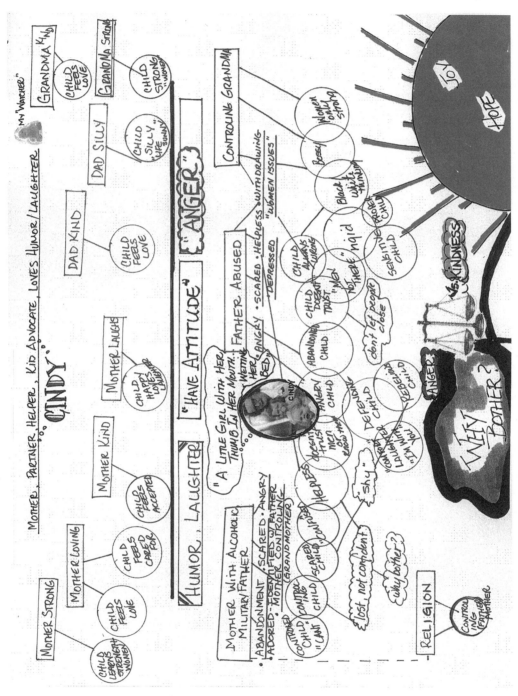

Figure 4.4. Cindy's Inner Community. This inner community drawing was originally done in color. In the unempathic lower regions, the predominant color is red—mainly down the middle in the anger and abused father zone. The regions to the left and right—the "why bother?" zone—are shades of blue. These same colors extend upward into the empathic zone for each person as well. At the lower right is a large yellow sun that seems to shine its rays of hope over the whole drawing.

Figure 4.5. Ben's Inner Community. This community was also originally drawn in color. Abstract and without words, Ben translated his layers into images drawn with his nondominant hand. He could easily do the exercise of placing his hands on the pairs even though his eyes couldn't identify the boundaries between inner community members with any certainty.

Chapter 5

Joining the Strands of Narrative

Marcus and I had spent a number of months connecting with one another to create a well-knit neural foundation for securely entering the right-mode jungle of his unpredictable, fragmenting childhood. During parts of our process, he felt impatient because he longed to be in an intimate relationship, but observed that his life wasn't moving in that direction in spite of our work together. As we continually invited his inner world to take us in the direction of his obstructions to easy connection, memories and states of mind emerged to be met with experiences that were containing, warm, and secure. At one point, we were drawn to interact with his internalized father, a man whose rage continued to unsettle Marcus's relational experiences, sometimes pushing him to become easily angry at small slights, sometimes leading to contraction and fearful disengagement in the face of any kind of confrontation—all outside his conscious control. As we moved through this particular patch of work, Marcus said, "This is a strange sensation, but I literally feel as though the ground is more solid beneath my feet." He went on to describe how he could recognize in his body when his internal father–frightened child pair was becoming active and could now "reach inside with a hand of reassurance so that I don't respond from those feelings." Together, we recognized that this was a clear indication that his inner narrative was changing, that his felt sense of his own presence and place in the world was shifting from tentative and defensive to solid and internally conscious. Together, we held these new foundations in our awareness while we continued to work with the pair toward full resolution. Marcus reported increases in stability week by week, with the therapeutic work flying along at this stage. He said he felt that it had "a life of its own," reporting his subjective experience of the momentum of neural integration. As his new awareness of solidity emerged, his outer relational life became richer as well.

The Neurobiology of Narrative

We are storytelling beings; the propensity for meaning is written into our genes. Our brains drive us to make meaning of our experiences, resolve conflicts, and prepare for the future. It has also become clear that this activity does not begin when we consciously shape experience into language. The internal process of knitting together neural networks related to our history and its impact on what we will do next goes on all the time, below the level of conscious awareness. The distinct set of circuits dedicated to this endeavor accounts for 60–80% of all energy used by the brain (Raichle, 2010). When our minds become occupied with a task in the external world, these circuits dim a bit, but the energy required for the outer task only amounts to about a 5% difference, so the internal weaving process continues even when we are consciously busy (Raichle, 2010).

The circuits involved in this integrative process include the medial parietal cortex (an area involved with remembering events relevant to our personal life), the medial prefrontal cortex (a region devoted to self-reflection and autobiographical memory), and the posterior cingulate cortex (a highly integrative region near the back of the brain) (Buckner et al., 2008; Raichle, 2010). Taken together, they do the job of weaving the strands of experience into the felt story of our lives (Mason et al., 2007). This knitting together also happens as we fall asleep, possibly during dreaming, and under anesthesia (Greicius et al., 2008; Raichle, 2010). In fact, the effort to interlace the old and new is such a pervasive human propensity that researchers have named these circuits the "default network" or "default mode network" (Gusnard & Raichle, 2001; Raichle, 2010).

Interestingly, these regions of the brain also become active when we are thinking about the past or future, or focusing on the internal world of another person (Buckner et al., 2008)—this latter activity culminating in creating a narrative of the other in our minds (Siegel, 2007). It is likely that this pattern of activity reflects our brain's continuing push toward integration and coherence within ourselves and with others in our world.

As tenacious as this network is in integrating everything available to it, it is likely that *circuits that remain dissociated from the overall flow of the brain stay literally out of the loop of the default network*. This is such an important understanding because it points the way toward the heart of therapeutic work. In the last three chapters, we have created opportunities for our brains to bring implicit neural circuits out of temporal isolation or dissociation, encounter new information, and enter the flow of our integrating brains. Such a process opens the way for both our lived and spoken stories to change. To deepen our understanding of this integrative process, we begin by looking at possible ways in which our narratives may have been shaped by our early and ongoing relational experiences.

How Relational Experiences Shape Narratives

In general, if the raw materials of the story—our lived experiences—are *fragmented*, then our inner tale will be similarly choppy. If the raw materials are *well knit together* and emotionally resolved, our narrative will convey a sense of flow and ease. More specifically,

- If our early relational experience *lacked the crucial glue of emotional vividness*, our story will likely be peopled with cardboard cutouts and factual events with little or no meaning.
- If our early experience was *mostly chaotic*, our story will often be jumbled, and we will have difficulty sorting out past from present.
- If our inner world is *awash in a sea of implicit pain and fear*, the underlying themes of our story will be colored with this palette in ways that often escape conscious detection.
- If we have had positive relational experiences interspersed with deeply painful, uncomforted times, *pockets of dissociated memories and states of mind* will create some troubling gaps in the flow of our story.
- If, for whatever reason, we are currently *receiving an impoverished flow of information from our right-mode processes*, which provide the energy and information for crafting a subjectively true story, then the left-mode may simply make something up out of random pieces of unrelated experience in its effort to make sense and meaning of life.
- If we had parents whose own mental health gave them the capacity for attunement, they likely *helped us tell our stories when we were small*, co-narrating their way through experiences that scared or hurt us, in a process that knit our brains into networks that support the ongoing formation of a full and meaningful inner narrative.

While these are some of the main patterns we see in therapeutic work, each of our narratives is unique, and many of us will move between patterns depending on the subject matter.

Let's check in for a moment. Settling into your caring observer, reread each sentence in the list above in a leisurely and receptive way. Notice your body's response to each of the patterns. Does your deeper mind resonate with some more than others? Does your mind want to pull away from some patterns? Also attend to any judgments—positive or negative—you may have about how you are paying attention or about being asked to do this kind of noticing. Write a few descriptive words about your bodily and emotional responses. You may also notice how these responses impact your perceptions of yourself, your relationships, and your world at large.

_____

_____

_____

_____

_____

_____

_____

_____

_____

_____

We may often think of our narrative as the story of our lives in words. Indeed, this is the culminating (and constantly emerging) stage of narrative. However, as we saw in Marcus's story, prior to that, we create a lived narrative out of the basic stuff of our experiences. The trajectory of this narrative shows up in how we relate with one another, how we speak about ourselves in the privacy of our mind, what we choose to do for a living, how we respond to stress, and whether we find life to be hopeful or grim. Our story tells itself to us in the flows of feeling that are most ingrained in our bodies, nervous systems, and brains, and in the behavioral impulses that arise in our muscles without our conscious bidding. Take a moment here to listen to your body's story of _this_ moment. What sensations and impulses to move are arising? Where is there tension or ease in your muscles? What flows of feeling accompany your body's story? What are you saying about yourself as a result? Listen with kind attention and then give words to your experience with as much descriptive detail as you can.

_____

_____

_____

_____

_____

_____

_____

_____

_____

_____

_____

In many ways, this felt and lived part of our moment-to-moment narrative is anchored in the complex activity of right-mode processing:

- In the mostly wordless reception area where the amygdala takes input from the thalamus and assesses the meaning of incoming experience, a layer of implicit memory is created, significantly influenced by what was previously encoded in this meaning-making, safety-assessing region of our brains.
- When conditions are sufficiently stable, this flow of energy and information integrates with information coming from the hippocampus, creating an explicit memory—a story with a beginning, middle, and end.
- When there is no obstruction, this story is passed along to the integrative circuits of the middle prefrontal region, adding the dimension of autobiographical awareness and meaning—the feeling that may eventually become words such as "*I* am having this experience now, and it *means* that my life is. . . . "
- At the same time, the neural streams from our muscles and joints, belly, heart, and nervous system contribute to the flow of information creating the moment's story.
- Sensory input and representations from previous experience add cortical voices as well.
- Over time, this experience is added to our ongoing story through the action of the default mode network.
- Mirror neurons and resonance circuits "reach out" to incorporate the other person into the story throughout the experience as well.
- However, at the root of the story we tell ourselves resides the coloration given by the initial response of our limbic circuits to the internal or external encounter.

Let's take a moment to see if we can discriminate these various flows of energy and information by stepping into our caring observer and entering a pleasant or meaningful moment in our history. Invite awareness of the initial response to the experience—eyes, face, full body, energy, surge of emotion. Then sense how these elements gather into an explicit story, and then into a story with "I" at the center. Notice the messages from your muscles, joints, belly, heart, breathing, and level of activation. Notice the presence of one or more other people in each element of the accumulating story. Then settle into the complete experience—like a guitar chord fully strummed and now enjoyed in all its harmonies. With kindness toward yourself, as best you are able, capture each individual layer in descriptive words. Then write about the meaning of the experience for you.

_____
_____
_____
_____
_____
_____
_____
_____
_____
_____
_____
_____
_____
_____
_____
_____
_____
_____
_____

Listening for Types of Narrative

With these last three practices, we are beginning to see the unique ways in which our lived narratives assemble within us, in preparation for consciously and verbally weaving the discoveries of the last three chapters into our spoken story. This movement from felt/lived narratives to spoken narratives often happens spontaneously, as we have said, because our brains are wired to create stories of personal meaning out of experience. However, depending on the relationship between the raw materials coming from the right-mode and the left-mode expression, we can recognize three kinds of narratives: coherent, cohesive, and fictional/defensive. Each carries distinct markers, both objectively and subjectively. As we move forward, it will be helpful to engage our caring observers so we can listen to our deeper minds talk with us about the ways each of these types of narrative may be part of our brains' meaning-making repertoire.

Coherent Narratives of Secure Attachment

Let's start with the experience of *coherent narratives*. As we receive such stories either from ourselves in the privacy of our own minds or as we listen to others give accounts of their lives, we may sense these unfolding pictures are *emotionally vivid*, held with considerable *equanimity*, filled with a *richness* that can contain both positive and painful aspects, and convey a sense of *wholeness*, both in terms of the overall story and the human beings who inhabit them—as though little is missing or hidden. Subjectively, we may feel simultaneously at ease and energized as we receive this flow of energy and information, which fosters both neural and interpersonal integration.

The capacity to create such narratives arises when our brains (sometimes combined with the brains of attuned others) have taken in experiences and passed them through the various stages of integration in the right mode (body, amygdala, hippocampus, middle prefrontal region—along with the many other circuits associated with these)—without encountering constraints that split off portions of the experience or block the conscious awareness required to encode explicit memory. Once the middle prefrontal region receives this energy and information, the flow to the left/linguistic mode picks up the naturally integrative process. The story may then take shape in conscious awareness and in words—a whole-brain event. We could argue that words can never fully capture the richness of the experience, but when words are buttressed with the presence of the felt experience, the whole can be passed to another person—who receives both the shaping of the words and the visceral sense of the experience through the dense interpersonal medium of mirror neurons and resonance circuits (Iacoboni, 2007; Siegel, 2007, 2010b). Words alone are truly dead, but words infused with felt reality are alive with meaning that extends throughout the body and the interpersonal world.

Securely attaching parents create the neural circuitry in which coherent narratives naturally develop. These parents are resolved enough in their own history to accurately see their children—a capacity that leads to a synchronous dance of attunement and regulation for all. By the time their children are 2 years old, parents have established the practice of co-storytelling, and when life presents challenges, parent and child share the story over and over until the youngster relaxes in resolution. This relational connection builds the integrated brain structure that supports coherent narratives.

All of us probably have parts of our history that are held as coherent narratives, arising from times when attunement was sufficient to support integration of the experience. The earlier practice of calling a pleasant or meaningful memory to mind culminated in expressing the memory in words—very likely a piece of our coherent narrative. Reflect again, for a moment, on the visceral feeling of this supportive memory. Do you sense both the fullness and the specific contours of the memory? Do you sense it connecting with other memories into an overall perception of life's possibilities? Or does this experience stand in contrast to so many other painful memories that your core perceptions are more defined by the troubling recollections? Write a few words about this.

_____

_____

_____

_____

_____

_____

_____

_____

_____

_____

Even in the latter case, if we continue to be attentive to our inner world and persistent in rescuing pieces of ourselves that have gotten caught in dissociation because of uncomforted pain and fear, our self-told story will continue to draw newly understood fragments into the integrating whole. It isn't so much that pieces of memory and parts of our selves have *become* dissociated, but rather that they *never achieve integration* in the first place, and thus remain locked in the timeless basement of the eternally present implicit past.

Lifeless Narratives of Avoidant Attachment

In these next few paragraphs, we are going to explore any narratives of insecure attachment that may be lingering in our nervous systems, bodies, feelings, and perceptions. Each narrative has a particular flavor of incoherence based on the way the circuits that lead to narrative were wired in our earliest relationships. It will be especially helpful to join with your listening partner in this process. You will have greater freedom to move deeply into your experience if you have an empathic and attuned companion.

Parents who are largely locked in their left hemispheres, in a world of tasks rather than relationships, can offer only *avoidant attachment* to their children. The resulting emotional deadness appears to come from a lack of integration between the two modes of processing, so that the left mode does not receive much enlivening, meaning-making input from the right. The resulting disconnection from the body's rich input regarding our emotional state and from the right-mode circuits that allow us to move in attunement with another means that we are stranded in an emotional desert. The implicit message that relationships don't matter is belied by heart rate measurements that show the nervous system activating when attachment is offered, but the signals stay out of conscious awareness (Siegel, 1999).

We might picture a mother devoted to helping her child complete homework, but unable to sense the need to comfort him when his best friend moves away. This pattern of response generates an attachment narrative in which staying in connection with people is equated with doing tasks well. One patient said to me, in a flat voice, "I have been married three times. I do everything my husbands want, and then they leave." It made no sense to her. When we talked about her early life, she reeled off a series of events that felt like dead fish slapped on a counter—that is the actual image that came into my mind. There were no living people in any of her stories. I felt empty and bored (a resonant response), then sad at the lack of aliveness and relational energy (a caring observer response).

Take a few moments to sense if your narrative contains relationships that have this quality. Sitting in receptivity and asking your inner world to take you to such times may open the door. Then write descriptively and share with your listening partner what you discover in your body, emotions, and perceptions as a result. As you listen to your partner, notice your own bodily and emotional responses, then enlarging your perspective to gather it all into your compassionate embrace.

_____

_____

_____

_____

_____

_____

_____

_____

_____

_____

Anxious Narratives of Ambivalent Attachment

Sometimes parents are partially overwhelmed by their own implicit unrest, and so offer periods of attunement interspersed with times when limbic activation sweeps them away into a world drenched in the past. This inconsistency and unpredictability are hallmarks of *ambivalent attachment*. A father delights in his 3-year-old daughter's earnest investigation of the bugs in the backyard. Their mutual curiosity draws them into a playful conversation with a snail—and attunement blossoms. Then she decides that rubbing mud on her face is a compelling and joyous idea. Her father, coming from an upbringing in which certain kinds of behavior are deemed the most valuable, loses contact with his playful self to scold her sharply for getting dirty. This kind of alternation between connection and rejection wires in anxiety and a sense of chaotic right-mode upset as the child waits for the next abrupt shift into rupture. For both of them, the right-mode circuits of regulation are fragmented and unreliable, so emotional balance, flexible responses to changing conditions, as well as attunement and empathy are sometimes off the table.

The narrative arising from such conditions often sounds like a jumble of events that scrambles the past with the present. Because the eternally present past of the dis-integrated implicit intrudes regularly on the integrated sense of past–present–future, the story embodies an anxious quality of dysregulated right-mode surging. My young patient, her eyes darting back and forth, breathing quickly, talked about her mother's death with a mixture of tenses. "She *died* a painful death, so scared. She *is* always like that, scared. She *was* so jumpy. If anything *scares* her, she *closes* up like a sea anemone when it's poked." Her sympathetic arousal touched my nervous system, raising my heart rate. Becoming aware, I was able to provide the disconfirming experience of regulation, first of myself, then of her. In childhood, her mother's escalation had set her own young sympathetic circuits on fire, so calm presence could now be part of the antidote.

Going back through your own history, do you sense important relationships that had this unpredictable, anxiety-inducing quality? Can you also sense the impact on your body, emotions, and perceptions? Then write about what you discovered, also sharing it with your listening partner. As your partner then tells you about his or her experience with this exercise, notice the impact on your body, feelings, and perceptions—then see if you can gather all of this into your caring observer.

_____

_____

_____

_____

_____

_____

_____

_____

_____

_____

_____

_____

_____

_____

Fragmented Narratives of Disorganized Attachment

Both avoidant and ambivalent attachment styles allow us to develop a coping strategy: strong development of the left mode at the expense of relationships, in the case of the former, or a cornucopia of tactics for gaining temporary regulation to relieve the anxiety, in the case of the latter. However, in the worst of circumstances, when we are terrified or utterly rejected on an ongoing basis, all capacity to cope fails. The person we depend on to keep our minds intact is instead the source of our *disorganization*, so we are left with the impossible choice of disintegrating through isolation or through our attempts to connect—what attachment researcher Mary Main (2000) calls "fear without resolution." These early and enduring impacts leave a vast implicit narrative sea in which we see ourselves as garbage, as monsters, as evil—a litany of perceived characteristics we use to explain the reason we are unlovable and destroy our mothers. At the level of our bodies, we may bounce from the severe sympathetic dysregulation of terror to the complete collapse of helpless fragmentation—or become trapped with both those responses raging in our bodies at once. This nervous system narrative of utter disorganization often overwhelms language entirely, leaving us with no story beyond the one unfolding in our physical being.

This nervous system narrative is paralleled by the earliest of implicit mental models encoding the compelling conviction that things can only go from bad to worse, that we should not exist, and that we must fail at everything we attempt—all of these rooted in our experiential inability to attract an attuned, affirming response from our mothers. These models can be so powerful that they guide every action in life, creating a circle of replication that appears to have no exit. It is as though we are fully locked in the implicit underground, unable to find even a strand of alternate experience in the present day to cast a different light on our beliefs about ourselves, our place in the world, and the nature of relationships.

We will speak more about these particularly tragic circumstances in Part II, letting interpersonal neurobiology add to the picture of hope for recovery even in these cases. In the presence of such negatively embodied narratives, our

The Brain-Savvy Therapist's Workbook

mirror neurons and resonance circuits may vibrate with intense disruption. Our thoughts may become fragmented or simply inaccessible. We may be overcome by feelings of helpless, hopeless despair and anguish. Images of physical fragmentation or dismemberment may even form in our minds. Picturing the brains and minds of our patients can help us provide a stable container for the bodily, emotional, and perceptual flood being experienced by them and ourselves.

For now, reflect for a few moments on any times in your life when you experienced this kind of terror or utter repudiation, sensing if there are any disorganized pockets within you as a result. These rise up in the nervous system, body, and mind as rapid breathing or holding the breath, behavioral impulses to pull away from offers of attachment, a sense of helpless collapse, inability to form a coherent sentence, profound confusion, self-disgust, and a host of other severely disruptive experiences. If patches of upset emerge as you open to these inner dimensions, allow you and your listening partner to hold them with compassion and kindness. Then, as you emerge from the disorganization, write and share your feelings and perceptions about those places, providing your partner with an opportunity to do the same.

_____

_____

_____

_____

_____

_____

_____

_____

_____

_____

_____

_____

_____

_____

_____

_____

Unless we have been raised in monochromatic families where everyone's attachment was the same, we likely have bits and pieces of all the styles, with perhaps one pattern we express most often. Being sensitive to our various relational responses, particularly noticing which comes up in what circumstances, can add a layer of awareness and processing that will help us integrate the neural nets into a pattern of greater security. We can know that when there are dissociated pockets, our acts of awareness, disconfirmation, and comfort spring the locks and invite these neural nets into the flow of time and the company of parts already liberated. As our narrative grows fuller with the addition of each new parcel of energy and information, in addition to an ever-more coherent narrative, we may well find an exponential increase in depth of awareness accompanied by a growing sense of flexibility and freedom from automatic responses. With what we know about how much neural firing takes place out of conscious awareness compared to what actually reaches consciousness, it is clear that our well-being and relational capacity depend on our brains being as integrated as possible—a lifelong task that can become a joyful part of our human experience.

The Cohesive Narratives of Insecure Attachment

Each of the insecure styles of attachment generates its own particular kind of *cohesive narrative* (Siegel, 2007)—meaning that each is based on a partial picture of our history due to what is and isn't wired together in our brains. As we know, in the big picture, our verbal left-mode processing depends on the autobiographical flow of energy and information from right-mode processing as the raw material for the emerging story. When that flow contains a limited and unhealed piece of energy and information, we can only tell ourselves the story that makes sense of this sliver. In fact, we will often have more than one story based on different and not-yet-integrated pieces of the experience held by various states of minds.

Let me share an example. My patient was witness to daily yelling from her second year of life when her father returned home from the trauma of the Korean War. By the time she saw me in her 30s, she had three stories about that time and her life in general. One was a compassionate adult narrative that reflected her understanding of her father's trauma and resulting rage. The second unfolded via her contracted, agitated body whenever she was in the presence of intense energy; her nervous system was unable to discriminate between angry and joyous intensity, so reacted in either case. The third gave voice to these lingering effects of the dissociated neural nets and implicit flow of these experiences with her father, although she was not consciously aware of its origin: "I think, by nature, I am like a delicate flower who needs to be sheltered from this dangerous world. I do better by myself, at home, even though it gets lonely at times." I believe she sought therapy so that she could have a safe companion to ease her loneliness. The third narrative gave explanatory voice to the second and remained dissociated from the mature, coherent

The Brain-Savvy Therapist's Workbook

understanding about her father's tragic situation. In terms of her life, the narrow, self-guarding narrative ruled her days.

We can ask, "Which of her narratives is true?" The answer depends on whose shoes we're occupying. In reality, all we ever have is our subjective truth—or truths—and these can be ones that lead toward bondage to old experience or toward the freedom of being able to see with wide-ranging eyes. For her child self, both her fragility and the danger of the world are subjectively true, and for her adult self, the intergenerational tragedy is subjectively true. The difference is that her first narrative could take in a broad range of information, allowing her to develop a compassionate understanding that included her experience as well as her father's, whereas the second and third are based entirely on a narrow strip of energy and information rooted in the implicit flow of her experiences with her father and mental models resulting from that flow. These were also held separate from the larger narrative—literally prisoners of war—until we began to work for their release.

This is the hallmark of cohesive narratives: They are *neurally bound to isolated, unresolved previous experiences*. A small piece of neural real estate in right-mode processing integrates bilaterally (across both hemispheres) with the meaning-making left mode, creating a story based on very limited information. In addition, because the roots are dissociated from the larger flow of the coherent part of our story, we are unable to take in new information that could change the narrative. These memories are effectively locked in a timeless box. In the last three chapters, we have worked to open some of those dissociated pockets and address the time-trapped implicit flow, in preparation for expanding our narrative toward a coherence that more fully supports well-being and attuned relationships.

Fictional/Defensive Narratives

Exploring the final type of narrative, we find that sometimes our minds have difficulty creating either a coherent or cohesive narrative and instead give us a *fictional verbal explanation* of the way we need our world to appear. If we are *not prepared to consciously face the flow of energy and information from the right*, or if that flow is *so diminished that our left-mode processing is getting little input*, or *if we simply aren't paying attention internally*, then our minds will simply make something up to fulfill our need to create story. This made-up narrative can come in the form of a defense—for example, "I'm the most brilliant person in my class, but I don't take tests well"—when a more comprehensive view of the situation would reveal a young women with a mid-range intelligence level that is unacceptable to her parents. It may also show up as a complete fiction to avoid awareness of a lack of information—for example, "We were in San Francisco over the weekend," when the person has no recollection of where he was because the multiplicity of his inner world means that his parts aren't aware of one another. These stories are so convincing that people with strongly separated inner communities do not perceive them as tales designed to cover gaps. With repetition, the neural net of listening to fiction as though it were reality can become that strongly developed.

Although this is an extreme example, most of us can look back at times when we used this strategy, often without conscious decision, to create a sense of continuity in our lives because we either didn't have enough information from our inner flow or we had not given sufficient attention to that inner flow to be speaking from a coherent, whole-brain place. When my neighbor asks, "How are you?" and I say, "Fine!" without checking my actual state, I am participating in a mild form of this activity. Because of our brain's architecture and our need to make verbal meaning, many times a day we may create explanations for our felt state without being connected to the implicit internal source. In order to process the enormous quantity of information flowing into our senses and within the brain, many memory systems operate in parallel, without direct connections to one another, and particularly without connection to the few circuits in the brain dedicated to conscious awareness and language (Milner et al.,1998; Rumelhart & McClelland, 1986). With attention, more of our implicit patterns can come into explicit awareness, connecting the limbic circuitry to the neocortex, which allows us to create coherent, resolving stories across these systems of memory and expression.

It will be helpful to spend a little time reflecting on moments when your storytelling mind made up something large or small to fulfill its need to create a narrative. Rather than seeing this as a character flaw, we can understand it as a symptom of incomplete integration, and hold it with kindness. As times of such storytelling come to mind, write a bit about the circumstances and meaning of the experience here.

_____

_____

_____

_____

_____

_____

_____

_____

_____

_____

_____

_____

_____

_____

_____

Exploring Our Changing Narrative

As we have undertaken our inner explorations in the previous chapters, we have created opportunities for our narratives to become more comprehensive. Formerly cohesive narratives may have dissolved as we have taken in enough new information to have a more coherent picture of the meaning of an experience. This can result in a broader, more comprehensive and compassionate understandings about ourselves and what we can hope for in the world. When I was in the midst of internalizing interpersonal neurobiology (as opposed to learning it in left mode)—a process that was the precursor for many of the practices in this book—I became aware of an internal softening toward strangers who were behaving thoughtlessly in all kinds of daily settings. Instead of tension and impatience, I began to find curiosity and even kindness spontaneously arising more often than not. After a little reflection, I realized that my internal narrative had changed from one that talked to me in a stern, judgmental voice about consideration and selfishness (applied to all beings, including myself) to one that was convinced, at a root level, that we are all doing the best we can, given the state of our brains, minds, and relationships. Over time, that softening extended to myself as well—definitely a harder sell because of my ongoing implicit bath in the waters of parental criticism from toddlerhood through high school. Doing consistent internal work with the memories and states of mind that anchored the self-judgments gradually changed the story I told myself as well. Most interesting, the new narrative of nonjudgment has continued to expand, becoming the centerpiece of all my work as a clinician and proponent-at-large on behalf of interpersonal neurobiology.

As we move down the integrative path, we can now ask how our lived and spoken narrative has changed as a result of the work we've done so far. First, we can begin to shift from the left-mode learning focus that the last few pages may have activated to a more right-mode awareness of listening internally. Now, let's go back to the work we did in Chapters 2, 3, and 4, gathering together the implicit streams, memories, and inner community pairs with whom we have spent conscious time so far. Some will appear in notes in this book, others may have needed the larger space of your journal for a more extended reflection in writing and drawing. Set aside an hour or two to gather these transformed flows of energy and information into one place in preparation for writing a paragraph about what you discovered with each experience. It might read something like this entry, which is adapted from a patient's journal.

> Following a feeling of fear in my body, I saw and felt myself as a child of about 6, with my older brother and father yelling at each other, until my father hit him hard enough to knock him down. I was with the younger part of me, helping to calm and regulate his fear. As I got closer to the child, I could feel how much I believed then that I should be able to stop them, and how my nervous system was running way too fast. Then I just shut down and went away. When my child was quiet and could really feel me with him, we moved toward both my brother and father, asking them what was hurting or scaring them inside so much that they had to fight. My internal father refused to talk with us, but I could feel both the anger and fear inside him. My internal brother was more able to allow us to help him with his big fear of my father and his feeling of needing to protect me. At the end of our work, my body was much calmer, and I was aware that I would need to return to this internal trio to help my father.

Following the example of this kind of healing narrative, it may be possible for us to explore our implicit and explicit stories before and after the healing work we did with a flow of implicit energy, a particular memory, or an internalized relational pair. The man in this example was able to sense how, throughout his life, he had easily felt at fault whenever he was unable to resolve any conflict that happened in his vicinity, whether it was reasonable for him to do so or not. His felt narrative included a tight body, followed by a sunken chest and a desire to get away as a means of skirting around the feeling of shame. Upon reflection, he realized how many times he'd said, "I'm sorry," and how bewildered others felt when he apologized at times that seemed unnecessary to them. As he reflected on these experiences, he felt the impulse to be critical of his apologetic ways, but then was able to hold that experience with kindness and with emerging wisdom about the origin of his automatic self-blame. This shift, based on the increasing availability of his caring observer, represented a substantial change in his narrative.

We worked some more with his internal father in the next few sessions, until we were able to move more deeply into the intention and emotion behind his rage. This led to a sense of deep calm, coupled with my client's ability to look back through the generations to see the legacy of terror and rage that flowed from one male in the family to the next. He said, "No wonder my father was so angry. He never felt like he mattered to anyone. That's how my brother feels now, and I've felt so afraid, whether I mattered or not wasn't even important to me. Now, with a lot less fear, I see that I used to feel that underneath, but now I just feel sad for all of us." Shortly after that, a new felt narrative made its way into his conscious awareness. Two members of his staff got into a heated argument just outside his office door. He felt his body start to tense, and just as his head was about to turn away, he was able to follow *a new behavioral impulse* to watch what was happening with curiosity and kindness. Since it was his job to manage these people, he made a conscious decision to intervene, knowing that he might or might not be able to help them reconcile. When he came to see me, he said that the outcome was unimportant and didn't share what it was. Instead, he was able to sit quietly with the new story in his body, emotions, behaviors, and words. We talked about how his implicit template of the meaning of conflict had changed, allowing for a new behavior to naturally emerge.

We can see that once the process of change is initiated, shifts in the felt/lived and spoken narratives spontaneously support and build on each other in sometimes surprising ways. This is the nature of neuroplasticity as our brain seeks greater coherence, once hampering constraints are removed. Now, calling on your caring observer and inviting some guidance from right-mode processing, take a leisurely time to write a paragraph in your journal about each of your experiences in Chapters 2, 3, and 4. This is another one of those times when our minds may grow impatient at the slow pace of the work. If you feel a familiar push to move on without writing and reflection, see if you can sit with that behavioral impulse and trace it back to its roots in previous experience—many of which may be cultural as well as personal. Doing this without judgment may be difficult, but the effort to do so will build the very circuits that can offer a safe haven for any aspect of your or your patients' inner worlds. Often, an unintended consequence of our impatience with our own process can be either an implicit or explicit expectation that our patients should also move at a certain pace, robbing us—and the healing environment—of attunement, acceptance, and the solid foundation conferred by our confidence in the brain's natural integrative flow.

When you finish this more extended writing, notice—without judgment, as best you can—which experiences have the most life and which seem especially meaningful. Then select one for particular attention right now. Let's begin by looking at this event from the viewpoint of being *within* this experience before it was fully known, embraced, and integrated. What felt/lived narrative did it generate then? You might notice the answer to this question via bodily sensations, behavioral impulses, surges of emotions, or perceptions of yourself and others. In addition, core assumptions about the world of relationships might float into your awareness. Write about these now.

_____

_____

_____

_____

_____

_____

_____

Was a spoken narrative generated from this inner story? Sometimes this type of narrative is a cohesive shaping of partial energy and information from right-mode processing, and sometimes it is a defensive or fictional one that protected you from having to come into contact with something too painful or frightening at the time. A small example of the latter may help. When I felt the developmentally appropriate urge to think deeply about the meaning of life in my later teenage years, my mind told me scornfully that it was stupid to do that. I now realize that this internal response amounted to an attempt to protect me from thinking too deeply about the impact our family's traumatic circumstances was having on each of us. As a result, my mind simply shut off that avenue of inquiry until I was in a solid therapeutic relationship that gave me the safety to come in contact with the destructive impact. In the case of cohesive narratives, our minds help us make sense of a sliver of emotionally vivid experience that isn't available for modulation via a whole-brain process; in the case of defensive narratives, for complex reasons we cannot fully explain neurobiologically yet, the mind determines the time is not ripe for integration of some area of experience and so directs our awareness away from those neural nets, perhaps until sufficient support is available. Often, only in retrospect, when we view the experience from the broader perspective granted by incorporating this piece into our coherent story, can we tell the difference between these two kinds of narratives. Write here about the spoken narrative—either cohesive or defensive—that emerged from your unhealed narrative.

_____

_____

_____

_____

_____

_____

_____

_____

_____

_____

Now, let's look at how the healing work you have done has influenced this particular narrative. Do you sense that either your felt/lived or your spoken narrative—or possibly both—have changed since doing some integrative work with this implicit flow, particular memory, or internal pair? Notice with kindness any widening of your perspective: Does your narrative encompass more aspects of the situation? Do you feel some settling in your nervous system when you think about the event or the inner people involved in the experience? Any difference in behavioral impulses? Any other changes that come to you as you listen internally from your caring observer state of mind? If you don't notice a lot of change yet, we can assume that some constraint is holding your implicitly informed cohesive narrative in place. As you settle inside, allow nonjudgmental awareness of these inner blockages to come forward as well. Our experiences always make good neural sense, so when we are unable to move forward into greater narrative coherence, it is simply our mind telling us that there is more to be done. After leisurely reflection, spend some time writing about whatever you discovered in this process.

_____

_____

_____

_____

_____

_____

_____

_____

_____

_____

_____

_____

_____

_____

_____

_____

It will be most helpful to spend this kind of time with each of the experiences from the earlier chapters. Bringing these inner shifts into conscious awareness means that we will be able to strengthen the new neural nets by directing our attention toward the changes—a process that fosters the integration of our narrative. *Where attention goes, so goes neural firing*—a most important principle to remember in maximizing neuroplasticity in the direction of greater coherence. Bringing in the interpersonal dimension by including your listening partner at this point will also strengthen these new nets and possibly make room for a second angle of vision that may open new possibilities within you—another example of how the various levels of integration, from neural nets to relationships, shape the brain.

As this chapter comes to a close, we can pause to sense the outlines of the unfolding process that is fostering smooth lines of communication between body (including our muscles and joints, gut, heart, and nervous system), mind (thoughts, beliefs, and feelings), and relationships (internally between our parts as well as externally). At this point, we may be able to sense how entering the inner stream from any angle—via implicit flow in the body, memories, or states of mind—creates a neuroplastic opportunity for the other streams of energy and information to gather and be transformed into a more comprehensive and meaningful sense of our lives. The last chapter in this section fosters movement in that direction.

Chapter 6

Practicing the Art of Compassionate Release

About 4 years into our work together, Jack arrived in a contemplative mood—unusual for him. As soon as he came in, he slowly and quietly said, "I was sitting on my front porch last night, and I saw—literally saw—the generations of men in my family all suffering from the same hostile, abusive treatment as children, and then passing it down to the next boys to come along. These grown men were helpless. They had no choice; they had no help; they had no understanding—like a bad root that got planted in time of out of mind and just kept sprouting. I lost track of time sitting there and realized that my chest was too heavy to move, feeling the weight of all those lost boys, including me and my brothers. You and I have talked about it, and I've known all this in my head for a long time, but in that moment I knew it in a different way that leaves me so sad and peaceful at the same time. It makes sense and it's tragic all at once." We sat together calmly with his sorrow until it lifted of its own accord, ameliorated by our acknowledgment and presence. Then Jack said, "What a relief to not have to hate anyone anymore—not even myself!"—chuckling, smiling, then settling again into a beautifully regulated calmness that was new for him.

His former agitation returned by the following week, so we traced it inside to memories and internal pairs still caught in chaos. However, as we continued to do this now-familiar work week by week, Jack also began to have more frequent spontaneous experiences of broad, deep understanding, accompanied by noticeable increases in compassion. We had a new rhythm in therapy, one we would pursue for another year. In his family, Jack had been known as the "clueless" one, skateboarding out of harm's way when he could, putting a layer of sarcastic humor between himself and the chaos the rest of the time. Of course, the whole disruptive family environment was implanting itself in Jack's implicit memory whether he was paying conscious attention or not. As a result, his adult relationships were train wrecks, and these failures eventually drove him to seek help. Now, after considerable courageous work to change his pattern of self-protection, haul dissociated neural nets into awareness, and be vulnerable enough with me to change his implicit relational expectations, he was becoming a stable haven for his troubled brothers.

The Visceral Experience of Forgiving

Let's pause for a moment to sense our inner response to the suggestion that it would be good to follow Jack's path and forgive—compassionately release— those who have hurt us. Even if our moral principles suggest that we be forgiving, our bodies and emotions may have a different reaction. Notice with kindness your bodily sensations, behavioral impulses, and surges of emotion in the presence of this thought—then write a bit. If you find visceral resistance to the prospect of feeling compassion for yourself or others, ask your deeper mind to share what it fears will happen if you grant this much grace. Then write a bit more.

_____

_____

_____

_____

_____

_____

_____

_____

_____

_____

_____

_____

_____

_____

As we ease into the visceral experience of forgiveness, we may find that Jack's is a hopeful story, and one with useful pointers for our own process. The passage from blame, hatred, shame, anger, jealousy, excuse-making, victim-

ization, and other relationally miserable states of mind to compassionate release of ourselves and others is not a smooth process that is accomplished
once and for all. Instead, this latter state emerges in gradually expanding waves
as more pieces of our well-differentiated coherent narrative link to form a story so rich in visceral understanding that increasing nonjudgmental acceptance
and compassion are the natural outcomes. In my view, the healing process is
not complete until our inner world is moving steadily toward this broadly accepting state of mind. Because we know that the people who harmed us also
dwell within us, because of our mind's powerful internalization process, until
we resolve these internal relational conflicts, constraints will hinder our integrative efforts. In terms of our subjective well-being, it may be impossible to
get truly comfortable in our own skin until we secure this kind of internal
peace.

As we progress in this direction, we will likely have more moments when the
intergenerational panorama comes spontaneously to our awareness. This
makes sense because neural integration occurs via a process of differentiation
followed by linkage (Siegel, 1999), as we noted earlier. As we make ourselves
available to all aspects of a particular memory, for example, the differentiated
pieces of the experience (body, emotions, images, internalized other) link and
integrate into a whole experience—which then becomes a differentiated piece
that is ripe for integration with the ongoing flow of the brain. Over time, as we
hold and inhabit them, these islands in the stream begin to coalesce into solid
ground on which we can stand to gaze with warmth and kindness on the flow
of our history. From what may have felt like a box of confusing puzzle pieces
gradually emerges the meaningful pattern of the whole.

Let's pause again for a few moments to see if our minds are ready to bring us
this kind of experience. From the viewpoint of your caring observer, bring your
family of origin to mind. Compassion can come in two distinct flavors, as Jack
noticed: the flavor of understanding and the flavor of empathic identification.
The first has a bit of protection in it because we aren't fully connected to our
body's felt knowing of the impact of this history, whereas the second exposes
us to a felt oneness with the family stream. Research has shown that distinct
circuits correlate with each of these experiences (Singer, 2006). If you have had
a generally secure childhood, it will likely be easier to connect with both kinds
of compassion; however, if your childhood was imbued with considerable
pain and fear, both the panoramic view and the empathy-based compassion
may wait to unfold until your earlier experiences are sufficiently soothed and
your brain has accumulated enough integration to take this next step. This
is one of those places where unhelpful judgments may arise if our minds
aren't ready to give us the full experience. If you can, meet any judgment with
kindness and continue to sit in the presence of your inner family—then write
a bit.

_____

_____

_____

_____

_____

_____

_____

_____

_____

_____

_____

_____

_____

_____

_____

Practices That Foster Compassion

Although this kind of integration will move forward on its own as we are attentive to our healing process, certain additional practices can foster the expansion of our capacity for compassion. One that has proven particularly effective is lovingkindness and compassion meditation (Salzberg & Kabat-Zinn, 2008; Germer & Salzberg, 2009). In lovingkindness practice, we wish goodness for ourselves or others, and in compassion practice we wish for the cessation of suffering—both being altruistic responses to our awareness of the inner state of ourselves or another. The meditative literature uses the word *wish*, but in reality, these practices activate a flow of energy and information that is far more substantial than is connoted by *wish*.

While this meditation has been practiced in the Buddhist tradition for 2,500 years, recent research is revealing how focusing the energy of kindness increases activity in the neural circuitry of compassion—that is, in the anterior insula, a pathway delivering information from the body that provides the emotional meaning of our state or that of another; and the anterior cingulate cortex, which weaves together thought and feeling and is strongly connected to the amygdala (Singer, 2006; Lutz, Brefczynski-Lewis, Johnstone, & Davidson, 2008). Significantly, this activation takes place primarily in the circuits of right-mode processing, our interpersonal brain. In addition, activation also increases in areas of the brain that have been identified as part of our resonance circuitry.

This brings us to the question of whether or not compassion can be developed. Lutz and colleagues (2008) explored the possibility of cultivating such a state through practice, using both experienced and novice meditators. The results revealed that activation of empathy circuits was greater in experienced meditators. In addition, in nonmeditative resting states, the resonance circuits of experienced meditators showed increased activation in response to all voices, indicating a greater sensitivity to others. Since it appears that the capacity for lovingkindness and compassion can be developed with practice, it is possible that the flow toward these states of mind might become stronger than our genetically supported impulse to protect ourselves. This latter focus separates our parts internally and blocks compassionate connection externally. When consistently nurtured, the states of lovingkindness in good fortune and compassion in misfortune may become traits of being with profound consequences for our individual well-being and the health of the planet.

We have already practiced the preliminary parts of this meditation each time we became inwardly focused and unconditionally accepting of whatever experiences arose. From this quiet place, the practitioner of lovingkindness extends goodness toward him- or herself, perhaps using statements such as "May you be well. May you be safe. May you be at ease." If we follow traditional practice, we will say these statements only to ourselves for weeks or months, before radiating this energy to others. This makes sense since as our self-acceptance increases, our ability to understand and hold whatever others bring will expand as well, allowing for a more unimpeded flow of compassion and lovingkindness.

Let's practice. Finding a quiet place and sitting in a comfortable position with feet flat on the ground or cross-legged in a chair or on the floor, invite your caring observer state of mind to notice, without judgment, what bodily sensations and emotions are present. Take your time here as you settle into interiority. Then, as you prepare to extend lovingkindness, you might want to place one or both hands on your heart, an action that connects us to our inner world, possibly through the neurons nested in the heart. Notice, again with kindness, your inner response to placing your hand(s) there. This gesture of connection can bring on a powerful response of many different flavors even before beginning the rest of the practice. Notice the influence on your body and feelings of doing just this much. Then write a few descriptive words.

_____

_____

_____

_____

_____

When you feel ready, radiate wishes for goodness throughout your internal world, saying whatever words of reassurance feel most suited to your state in this moment: "May you be safe"; "May you be well"; "May you be joyful"; "May you be at ease." As you continue the practice, other thoughts may intrude, including judgments about what you are doing. As best you can, *observe, observe, observe* while you continue to radiate lovingkindness to your inner world. If a feeling of suffering arises, you can meet it with compassion—"May you be comforted. May you be free from suffering"—or words of your own choosing. At the beginning, you might do this practice for 10 minutes and then extend the time until you are cultivating this state of mind daily for at least 20 minutes.

After this initial practice, attend to your body, emotions, and perceptions—then describe any changes you notice between your initial state and now. If there are judgments about how you practiced, sense their impact on your body and mind, then release the judgments and notice what shifts. Write a bit about both the meditative experience and the judgments.

_____

_____

_____

_____

_____

_____

_____

_____

_____

_____

_____

_____

_____

_____

The feeling that it is selfish to focus only on ourselves comes up frequently at the beginning of practice, sometimes so viscerally that it is hard to keep hands on heart. If that happens, there may be a root experience somewhere within us that told us it is wrong to have equal regard for ourselves. It can be very helpful to approach this constraint as we did in Chapter 4: by focusing on

The Brain-Savvy Therapist's Workbook

the sensations in our bodies brought on by the resistance and asking our deeper mind to take us to the internal pair that holds this implicit knowing.

At the same time, we have already cultivated another ally that can help us overcome this resistance to wishing ourselves well. The differentiation we have experienced by practicing being the caring observer of our inner processes can give us the ability to stand in two places at once, making it easier to send well-wishes inward to all the members of our inner world. Often, this practice will create sufficient safety for even unseen members of our inner community to come out of hiding/dissociation into this richly healing environment.

Experiencing the Phases of Integration

We have actively participated in quite an adventure since our initial meditation practice in Chapter 1. We may notice that our path traverses the domains of integration that Daniel Siegel (2007, 2010b) articulates. We have prepared our minds to attend to our inner world (integration of consciousness) and rounded up a listening partner to help us regulate our experience and shape our implicit memories (interpersonal integration). After attending to the whisperings of our implicit world (the beginning of vertical integration), we invited dissociated memories and inner community members into awareness to receive the care and understanding that can allow them to move into the integrating flow of the brain (vertical, memory, and state integration). We then observed that our lived and spoken narrative began to shift in response to these inner changes (bilateral and narrative integration), and we supported that process by attending to it in our bodies and giving it words. Finally, we noticed that our minds were moving toward a broader, more compassionate perspective (perhaps the leading edge of temporal and what Daniel Siegel [2007] calls transpirational integration—coming to terms with impermanence and experiencing interpersonal oneness as a lived reality).

We have experienced two phases of temporal integration, the first of which is part and parcel of the implicit becoming explicit. As we have discovered in our bodies and our minds, hurtful and frightening implicit memories imprison us in the eternally present past until they are brought to consciousness and given the integrative time stamp that allows them to be experienced as truly past. In this way, more aspects of ourselves become integrated with this present time. Later in our process, our maturing minds come face to face with the other aspect of time—the underlying existential reality of our mortality and the frequent experience that all things are impermanent. Each of us may or may not choose to look at this directly. As I am growing older (and presumably more integrated), I sometimes have the visceral sense that I don't live in just one body. Instead, those with whom I have shared strong energy carry aspects of me, as I carry aspects of them. I am spread out in time and space, while still living solidly in my own body. It is hard to capture this experience in words, but when it is available, it brings a powerful sense of continuity and communion, and in some way, dismisses death as the final truth.

This sense of interpersonal oneness may also be the beginning of transpirational integration (Siegel, 2007), a state of unity where the words that anchor us to duality begin to fail us. Maybe it is enough to say that we will know it when we experience our departure from the "optical delusion of consciousness" (Einstein, 1950) that enforces the perception of duality, followed by our arrival at the felt conviction of our enduring interconnectedness.

We have each experienced the natural unfolding of these many integrative processes in our own unique way as we moved into greater cooperation with our brain's intrinsic flow toward greater coherence. Quite an accomplishment—and also the first movement in a lifelong integrative symphony. If we take up the practices of lovingkindness and compassion as part of our daily life, we have the opportunity to continue to foster neural integration and expand our awareness of oneness, should we wish. At the further reaches of exceptional mental health, the Dalai Lama (2008) speaks of the leap from empathy for those with whom we are naturally affiliated to universal compassion. He believes that this expansion comes as a result of conscious choice and practice; it does not arrive automatically through increasing neural integration. Several forms of meditation open the door to experiences that may provide the springboard for that leap. Newberg and colleagues (Newberg, d'Aquili, & Rause, 2001) suggest that during deep meditation, the parietal lobe grows quieter, allowing the differentiation between self and other to diminish, so that the meditator has an experience of oneness (Shapiro, Walsh, & Britton, 2003). Whatever we may believe about the origin or meaning of such experiences, they do confer the tangible benefit of shifting our perspective in a visceral way, perhaps similar to the shift experienced by many of the astronauts who have viewed our planet from a great distance and sensed the Earth's wholeness. If this transcendent experience rests on the solid ground of neural integration, it can become bedrock for an internal state of ongoing compassion that generates acts of kindness.

Now, our challenge is to support the ongoing work of integration as part of our daily commitment to ourselves, our families, our patients, and society at large. Fortunately, it is heartwarming and head-clarifying work. As we move into Part II, we will bring this newfound embodied wisdom to the project of talking with ourselves and our patients about the dance of brain, mind, and relationships on the road to increasing mental health.

A Brief Review of Brain Basics

This brief section provides basic information about the architecture and con-nectivity of our brains. Some of the information is drawn from *Being a Brain-Wise Therapist: A Practical Guide to Interpersonal Neurobiology* (Badenoch, 2008), supplemented with new discoveries and a greater emphasis on the *embodied* and *relational* brain. We are at the very beginning of understanding basic neural processes and the function of various brain structures, both as individual groups of neurons and as part of the brain's complex process of interconnectivity. Here, we look at those regions that are most crucial to the therapeutic endeavor with the humble thought that much more will be known by the time this workbook is published.

Let's begin with a short visit to the micro level. The brains of adult humans have about 100 billion *neurons* that, on average, have between 7,000 and 10,000 synaptic connections to other neurons, creating 2 million miles of neural highways in our brains (Siegel, 1999). These neurons connect via *synapses*, which are actually very small spaces between sending and receiving neurons, called *synaptic clefts.* Communication between neurons is accomplished by a large number of neurotransmitters, produced in presynaptic neurons and carrying messages that increase (excite) or decrease (inhibit) electrical activity in the postsynaptic neuron. Increases and decreases in these neurotransmitters can have a dramatic impact on thought, mood, behavior, and relational style. An army of *glia* (Greek for glue), tiny cells outnumbering neurons at least 10–1, have long been known to wrap axons in *myelin* to provide stability and speed connection between neurons, to act as the maintenance crew for neural debris, and to provide nutrition.

The familiar (and now, we realize, much simplified) picture of the neural communication network shows us that neurons are composed of a cell body, with a forest of beefy *dendrites* at one end and one long, willowy *axon* (often with branches) at the other. The old story was that the electrical impulse moved down the axon, releasing neurotransmitters into the synaptic cleft, where they made the short trip to a receiving dendrite on another neuron. Now we know that the electricity occasionally flows the other way, with dendrites sometimes sending and axons receiving; that a whole class of neurons communicates very rapidly without neurotransmitters; and that the ubiquitous glial cells are not limited to a maintenance role, but are also implicated in the communication network by influencing the way neurons fire (Fields, 2006). Currently, there is even the suggestion that perhaps neurons are in the support role and that glia, through the calcium waves they generate to communicate with one another and with neurons, may be the source of our creativity (Koob, 2009). This is both strong evidence for what we *don't* know, and an invitation to follow a gripping story that is unfolding at this moment.

To handle the unfathomable amount of information offered to us by external sources and internal events, our brains operate as parallel distributed processors, which means that many operations are going on simultaneously, gathering together into larger networks at a later stage in processing. Both experientially created constraints and the sheer volume of information mean that not all neural nets become linked. However, in the course of therapy, we can cooperate with our brain's tendency toward complexity by relieving the constraints that keep parts of our brain in conflict with one another in ways that harm our functioning.

The flows of energy and information across the brain and throughout the body, flickering in and out of conscious awareness, are fully responsible for the subjective quality of our lives. As we grow familiar with experiencing our brains as extending throughout our bodies and even outside our apparently containing skins, our angle of vision shifts and widens—perhaps giving us a different perspective on what it means to be human. Let's start with gaining a sense of how our brain is distributed throughout our body proper (see Figure A1).

Somatic Nervous System

The *somatic nervous system* includes our skeletal muscles, skin, and sense organs.

• The skin and sense organs bring information from the outside world into our embodied brains.
• Our skull brain sends messages about relaxing or contracting our muscles, sometimes configuring our bodies according to nonconscious neural events.

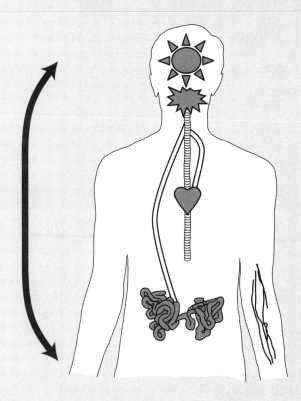

- Brain in Skull
- Brain Stem
- Spinal Cord

- Heart Brain
- Autonomic Nervous System

- Gut Brain
- Somatic Nervous System
(muscles, skin, sense organs)

Figure A1. Cartoon version of streams of energy and information flowing in the embodied brain. Each stream is bidirectional, with the skull brain informing the body and the body shaping the flow in the skull brain.

If a memory of being hit is activated, with or without conscious awareness, our muscles may respond by moving into the pattern associated with that memory.

• On the other hand, when our muscles contract or relax in response to a current day event, a memory of the same or a similar tension or position that is associated with a past experience may be reawakened. There is then some probability of other aspects of that old memory being activated as well.

Enteric Nervous System

Moving more into the center of the body, let's consider what is called the "gut brain," the *enteric nervous system*.

• It is composed of about 100 million neurons and attendant cells, located in sheaths of tissue lining the esophagus, stomach, small intestine, and colon (Gershon, 1998).

• The same proteins and neurotransmitters run the show below, as above.

Perhaps this is because the gut brain and central nervous system differentiate from the same embryonic tissue, but then perform their core functions independently.

• At the physical level, this neural community is responsible for all aspects of digestion and can learn, remember, and even generate new neurons (Liu, Kuan, Wang, Hen, & Gershon, 2009).

• It also receives information from the skull brain, particularly in regard to stress (10% of the information flow), and sends information, particularly in regard to our inner sense of how safe we are (90% of the information flow) (Brown, 2005).

• Paying attention to the sensations flowing from this brain lets our conscious mind have a gut sense about whether to be on guard or remain relaxed.

Autonomic Nervous System

The brains in the head and gut are connected via a bundle of a thousand or so nerve fibers that comprise the vagus nerve, tying the gut brain to one branch of our *autonomic nervous system* (ANS).

• The three branches of these peripheral nerves (meaning, outside the central nervous system) regulate the activities of our so-called hollow organs, such as the heart, stomach, kidneys, and others.

• They also respond to what Stephen Porges (2007) calls our neuroception of safety, danger, or life threat. As we will see, our range of possible behaviors is influenced, perhaps even determined, by the status of our ANS.

• When we "neuroceive" that we are safe, the ventral vagal, the speedy myelinated branch of the parasympathetic, activates and we become available for social connection.

• If we begin to neuroceive threat in response to internal or external changes, our nervous system responds by activating the sympathetic branch in the interest of survival.

• If we neuroceive a threat to life, the unmyelinated dorsal vagal branch of the parasympathetic helps us feign death to avoid death, much like a possum. We revisit the ANS in more detail in Chapter 7 as we consider how it may influence our view of the beginning stage of therapy.

The ANS also connects to the *brain in the heart*, as the socially engaging ventral vagal has strong connections there.

• The heart contains about 40,000 neurons with accompanying neurotransmitters, proteins, and support cells, engaged in learning, remembering, feeling, and sensing (Armour & Ardell, 2004).

• Just as the heart brain receives information from the ANS, whose activation includes inputs from the skull brain, the heart brain also sends a continual flow of information to the brain stem, participating in the regulation of the ANS, and also communicating with the limbic and cortical areas in ways that influence perception and all other aspects of mental and emotional life. This seems to mean that by attending to the messages from this neural circuitry, we can learn about our perception of connectedness in the moment (Armour & Ardell, 2004).

• Interestingly, the heart brain and gut brain can send streams of information with different messages simultaneously, attesting to our embodied, relational brain as a parallel processor, with various modules operating independently, yet in communication with the whole (Armour & Ardell, 2004). To get a sense of this, we might imagine both the gut fear and heart attraction often felt by a person in an abusive relationship.

Spinal Cord

Now we arrive at the *spinal cord*, the main conduit of messages between the body brain and the skull brain.

• A layer of the spinal cord called lamina 1 gathers the flow of energy and information from the gut and heart brains, muscle tension, facial expressions, and pain signals (Siegel, 2010b).
• It also provides a bridge to the outside world by channeling messages from the senses to our embodied brains.
• This bundle of nervous tissue and support cells is about 17–18 inches long, so it does not extend the full length of the spine.

Brain Stem

This gathering information is delivered to the *brain stem*.

• This gateway to the skull brain is crucial for survival; it is involved in controlling heart rate and respiration, vessel constriction, temperature regulation, sensitivity to pain, and cyclic variations in alertness and consciousness.
• In full-term babies, this part of our brain is fully wired at birth because so many of its functions are related to basic survival.
• Because the brain stem is intimately involved in the rapid mobilization of energy, it also deals with whether we are reactive or receptive to new information—whether we go into a fight, flight, or freeze response—working in concert with the limbic region, in particular.
• The brain stem is also a major relay station between the body and the skull

brain, a bidirectional system that both sends regulating information to the body and receives information from the higher regions.

• As part of the motivational system, our drive for survival basics—food, shelter, safety, and reproduction—is supported by activity in the brain stem as well.

Cerebellum

At one time, we thought the *cerebellum* was mainly responsible for coordinating our movements in time and space.

• However, studies are now showing that the robust flow of energy and information into this region from the cortex is processed and then redirected to many areas of the brain.
• This redirection to many areas of the brain makes the cerebellum central to coordinating complex mental as well as motor processes, including the allocation of attention and problem-solving functions (Allen, Buxton, Wong, & Courchesne, 1997).
• Unlike the brain stem, the cerebellum is largely undeveloped at birth and accumulates information throughout childhood and adolescence, building its capacity for continual prediction and preparation in response to changing internal and external conditions (Courchesne & Allen, 1997).

Thalamus

Directly above the brain stem and near the center of the brain, we find the *thalamus*.

• This region relays sensory information to the neocortex and facilitates communication between cortical regions.
• The decision about which information is relayed seems to be made in accord with current attentional demands (Guillery & Sherman, 2002).
• One theory about the origin of conscious awareness is that it is mediated by the 40-cycles-per-second thalamic–cortical sweep from back to front that connects groups of neural nets into a whole and delivers them to the dorsolateral prefrontal cortex, the chalkboard of the mind, producing the sense of continuous experience from the disparate processes unfolding in the brain (Crick, 1994). This "sweep" occurs in both halves of the brain, possibly delivering information to both the right and left dorsolateral prefrontal cortices and thereby mediating awareness of the distinct kinds of information processed in each hemisphere (Siegel, 1999).
• Some pathways connect the thalamus to the amygdala for rapid assess-

ment and response to incoming information, and complex connections between the thalamus, anterior cingulate, and hippocampus help focus attention on emotionally relevant new information.

• Overall, the thalamus offers more than delivery services; it also processes new information and possibly assists in the integration of information that is already flowing within the brain.

Limbic Region

In intimate interaction with the brain stem and all other parts of the brain, the *limbic region* is the social–emotional–motivational nexus of our brain. Neurons located here project to every region of the brain. Although there is likely some encoding of the limbic region in utero, it is still largely a sea of neurons at birth, waiting to be linked by relational experience (see Figure A2).

The limbic structures that most concern us as therapists are the *amygdala, hippocampus*, and *hypothalamus.*

• The amygdala encodes a number of emotions that we consider to be negative into long-term implicit memory: fear, anger, and sadness, in particular (Adolphs & Tranel, 2004; LeDoux, 2002; Phelps & LeDoux, 2005). It appears that emotions we consider to be positive tend to encode differently, integrating throughout the brain (Adolphs & Tranel).

• These long-term implicit memories are encoded as bodily sensations, be-

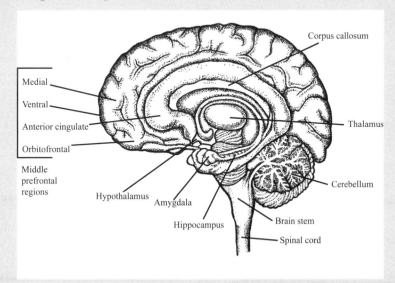

Figure A2. Right-Hemisphere Limbic and Middle Prefrontal Regions. Fostering neural integration of these two regions is the foundation for effective psychotherapy. The corpus callosum, bands of fibers carrying information between the two hemispheres of the brain, and the thalamus, a central relay station for incoming sensory information are also shown, together with the spinal cord, brain stem, and cerebellum. Art by Ron Estrine.

havioral impulses, emotional surges, perceptions, and sometimes as fragmented images. When they are reawakened, we have no sense of remembering,
but we feel as though they originate in the present moment.

• Our first assessment of the meaning of an experience also occurs in the
amygdala, which makes a judgment about the safety of a given person or situation (Adolphs, Tranel, & Damasio, 1998). The new input is compared to what
is already encoded and if there is a match, the old perception is activated,
along with the protective behaviors associated with that perception. This happens below the level of conscious awareness, although when attended, the implicit world can become explicitly known.

• The hippocampus comes online gradually when it is genetically nudged to
integrate with the amygdala at approximately 10 months. Its integrative capacity develops over time until it achieves a more reliable capacity by 4 to 5
years—about as far back as mentally healthy adults can gain a sense of continuity about their explicit memories.

• It has been called the cognitive mapper because it integrates the fragments
of implicit memory into an explicit whole and places a time stamp on the experience. Then, when we recall an explicit memory, we have the visceral sense
that the event happened in the past.

• The hypothalamus, working with the pituitary, controls the neuroendocrine
system, releasing neurotransmitters and hormones throughout the body and
brain in response to input from the brain stem (where bodily inputs converge)
and limbic region as our assessment of safety in the moment fluctuates.

• When we neuroceive (become aware, but not consciously) and perceive
(become consciously aware) a stressful situation, the HPA axis (hypothalamic–
pituitary–adrenal axis) prepares the body for its next moves to ensure survival.

Taken together, these three aspects of the limbic region are central in our
ability to attach, to protect ourselves, to successfully handle sudden stressful
situations without conscious awareness, to create and sometimes to retrieve
implicit and explicit memories, and to feel alive in the midst of our experiences.

Middle Prefrontal Cortex

Because of the intimate interface between the limbic region and the aspects of
the *middle prefrontal cortex*, we are going to consider them next (refer again to
Figure A2 to gain a sense of their location).

• Traditionally, the *anterior cingulate* has been considered part of the limbic
proper, more because of its connectedness to those circuits than its location.
The entire cingulate cortex, all of it integrative in a variety of ways, lies be-

tween the cortex and corpus callosum. The anterior portion is adjacent to other regions of the middle prefrontal.

- Although it has many functions, two that are particularly important for our endeavor are its capacity to focus attention, allowing us to use our minds to shape our brains in the direction of regulation; and its capacity to weave together thought and emotion to allow us to make the best decisions for our particular situation.

- The *medial prefrontal cortex* seems to be the gathering place for our sense of self. As various inputs integrate, our felt autobiographical narrative emerges here (Gusnard, Akbudak, Shulman, & Raichle, 2001).

- This region is part of the default mode network that continually integrates information flowing through our brains. It is also active when we form images of others within our minds (Raichle, 2010).

- The *ventromedial prefrontal cortex* appears to weigh various options in light of our meaningful narrative, leading to decisions based on our ever-evolving history (Fellows & Farah, 2007).

- The *orbitofrontal cortex*, with the closest connections to the limbic region—so close that some researchers consider it part limbic, part cortex—is strongly correlated with our capacity to form rich attachments (Schore, 2009a).

- Sending gamma-aminobutyric acid (GABA)-bearing synapses to the amygdala, this part of the middle prefrontal region is crucial for self-regulation and response flexibility (Siegel, 2006).

- When mothering people are in attunement with their infants, this region begins to fire and wire in the months before integration with the limbic regions commences (at about 24 months).

Working together, these regions integrate information in right-mode processing, creating a bridge for the materials of our felt narrative to move into left-mode processing and become our spoken narrative. When the connections between the limbic region and middle prefrontal cortex are strong, nine capacities, identified by Daniel Siegel (2006, 2007, 2010a, 2010b), emerge: bodily regulation, attuned communication, emotional balance, response flexibility, mitigation of fear, empathy, self-knowing awareness connecting the past/present/future into a meaningful whole, intuition, and moral development. In short, these connections underlie personal well-being and relational goodness.

Insular Cortex

Also lying near both the limbic region and middle prefrontal cortex, one other aspect is of particular importance to our therapeutic process: the *insular cortex* (or insula).

• The bidirectional flow in various parts of this region allows us to map our own internal state and that of another, both consciously and out of conscious awareness.

• This is the main pathway between body, brain stem, limbic, and cortex, allowing us to resonate with others and become aware of the emotional meaning of bodily states.

• A crucial part of our resonance circuitry, the insula ferries information received from the outside world by our mirror neurons through the corridors of our inner world until we can become conscious of another's intentions and emotions (for a full review of these circuits, see Siegel, 2010b).

Neocortex

Now, let's look at the *neocortex*, beginning with its overall structure (see Figure A3).

• The neocortex is composed of six horizontal layers, each about one business card thick. The top two carry invariant representations built by experience, allowing us to anticipate what comes next. The bottom two take in new information, giving us the opportunity to attend to novelty (Hawkins & Blakeslee, 2004). A creative neural event can unfold in the middle two layers as the expected and the novel meet.

• This sheet of neurons is also organized in vertical columns. On the left, these columns have few interconnections between them, whereas the right is rich in cross connections. This correlates well with orderly left-mode processing and the more global embrace of the right mode.

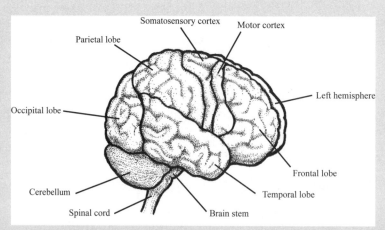

Figure A3. The Cerebral Cortex. We are looking at the right hemisphere, with the back of the brain at the left. This cortex, particularly the frontal lobe, is most extensively developed in human beings. Art by Ron Estrine.

Considering the individual lobes, we'll begin at the back and move forward to meet the middle prefrontal regions we have just discussed. An integrative flow emerges as our brains take individual pieces of energy and information and link them.

• The large cortical structure extending across the back of the brain is the *occipital lobe*, dedicated to integrating bits of visual information into whole images in sighted persons. For those who are blind, this area can be recruited for touch and sound and possibly other tasks (Amedi, Merabet, Bermpohl, & Pascual-Leone, 2005).

• The *parietal lobes* process information about touch, pressure, temperature, pain, where we are in space, sensory comprehension, understanding speech, reading and visual functions; the *somatosensory* strip at the front of these lobes receives information from the spinal cord about touch, position of body, and other matters. These lobes have two functional regions: one involves sensation and perception, and the other is concerned with integrating sensory input, primarily with the visual system. In this way, sensory information is drawn into a single perception, and a spatial coordinate system develops to map the world around us.

• The *temporal lobes* at the side of the head process complex information about smells and sounds and have many integrative functions relating to memory. The primary auditory cortex resides here, with these lobes taking in the sensory information and linking it with other streams of information. Just inside the temporal lobes, in the medial temporal cortex, we find the hippocampi, the limbic structures most involved in explicit memory creation and retrieval. Damage to the left temporal lobe can result in decreased recall of verbal and visual content, including speech perception, and damage to the right lobe can impair recognition of tonal sequences and visual content, such as faces.

• Finally, moving from back to front, the *frontal cortex* contains regions for motor control of voluntary muscles and motor planning (motor and premotor strips) as well as for concentration, organization, reasoning, judgment, decision-making, creativity, abstract thinking, emotion, and relational abilities (to name a few). If we move to the bottom-most area of the frontal cortex, we return again to the highly integrative prefrontal region, a crucial area for healthy functioning in our relational lives.

• One other area of the prefrontal region is central to the therapeutic endeavor: the *dorsolateral prefrontal cortices*. Located at the sides of the prefrontal lobe, they are considered the home of working memory, the "chalkboard of the mind." When something comes to conscious awareness, these cortices are involved. Neuroscientists believe that on the left, explicit information in words comes into conscious awareness, whereas on the right, conscious awareness of felt experience in the body and spatial awareness, sometimes accompanied by poetic, metaphorical, or fresh language, likely emerges.

Hemispheric Divisions

In addition to the partition of the skull brain into brain stem, limbic, and cortical regions, it is also divided into two hemispheres that are so autonomous, both in terms of structure and function, that some people consider them to constitute two brains. Were it not for the *corpus callosum* (the band of tissue right beneath the cingulate gyrus in Figure A2), the major highway of communication between the two halves, along with a few other smaller bands of fibers (called *commissures*), this would be largely true in the anatomical and functional sense. For example, the anterior commissure connects the right and left temporal lobes and the amygdalae to one another. Even though there are similar structures in both halves of the brain (two amygdalae, two hippocampi, two temporal lobes, etc.), the way they perceive experience as well as the information they process and their means of processing that information are quite different (Schore, 2007; Siegel, 1999). At the same time, it is also true that due to complex interconnections across the brain, many processes incorporate both hemispheres (Siegel, 2010b). (See Figure A4.)

Left-Mode Processing		Right-Mode Processing
Logical		Holistic, spatial, nonlinear
Linear		Prosody, eye gaze, touch, gesture
Literal		Circuits of attachment
Practical language		Regulation
Making sense		Integrated map of the body
Factual memory		Affective experience
Social self		Experience of the self
Spoken narrative		Implicit memory
Analytical problem solving		Autobiographical memory
Handling the familiar		Intuition
Moderate levels of stress		Fresh, metaphorical language
More defined neocortical columns		Rapid processing of novelty
Yes/no		Severe levels of stress
		More integrated cortical columns
		Both/and

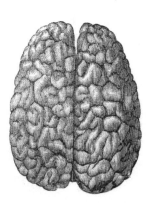

Figure A4. Functions of the Two Brain Hemispheres. Although many of our brain processes involve activations on both sides of the brain, the left mode or right mode may provide the crucial input for a particular kind of experience. Throughout this workbook, we have used the word *mode* rather than *hemisphere* because a percentage of the population has reversed hemispheric functions. Following Daniel Siegel (2010b), this designation also honors the reality that many processes are not hemispherically bound. Brain hemisphere image licensed from iStockphoto.com.

Checking with ourselves, we can verify the independent operation of the two modes. We can hold a left-mode explanation for why we do something or judge our actions as stupid or meaningless, while at the same time, there exists within us a right-mode implicit reason that requires the behavior (Toomey & Ecker, 2007). At other times, the values of our logical mind may be in conflict with the unseen and unattended needs of our right-mode yearnings. Some of these distinct knowings will always exist, but those that harm our functioning are the focus of the resolving activities that unfold within the therapeutic relationship.

We began our walk along the neural path with information entering our brains through the senses, ambled along the byways of the embodied brain, coming back now to how others in the outside world influence our neural firings. In Chapter 8, we discuss mirror neurons and resonance circuits in detail, so I won't repeat that here. In very brief summary, through the complex feedback loop that begins with mirror neurons and culminates in the middle prefrontal cortex, we dance internally and externally with those around us, sometimes consciously, most often out of awareness. We incorporate one another into our very being. In this sense, we have no privacy. Our minds are open to everyone, and we are all part of each other.

And yet, in another way, we have only the privacy of our minds. As sophisticated as our neural processing is, we actually encode a miniscule percentage of what is presented to us via our senses, in our own unique way. The portion of this that becomes conscious is another tiny fraction unique to each one of us. Privacy intensifies because our prior encodings alter our perceptions, which influence what we are encoding in this moment, most dramatically in regard to what an experience means. You and I might have an interesting discussion about the exact shade of green a particular tree is lavishing upon us, with our varying perceptions based on the uniqueness of our rods and cones. However, when it comes to the meaning of that tree, our responses may become profoundly idiosyncratic based on the many experiences we've each had involving trees. Somewhere in this balance between interpersonal oneness and absolute uniqueness lies what it means to be one human being among others.

Part II

Weaving the Brain into the Flow of Therapy

From First Contact to Transition

Introduction

We now bring all that we have generated in our bodies, minds, and listening partner relationships into the process of translating brain wisdom into *presence*, *words*, and *actions* for the benefit of our patients. Although it is important for us to speak about the brain with clarity at the right empathic moment, another kind of conversation precedes that one and is equally significant. How will we now talk *with ourselves* about the healing process with the brain in mind? As therapists, we are always having an interior conversation about the healing process. In essence, we prepare a space and a meal for our patients according to what we implicitly and explicitly believe about how people are wounded and how they heal. If there is sufficient resonance in the therapeutic relationship, our patients will either join us at the table we have set, or, if we become implicitly entangled, we may find ourselves sitting at their family table instead. Because of the reality of mirror neurons and resonance circuits, we can't help but enter each other's worlds.

One therapist told me about working with a woman whose history of abuse only came to light after a few months of meeting. The flood of dysregulation that followed her willingness to disclose her traumatic history frightened him, but his compassion for her suffering also led him to see the harm in abandoning her at the height of this struggle. As she felt her therapist's fear rise—a state of mind with which she resonated because her mother was terrified of her father—she began to find ways to soothe him. She talked in a quiet voice, pushed away the rising terror within her, brought him the occasional latte, and noticed that he was growing calmer. Frequently, images of her comforting her mother over a cup of tea swam into her mind, but she didn't tell him for fear that he would say, "No more lattes," and return to his frightened state.

For his part, he interpreted her apparent increased calmness as indicating that they had done enough work for her to begin to regulate more easily. Only later, when her chaotic nervous system burst to the surface again, as a series of external events overcame her pseudo-regulation, did he begin to question what had happened in the relationship—a sterling example of humility and self-honesty. As he mulled her history, he realized that he had fallen into her implicit relational world rather than drawing her onto the safe ground of his integrated mind. The story has a good ending because they were able to talk about what had happened, making the implicit interaction explicit. He then got some therapy of his own, uncovering and healing the roots of his fear of her dysregulation, a process that established within him the needed solid space to now contain her upset when it blossomed.

As our brain-wise perspective deepens, it brings two significant gifts. The first is a profoundly increased reservoir of nonjudgment and compassion as we viscerally understand why people think, feel, and behave as they do. This open and empathic space allows our mirror neurons and resonance circuits to vibrate with the full-bodied experience of the other person's suffering. The vulnerability conferred by this state of mind can draw us into our patient's relational patterns, as the good-hearted therapist in our story experienced. However, the second gift, the capacity to understand with clarity—to actually form pictures of what is happening in our brains and minds, and those of our patients—gives us a greater likelihood of keeping or quickly regaining our feet as our compassion increases. In fact, when these two capacities grow in tandem, we give our patients a space and a meal rich in both nurturance and grounding wisdom. Fostering this kind of development is the goal of the second and third parts of this book.

We are going to begin by exploring what interpersonal neurobiology tells us, from a broad perspective, about the nature of brain, mind, and relationships—whatever our therapeutic paradigm. As we proceed through Part II, these core principles that emerge from the science can guide our conversation with ourselves. They are not the only principles that can be drawn from the science, but they make a useful group for our purposes. Here we are formalizing the awareness we have been building in our bodies and relational brains thus far. In the natural pattern of integration, we are inviting what we have experienced within ourselves to flow into our spoken narrative about the healing process.

Following is a list that provides a summary of the points we will discuss below in this introduction; it can serve as a reference to which we return as we practice conceptualizing the inner worlds of our patients throughout Part II.

1. Our early attachment history matters.
2. Our bodies are part of every memory.
3. Our brains can and do change all the time—neuroplasticity is real.

4. Neural integration is the foundation for increasing well-being and can be fostered in interpersonal relationships.
5. Our brains are always on the path toward greater complexity and coherence, hampered in their natural course only by constraints, many of which can be changed, particularly within empathic relationships.
6. Healing as well as healthy living requires the presence of both right-mode and left-mode processing.
7. Mindful attention is one key agent of change.
8. Interpersonal oneness is real, and the therapist's mental health matters.

In keeping with our integrative practice of noticing how our thoughts resonate with our implicit knowings and touch our inner community, let's sit with each of these eight principles, paying kind attention to what happens in our bodies, nervous systems, feelings, and perceptions as we invite our right-mode processing to be present in this conversation. Are some principles more comfortable than others? If there is discomfort, we can ask, "Who inside feels upset by this idea?" If there is a particularly strong positive resonance, we can ask the same thing—"Who inside feels uplifted or energized by this thought?" After spending some leisurely time in this investigation, write a bit about those principles that particularly touch you, both describing your experience and reflecting on the meaning. Feel free to continue the conversation in your journal if you run out of room.

_____

_____

_____

_____

Now, let's look at these principles a little more deeply.

• *First, our early attachment history matters.* As we discovered in Part I, the implicit sea inside contains flows of ever-present energy and information established in our earliest relationships, as reinforced or modified by later experience. These core knowings are our eternally present past, made visible to us in our relational patterns and firmly held beliefs about who we are, and often influencing our vision of possible futures. However, the roots, firmly planted in the distant past, are often invisible. As we become intimately familiar with these flows within ourselves—as our implicit becomes explicit—we develop the ability to see and feel our way into the depths of our patients' inner landscape as well. As our skill builds, we may often begin to recognize how their implicit flows create energy patterns and pictures in our minds and bodies unbidden, messengers that allow us to hold and therefore shape those flows in the direction of regulation and integration—a process that Daniel Siegel (2010a, 2010b) calls *mindsight* and that Allan Schore (2003b, 2009a) points to in his discussions of the continual micro-second right-mode to right-mode exchanges between patient and therapist. As these early attachment patterns are rewired into pathways of increasing security, outer life will begin to take a similar shape. *The implicit ground establishes the foundation on which the house of thoughts, feelings, and behaviors is built.* Part of how we make sense of our patients' lives is to clearly see the deep roots beneath the current circumstances, discovering the coherence between implicit patterns and current manifestations (Badenoch, 2008; Ecker & Hulley, 1996, 2000a, 2000b, 2008). Without this guidance, we sometimes wander in a wilderness of confusion about why, for example, an obviously intelligent and competent woman believes that she is stupid and worthless, and all our efforts to use cognitive means to help her to shift this erroneous belief lead nowhere.

• *Second, the body is part of every memory.* We have spent a good deal of time getting familiar with our body's language—the ebb and flow of intensity in our nervous systems, the way our muscles and organs tense and relax, behavioral impulses that surge up from the depths, changes in the rhythm of our breathing. These upwelling messages have guided us toward our inner world as they tug on strands of physical experience that, in turn, activate the rest of a particular neural net, providing a first step in linking the pieces of memory together. As with any developing skill, becoming more sensitive to our own bodies makes it more likely that we will include this dimension in the therapeutic process as well. Since the heart of attunement is following our patients wherever their integrating brains take them, our growing awareness of their bodies' messages increases the range of our tracking. Their felt sense of being seen and understood, even without words being exchanged, amplifies the healing possibilities.

• *Third, our brains can and do change all the time—neuroplasticity is real.* This hope-instilling message of change can be powerfully sustaining for clients whose inner worlds lead them to predict more of the same misery in the future. Such pessimism is a result of how our brains work. Because one of the brain's central functions is anticipating what comes next—a valuable capacity for survival—it continues to shape implicit pictures of the future based on what we have experienced so far. Even if our patients consciously hold positive images that are different from the unseen beliefs of their deeper mind, the implicit tug will say more about what they do next. As we work with them in therapy, our patients' implicit ground will change. Until that change has solidified, however, our intellectual conviction and personal experience of neuroplasticity, both as we hold it internally and speak about it with our patients, can help them plant one foot of hope in their left-mode processing while creating an atmosphere of optimism that quietly bathes their right-mode visceral experience.

• *Fourth, neural integration is the foundation for our increasing well-being, and can be fostered in interpersonal relationships.* If brain science makes anything clear, it is that our quality of life is strongly influenced by the degree of integration between our body, limbic region, and middle prefrontal circuits. Without enduring connections between these three areas, particularly in the hemisphere supporting right-mode processing, we are often at the mercy of speedy reactivity before we have the opportunity to make a decision (Damasio, 2000). In a real sense, dissociation of these circuits takes away choice. We also have diminished capacity for empathy, attuned communication, intuition, and even moral action (Siegel, 2007). As these right-mode circuits become more linked, other forms of integration—memory, state, and narrative, for example—naturally emerge as an inherent part of the brain's self-organizing ways (Siegel, 2006, 2007, 2010b). The best news is that attuned relationships pull these circuits together (Schore, 2003a, 2003b, 2009a). In our therapy room, just as at the beginning of life in the dance between parent and child, our patients' prefrontal circuits can pick up the rhythm of our integration. If we are able to hold a picture of these circuits knitting together, we can further enrich the interpersonal environment.

• *Fifth, our brains are complex systems, moving naturally toward greater coherence, hampered only by constraints, many of which can be transformed.* Not only do our brains change, but they change in a particular direction when conditions are right. We use the word *constraints* to talk about how established neural pathways and a host of other biological influences direct the brain's flow. These ingrained patterns of energy and information can constrain us in the direction of warm attachments and resilience or toward various shadings of painful attachment and despair. Genetics and temperament can also act as constraints on the system. The good news is that relationally established constraints can be modified in relationship as well. We can then begin to picture the therapeutic relationship as the medium in which this alchemy can occur so that the natural integrative process can resume its flow. This balanced view requires neither the therapist nor the patient to take full responsibility for the outcome, but rather locates the work in the interpersonal matrix where *the therapist's coherent mind meets the patient's integration-seeking brain*. Many therapists have said that the idea of partnering with the natural developmental process of their patients' brains allows them to be more relaxed—and therefore more coherent. In this case, neurobiological awareness initiates a lovely self-reinforcing cycle of integration for all.

• *Sixth, healing as well as healthy living requires the presence of both right-mode and left-mode processing.* One of the cultural constraints in the Western world is our privileging of cognition and reason, often at the expense of emotion—as though they were separable or that the former could control the latter. Rather than pitting the two modes against one another or judging their relative value, we can begin to understand how they operate together in many aspects of the healing process. As we have experienced, gathering up all aspects of a neural net involves touching the differentiated strands located in the body, nervous system, limbic region, and cortices so that the neurally ingrained experience becomes an integrated whole that can seek linkage with the brain's movement toward increasing complexity. Current research notes that in order to change implicit patterns, we must unlock the stored memories by coming into emotionally vivid contact with them while simultaneously providing an equally vibrant disconfirming experience to prepare for this energy and information to integrate into the larger flow of the brain (Pedreira, Perez-Cuest, & Maldonado, 2004; Rossato, Bevilaqua, Medina, Izquierdo, & Cammarota, 2006; Winters, Tucci, & DaCosta-Furtado, 2009). This movement from implicit to explicit requires processes beginning in right-mode processing and ultimately mediated by both hemispheres. As our brains become more integrated, the resources of both modes of processing are more easily available for everything from high-quality relationships to balanced decision-making and compassionate living.

• *Seventh, mindful attention is one key agent of change.* From the moment we hear our patients' voices for the first time, our minds may begin to reach toward understanding, forming pictures of the many layers being shared. This kind of deep listening is the beginning of mindful awareness in the inter-

The Brain-Savvy Therapist's Workbook

personal realm, a tender, curious openness to another person's body, nervous system, and inner world. In this caring observer state of mind, our more integrated activation can begin to weave our patients' brains into similar patterns, bit by unseen bit. In this way, our ongoing attentiveness also teaches our patients' minds the pathways of mindful awareness, and we will see their capacity for greater mindsight (Siegel, 2010a, 2010b) gradually emerge. As time passes, we may sense that our two attending minds are creating an environment in which neural nets holding old wounds may open to the safety and comfort being offered. In this way, we develop a foundation that can support whatever else may need to happen in therapy. As we will see, the addition of formal mindfulness practices can also deepen and speed our integrative process at times. However we approach the inclusion of mindfulness, the accumulating body of research tells us that sustained practice produces not only momentary functional changes in neural connections, but enduring structural changes as well. That is, states of mind that originally require effort can become effortless traits of being with practice.

• *Eighth, interpersonal oneness is real, and the therapist's mental health matters.* Many of the previous principles suggest that both of these are true, and what we are learning about mirror neurons and resonance circuits confirms them further (Iacoboni, 2007, 2009; Siegel, 2007, 2010b). These points bear repeating because they call us to radical responsibility for the condition of our brains and minds, not only as therapists, but as human beings influencing all those around us. We certainly do not need to be completely healed, but we do need to be as aware of our inner world as we can, vulnerabilities and all.

These core principles have been listed and numbered, perhaps inducing us to stay mainly in our orderly left-mode processing, except when we paused to mindfully sense our response to each short sentence. Let's pause again for a moment to be sure that we're bringing our right-mode along with us by asking: In reading through these principles, what body sensations might we notice? Any emotional surges? Any behavioral impulses? Changes in perceptions about ourselves or the therapeutic endeavor? Judgments about what we're doing? Returning to descriptive rather than explanatory language, write a few words about what you notice with each of these questions.

_____

_____

_____

_____

_____

_____

_____

_____

_____

_____

_____

_____

_____

_____

_____

_____

_____

_____

_____

_____

Why is this list of principles important in my estimation? When we are grounded in a set of principles, we can open our minds and hearts more thoroughly to our clients. Fewer of our resources are entangled in deciding what to do next, or even more distracting, in wondering if the therapeutic endeavor works at all, especially when we are stuck in the doldrums or the upset that can pervade the relationship at times. Being able to see where we are in the process and communicate that to our patients is bedrock for making our way through these difficult stretches. The other crucial point is that our left-mode knowledge of the brain and mind needs to be refined enough that we feel confident in our inner process and our outer expression of brain wisdom. Our capacity to weave these ideas into our unseen process of presence and into the conversation of therapy rests on that foundation.

Taken together, these principles suggest that we get the most bang for our neuroplasticity buck when we approach therapy as an attachment relationship unfolding in a milieu of mindful awareness, supported by a thorough knowledge of the processes of brain and mind. Now comes the next step—practice, practice, practice. In Part I, your listening partner provided containment and nurturance, helping your implicit patterns shift in the direction of security. Here, that person will become your indispensable sounding board for articulating what you are learning.

I teach a series of classes in the Interpersonal Neurobiology certificate program at Portland State University. The second in the series has a name similar to Part II of the book—"Weaving Brain Talk into the Flow of Practice." The students unanimously report that starting to talk out loud immediately illuminates what is fuzzy and what is refined in their brains. It also puts them face-to-face with fears about sharing this with others—

"Am I intelligent enough?"
"Do I know enough?"
"Will I be able to translate this into words they will understand?"
"Will they be interested?"
"Will I be able to tell when to stop?"

This last question comes up because some people find their enthusiasm for the subject carries them into realms beyond the tolerance of their audience. Approaching the process with humor and good will allowed these students to nurture one another through the rough spots. The interesting part was that practice became so compelling that they were seeking to form groups for ongoing practice after the class.

In the following chapters, we are going to make our way through the therapeutic process, beginning with first contact and finishing with thoughts concerning what interpersonal neurobiology suggests about the transition out of therapy. In each section, we explore the neurobiology of the topic from the viewpoint of what it means for our patients and the therapeutic process. Since we wish to support the inner and outer conversation, one experiential practice will involve writing about how these principles shape our interior dialogue about the therapy process. Then to prepare for the second conversation—the one in which we share the brain and mind with our patients—we are going to do some writing that translates the science into neurobiologically correct and manageable bites for our patients, who are likely new to the subject. Writing is an excellent steppingstone to speaking because it clarifies what remains slightly out of focus and what has taken up solid residence in our whole brain.

The final and indispensable piece is sharing what we are developing with our listening partners. These dialogues seem most useful when they take the form of actually speaking the words as though your partner is the client, rather than talking *about* the topic from a safe, intellectual distance. The listening partner can be most helpful by providing attentive presence unless the speaker requests input. At the end, if the speaker wishes, the listener can share his or her experience in a kind, nonjudgmental, and truthful way. The final step, as always, is for both speaker and listener to reflect on the process, listening to their bodies, nervous systems, feelings, and behavioral impulses, and to write or talk descriptively about these areas.

Each chapter also contains specific examples of using these principles with patients. These examples represent the way that my mind has guided me to employ the information. The most important part of this process is for you to find your own voice, both internally and externally, so although I think that the examples can be helpful illustrations, they are no substitute for what you will create out of your own personality and gathering experience. This book is not intended to be a "how to" in the sense of offering specific protocols. Each therapeutic relationship generates its own dance, timing, quirks, and patterns, and the art of brain-wise therapy is *letting the science flow in response to the empathic environment.* In my view, that is the principle above all others—that *whatever we do flows from attunement and supports deepening connection.*

The other core principle—kindness for self as the foundation of compassion for others—remains our constant guide and companion. Again, this is a leisurely process, aimed at developing solid, whole-brain neural nets that will accumulate into an embodied paradigm shift. From this emerging perspective, empathy and brain wisdom amplify one another to ground the therapeutic endeavor.

Chapter 7

Beginning—with the Brain in Mind

What would it be like to have the brain at the center of our attention from our first contact with a new patient? What brain systems would we particularly consider at this tender stage, and how would those reflections shape our inner space and guide our outer actions? The first brain system that springs to my mind is the autonomic nervous system (ANS) because it helps us think about how to create safety for our patients. Putting ourselves in their shoes as they call our voice mail, we can imagine them possibly feeling anxious, depressed, vulnerable, scared, needing help—all states of mind that potentially activate the sympathetic nervous system (SNS). Stephen Porges's polyvagal theory (2003, 2004, 2007, 2009a, 2009b), building on the legacy of Paul MacLean (1990), illuminates the connection between ANS activation and our ability to forge a therapeutic alliance.

How the Three Branches of the ANS Work

First, we're going to get a picture of the operation of the ANS. Traditionally, the ANS was thought to be composed of two branches: the sympathetic branch, as the accelerator, and the parasympathetic branch, as the brakes. From this perspective, the goal was to keep the two in balance. Instead, it turns out that the ANS has *three* branches that are hierarchically arranged so that with increasing neuroception of danger, one branch goes offline in favor of the next to ensure our survival. The word *neuroception* was coined by Stephen Porges (2003), as noted previously, to talk about how our nervous system, along with several other circuits, can detect danger without conscious awareness. Before we perceive danger, a conscious state, we can "neuroceive" it and act on that neuroception. The ANS does not operate alone, but works in conjunction with circuits that recognize faces, assess intention, rapidly assess threat, and carry emotionally relevant information from the body to the limbic region—in short, those circuits that tell us how safe we are with others and the environment (Adolphs, 2002; Critchley, 2005; Morris, Ohman, & Dolan, 1999; Winston, Strange, O'Doherty, & Dolan, 2002).

For we human beings, our nervous system's preferred way of finding and maintaining safety is via connection with others. Consequently, the first system in the hierarchy is the ventral vagal parasympathetic, a circuit that allows us to be still and stay engaged at the same time, a central requirement for secure attachment—what Stephen Porges calls "love without fear" (Porges, 1998, p. 849). This circuit slows the heart (the vagal brake), decreases our fight–flight response, and reduces the stress hormone cortisol (Porges, 2009b). In short, it prevents the sympathetic branch from taking over. Interestingly, this circuit also reduces inflammation and puts us in a state of growth and restoration.

Two people in this state can coregulate one another, even in stressful situations, largely because in the course of mammalian evolution, the ventral vagus became integrated with the circuits that control the muscles of the face and head. These neural pathways regulate eye gaze, prosody, ability to listen, and facial expression—in short, many of the nonverbal ways in which we communicate our connection with each other (Porges, 2009a). A calmly beating heart and relaxed yet animated face signals our readiness to engage. This calm, safe state rests at the foundation of the therapeutic alliance.

Take a moment to move this left-centric information into your body by seeing if you can call into vivid experience times when your ventral vagal system was at work. As that memory activates, what bodily sensations, emotional surges, and behavioral impulses do you experience? What happens in your feelings and your perception of yourself and relationships? Being able to recognize and call on this state is helpful as we prepare to meet our patients. It may become more identifiable in our awareness if we write a few words about its physiological, emotional, and perceptual markers.

_____

_____

_____

_____

_____

Many of our patients' life experiences may have left them without regular access to this calm state. Instead, they may be burdened with nervous systems that regularly respond to experiences we might perceive as neutral with a neuroception of danger or death threat, resulting in a move into one of the other two branches of the ANS. When our connection with others is insufficient to maintain a neuroception of safety, the SNS takes over. In a state of safety, we can experience fluctuating levels of sympathetic arousal that support an active pursuit of attachment, curiosity, play, sexuality, and other energized quests. However, as our neuroception shifts from an assessment of safety to danger, the ventral vagal brake on the heart is removed and the SNS is free to activate more fully to prepare us to defend ourselves (Porges, 2007). Mobilization takes the form of increased heart rate, release of the chemicals we need for action, and other metabolic shifts that prepare us for fight or flight. In the interests of survival, the circuits that connect us with others go offline so that we can focus on the threat, and, as a result, our capacity to take in new information is dramatically reduced. This means that others will not be able to regulate us until our neuroception of safety is restored.

From the viewpoint of our patients, our capacity to offer attuned presence may create a safe-enough environment to stimulate a neuroception of safety in them. As a result, it is important for us to recognize when we are *not* in that state. Take a moment to call to mind and body moments when you have experienced the shift into a fearful sympathetic activation. Recalling the circumstances, notice with kindness the response in your body and emotions as well as any shifts in perception. See if you can also recall what returned you to a calm, receptive state.

_____

_____

_____

_____

_____

_____

_____

_____

_____

_____

Now let's consider the third branch of the ANS. Under more dire circumstances, as our neuroception shifts from safety or danger to all-out life threat and helplessness, the sympathetic circuit turns off in favor of the other branch of the parasympathetic, the dorsal vagal, dramatically reducing heart rate, stopping digestion, and shutting down other metabolic systems to move into death-feigning behavior—a freeze state that may be marked by dissociation or a collapse into stillness (Porges, 2007). Our bodies release endorphins to ensure a less painful exit, as our entire organism prepares to die. Under extreme traumatic conditions, the SNS may not turn off completely as the dorsal vagal comes online, creating a state of extreme physiological stress akin to the strain on a car that results from revving the gas and slamming on the brakes at the same time. These two countervailing processes produce a state of mind and body that is difficult capture in words, but might be partially described as a state of unmoving, wordless terror.

As I work with survivors of trauma, their nervous systems sometimes fall into this state as the memories of extreme helplessness arise from the limbic depths. Given sufficient stress and no escape route, we can literally be frightened to death. Take a moment to sense in your body and feelings if there are any moments when you slipped into the frozen protection of dorsal vagal dominance. Then write some descriptive words about both the experience and what drew you back into a calm, connected state.

_____

_____

_____

_____

_____

_____

_____

_____

_____

_____

As we observe these different states of activation with kindness, we are building the very neural pathways that can help us find regulation even when our patients bring us the intensity of their inner world. If we are in attunement with our people, our mirror neurons and resonance circuits will light up our embodied brains with an ANS experience that parallels theirs, leaving it to our middle prefrontal circuits to provide the neural container that can regulate us first. This, in turn, sends a wave of activation and reassurance that begins to ignite our patients' prefrontal–limbic integration as well. Our mind can hold and shape their mind.

Now we're going to take some time to absorb the left-mode information. Translation from hearing to writing is the first step in moving the information from incoming (learning) to outgoing (sharing). After gathering up your journal, invite your mind and body to tell you what they remember about the three branches of the ANS. While it isn't necessary to know the proper name of every circuit involved, it is helpful to be clear about the relationship between the three subsystems, the characteristics of each ANS state, as well as how and why a person moves from one to the other. If any of this feels cloudy, feel free to review the above paragraphs.

When you have a fairly solid picture in your mind, write a paragraph in your journal to further integrate this information into your explicit memory. The elegance of the writing isn't important, but the feeling of *sharp clarity* about the topic does matter. Although we certainly don't have to be neurobiological experts, our ease with the broad outlines of key principles makes it more likely that we will be able to offer the information at the right empathic moment because we don't need to search around for the details in left-mode processing. Such clarity also makes it easier for us to use these embodied concepts effortlessly to guide our way of thinking about, and being with, our patients. Take as much time as you need to write a paragraph that brings you ease in mind and body.

When you finish writing, notice with kindness any judgments that arise about how you did the exercise and what that means about you as a person. It is so easy for many of us to slip back into criticism when we move toward learning something new or to renewing our acquaintance with something we haven't quite mastered. When we are easily able to be kind to our judging selves as well as to our learning selves, we will know that we are making significant strides toward being anchored in our caring observer. Take a few moments to write about the experience of judging and the ongoing challenge of seeking to let go of judgments.

_____

_____

_____

_____

_____

_____

_____

_____

_____

_____

_____

It is also helpful to start talking out loud about the ANS with your listening partner, developing ease in moving the concepts into spoken words. Speaking about it out loud a few minutes a day for a week will likely yield better results than one long session. You may even find yourself bringing up this topic in apparently casual conversations with friends and family—any venue will do.

Creating Safety for Our Patients

How does awareness of these three ANS circuits guide our initial interactions with the people coming to see us? We're going to move through this process in what may seem like small steps; however, if we follow along in our body and feelings, we may get the sense of how small decisions impact our patients' larger experience.

Voice Mail

You might begin your pursuit of creating safety for your patients by listening to the voice-mail message new people hear when they call you. When it is possible, it makes sense for patients to hear your voice rather than someone else's because so much is communicated by prosody and pacing, accompanied by a choice of words that conveys warmth and stability. We can imagine that their nervous systems may often be hovering between ventral vagal and sympathetic activation, on alert to see who will meet them at this crucial juncture. If they "hear" safety and move toward connection, their systems will also likely release oxytocin, a hormone and neurotransmitter that mediates attachment experiences and creates a feeling of well-being (Carter, Harris, & Porges, 2009), helping this person make a secure beginning with you. Ranging back over your own history, ask yourself if you have ever been in a therapeutic situation where you were met with an initial reception that helped establish such a connected state of mind in you, and write about the key elements of that experience here.

_____

_____

_____

_____

_____

_____

_____

_____

_____

Waiting Room

Now your new patient is in the waiting room. What experiences there might foster a neuroception of safety? Years ago, at our California agency, one of our young interns was quite introspective and so passed through the waiting room for breaks without really seeing who might be there. In a matter of weeks, all of us heard from several of our patients that this new person was "mean," "uncaring," "unsafe," "rude," and "stupid"—all reflections of our patients' perceptions of our intern's nonverbal messages. In reality, she was a deeply caring person who was still immersed in whatever had just happened with her previous patient. However, nonverbal messages so powerfully impact our relational right-mode circuits that they immediately get altered by our implicit coloration of their meaning.

This experience taught us that walking through the waiting room in a state of conscious, warm connection with all present helped maintain the neuroception of safety we also cultivated with comfortable, informal chairs; gentle music; art, travel, poetry, and science books side by side with *Time, People*, and Calvin and Hobbes (a perennial favorite). Some of our people began to come a little early to settle in, a few even dozing off. Mysteriously, new books showed up on the bookshelf to augment our collection. Perhaps they were leaving pieces of themselves with us for safekeeping; perhaps they were anchoring themselves to therapy by making sure they returned to read more from that particular book.

We also learned that our patients closely watched our interactions with one another. From our agency's earliest days, we knew we needed a safe environment to make the most of supervision, so we consistently cultivated respect, care, openness, and joyous good humor. Over time, we understood that the felt sense of these supportive relationships was forming a holding environment for our patients the way that a warm and stable extended family might. Many times we heard, "I feel like I'm coming home to the home I never had." While all of this has a sweet feeling to it, it also has an identifiable neurobiological component: We were consciously using the environment to begin to weave formerly disrupted neural nets into patterns of increased security.

After we had been in business long enough to afford a receptionist, we decided not to hire one because we wanted our patients' first greeting each time to come from their own therapist rather than from the business end of the office. This isn't feasible in every setting, but it does point the way toward building front office policies and providing training for staff that are based on the goal of fostering a neuroception of safety and secure attachment. Patients have told me about other therapy experiences, saying that a sterile environment resembling a traditional medical office leaves them feeling "generic," "impersonal," or "like a number or a file." In the real world, the best we can do is consciously build on whatever our current circumstances offer. Just our awareness of wanting to extend warmth and security will impact our patients' experience of the environment.

The First Session

Now, we welcome our patients into their first session, continuing our focus on safety and its relationship to the circuits of connection in both therapist and patient to support these first moments of engagement. As best we can, we offer calm, warm, caring presence, laced with curiosity about who this person is and respect for his or her willingness to seek help. Thanks to my own years in therapy, I have a healthy regard for what it takes to enter a situation where I am going to share the most tender aspects of myself with a stranger, coupled with the memory of being met with such warmth and concern for my well-being that it fostered enduring connection. Neural nets formed during conditions of emotional meaning and intensity have additional strength, and first meetings almost always offer abundant opportunity to forge these nascent connections. Then, if we are able to consistently offer this kind of presence, the new neural net embodying the experience of healthy relationship gains strength through repetition.

Through our mirror neurons and resonance circuits, we—therapist and patient—immediately influence one another's neural firing and autonomic activation. If my embodied brain is in an integrated state (middle prefrontal circuits online and ventral vagal system engaged), then I will be more able to both resonate with and regulate whatever dysregulation my new person may bring. At first meetings, my system has a quality of increased alertness that doesn't quite rise to the level of caution, but does give voice to my amygdala's awareness that something new is about to happen. When this is coupled with curiosity, my sympathetic activation can be used in service of connection.

Traditional wisdom says that rapport is the most important outcome of the first session, and we can see that neurobiological discovery supports that idea. To deepen this connection, we want to build on the wordless experience of safety we are offering to help our clients feel received without judgment through our *mindful attentiveness* to their primary concerns. This is often the first way that mindfulness enters the therapeutic picture—not as a formal practice or even as encouraging mindful awareness in our patients, but through their experience of being embraced by our caring observer. *As long as one person in the dyad is mindful, the regulating capacity of that state is present for the interpersonal system.* Although a high degree of regulation may or may not happen in the first session, we will begin to notice times when greater synchrony flowers between us and our patients (Marci et al., 2007). At those moments, we might picture the two of us in the hub of the mind (Badenoch, 2008; Siegel, 2006, 2007, 2010a, 2010b), able to direct our attention to any point on the rim (see Figure 7.1).

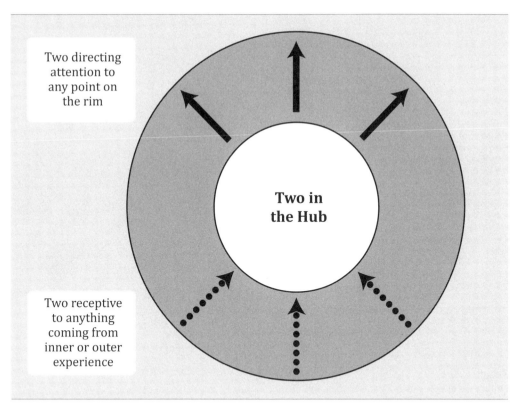

Figure 7.1. Two in the Hub. Therapist and patient in resonance with one another, able to direct attention to any point on the rim or sit in receptivity to inner and outer experience.

Holding this image in our minds from the first session can foster creation of that mindful space and extend an unspoken invitation to our patients, through resonance, to join us there, quietly fostering their capacity for caring self-observation. When those moments of synchrony occur, they often carry a quality that many have described as "sacred"—a hush that embraces both people in a sea of heightened awareness and goodness that is perhaps the subjective experience of powerfully enhanced neural integration. At those moments, it is a though the rim is surrounded and compassionately held by the hub (see Figure 7.2).

There is a subtle but important difference between observation of the rim from the hub and compassionate connection to rim experience. In the former, hub and rim can remain separate, while we often have the sense that we are more than what is occurring on the rim. People report calm observation of one part of the brain by another. The addition of compassion draws the rim experience into the embrace of the observing mind, likely activating our attachment circuits, drawing the orbitofrontal cortex and limbic circuits into closer connection. This can lead to greater integration between our caring ob-

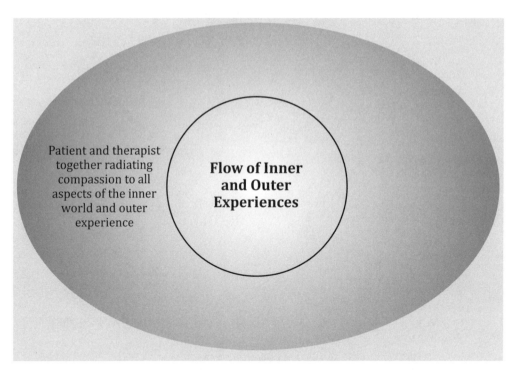

Figure 7.2. Two in the Compassionate Hub. Patient and therapist actively radiating compassion to all inner experience—thoughts, feelings, beliefs, sensations—and all outer experience entering through the senses.

server and the observed state of mind, and the hormones and neurotransmitters that knit people (and perhaps parts of our mind) together may flow more freely as well. These states do not always occur in this sequence, and often observation naturally leads to compassion. Nonetheless, it is helpful for us to be able to sense the shift that occurs in moving from one pathway to the other in ourselves and in our patients. Take a few moments to experience the difference between these two states—sitting in the hub and moving toward the rim, then shifting to receiving and embracing all experience with acceptance and compassion. Write a few descriptive words about both.

_____

_____

_____

_____

_____

_____

_____

_____

_____

_____

_____

What we talk about during that first session can also set the tone for the ongoing work. The first priority of receiving our patients fully sometimes opens the door to introducing the topic of brains and minds in the first session or two. I often begin with Daniel Siegel's hand model of the brain (first written about in Siegel & Hartzell, 2003) because it is tangible, portable, and begins to develop a strand of conversation that will be with us throughout the relationship (see Figure 7.3).

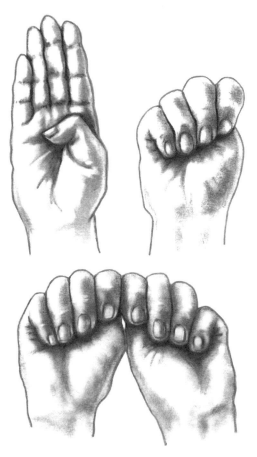

Figure 7.3. The Brain in the Palms of Our Hands. This portable brain is useful for making the brain visible and tangible for ourselves and our patients. Roughly, the wrist and arm are the spinal cord, the lower palm is the brain stem, the thumb is the limbic region, and the back of the hand from wrist to fingertips is the cortex. The two hands are the two hemispheres. If we picture an eye in front of the middle two fingernails of each hand, then we can experience our brains as gazing at us.

A young couple came in because they were having severe disagreements about how to raise their young child. With SNSs blazing, they insisted that I resolve their dispute by telling them which parenting style was right. For him, their child's freedom of expression was everything, and for her, good behavior meant they had done an adequate job as parents. Instead of casting a vote, I brought out the hand model, and, as I asked them about their early histories, I showed them how these patterns had been wired into their brains. Their hands were imitating mine, their eyes and posture were alert, and they moved easily out of sympathetic arousal into connection with me—so I knew they were listening with both their left and right modes. As we talked about the power of implicit memories, they could see why this had become a life-or-death struggle for them. In that first session, we also spoke about the process of attachment, neuroplasticity (without using that word), and how we humans are constantly influencing each others' neural circuitry. All of this exchange flowed naturally around their particular histories and concerns. When they left, they were using their hand brains to talk to each other in playful puppet voices.

When they came in for their second session, they were overflowing with enthusiasm about their brains, filled with questions, and reporting that they were fighting less because they quickly became curious about what was going on in each other's brains at those times. In our next few sessions, we got into emotionally vivid contact with the implicit reasons why they were each so invested in one parenting style. As their limbic tension resolved, with new connections springing up between the middle prefrontal and limbic regions (a process we traced with our hand brains), the door to parenting with their little girl's developmental needs in mind opened. This process moved with speed, grace, and excellent results, unfolding around our illuminating and regulating brain talk.

Bringing in the brain early, with the appropriate information offered at the right empathic moment and in ways that connect with the person's current concerns, adds a powerful strand to the conversation no matter the diagnosis or issue. Brain talk then becomes part of our narrative of healing. Here's another example. Last week, a man in his 40s came in for the first time, feeling dejected about his hostility toward his stepchildren. He said, "I just have bad character. What kind of man can't be civil to a pair of 8-year-olds? I'm so ashamed." I said, "I see how sad you feel about this. I want you to know that this isn't going to turn out to be a problem of character, but of neurobiology. The new brain science tells us that when we repeat behaviors we don't like, it's because the pattern is wired into our brains. The research also tells us that with focus, hard work, and a solid connection with another person, these patterns can and will change. I'm very glad you're here." The change in his posture and eye gaze let me know that he had heard me deep down and been able to let go of some of his shame.

When I work with people who have been severely abused, one ongoing concern is regulation because their nervous systems are often frayed and hyperreactive. As we look at what happens to the brain during trauma, right there in our hands, so to speak, patients begin to develop the circuits of caring observation toward their own mental processes. Then, when the memories pour in, at least some small percentage of their minds stands apart from the flood to understand what is happening. The increase in regulation is palpable, along with their growing sense that they have some control over the magnitude of the experience.

Let's spend some time reflecting on ways to bring the brain in during the first session or two. Think about a recent first meeting and imagine how this conversation might have begun. If you are introducing brain concepts regularly now, can you think of additional strands that might be added? Write about your experience here.

_____

_____

_____

_____

_____

_____

_____

_____

_____

_____

_____

_____

_____

_____

_____

This is one of those times when having a listening partner is particularly helpful. Spend some time brainstorming about recent first sessions. When and how might the brain and its interpersonal processes have come up? Play with the hand model, using one hand (for simplicity) or two (when talking about both hemispheres). Experiment with possible kinds of information you might share at an initial session. As you practice, notice the difference between delivering the information from left-mode processing only and from a more whole-brain, embodied state. What are the key ingredients that make the latter kind of sharing possible? Practice out loud with one another until you both feel settled in the experience of tracking the pathway from the needs your patients are expressing to a natural opening for conversation about the brain and mind. Developing this intuitive capacity takes a lot of consistent practice. While different aspects of brain functioning will be relevant in various circumstances, the hallmark of including brain information in ways that advance therapy, rather than detour us into left-mode-only territory, is enhanced empathy and connection. This will be a good page to dog-ear for future exploration as you add to your base of secure knowledge. As you and your listening partner work together, also notice if it is possible to be kind to yourselves in this process of developing increasing facility. Then write a few words here about how your practice of kind self-acceptance is coming along.

_____

_____

_____

_____

_____

_____

_____

_____

_____

What Our Patients Bring

How might we think about what our patients bring to this process? Neurobiology tells us that we human beings are primed for attachment and for neural integration as two primary biological imperatives. These are foundations on which we can rely as we begin. We can see our patients as ready and able to contribute to their healing path by virtue of these intrinsic twin tendencies. Take a moment to picture your patients as *embodied beings bent on healing*; then visualize them as *people with broken minds*. This shift in our perception can change the flow of energy and information in us—and therefore within the relationship—in a fairly dramatic way. Sense the difference in your body, feelings, and perceptions as you hold each of these in your mind. Then write descriptively about both.

Now, take this a step further and sense the influence these two states of mind may have on your patients as they resonate with the way you are holding them in your mind.

In addition to their basic human nature, our patients also bring their lived story—both their current concerns and their history—which they share in the way they hold their bodies, the pattern of their breathing, their level of activation, their degree of ease with eye contact, the tone and rhythm of their voice, as well as in their words. When we are able to attend to our resonance with these many flows of energy and information, the reach of our attunement expands. Sometimes, the particulars of the verbal story are the least informative, whereas the *relational patterns within the story, coupled with the body's symphony of clues,* tell us more. A quality of life disruptive enough to carry a person into therapy frequently contains elements that speak of early wounding. Attending to our bodies, we may find that we begin to create felt hypotheses about the points of disruption and dysregulation for this person, even though we know nothing of his or her factual history yet. As we accurately resonate with the messages our patients need us to hear with our bodies as well as our minds, we are expanding the foundation of safety, receptivity, and containment that encourages them to continue down the path of healing. Then when we ask, "How was this for you today?"—or something similar—at the end of the session, we may feel the wash of secure connection beneath whatever words they share about their experience with us. In my experience, this is a much stronger predictor of their returning for another session than any words they may speak.

Talking about the ANS with Patients

We're going to wrap up this chapter by thinking about the ANS beyond the initial session. Give yourself some time to reflect on your current patients, imagining who might most benefit from hearing about the interaction of the three branches. Once you have a clear picture of whom and when, spend some time writing a script of the imagined discussion in your journal. Then do some role-playing with your listening partner in which you speak the actual words you would share with this particular patient, rather than talking *about* what you might say. As you move through this process, you may find that other patients and scenarios come to mind easily—a clear request from your integrating brain to repeat this process until you feel ease throughout your body and mind with this particular information. Take a moment to notice any judgments that may have arisen about how you are doing in the role-play, extending kind acceptance to this part of your internal process as well, and writing a bit about that.

_____

_____

_____

_____

_____

_____

_____

_____

_____

_____

_____

Let me share an example of how talking about the ANS with couples in conflict can help shift the focus from fighting to curiosity about each other's inner worlds. Andrew and Maggie came for therapy because they were arguing so frequently that they had lost touch with the joy and playfulness that had filled their early days together, although they were both clear that they still loved one another and considered each other to be good parents for their two young children. Both expressed sadness and a strong sense of feeling helpless to make any change in this escalating pattern. We worked through family history to gain perspective on the roots of the mutual antagonism. Both had grown up in families that avoided intimacy and vulnerability through fighting, so the pattern was well ingrained at both an implicit (most important) and explicit level. I was impressed and heartened by how much empathy they could experience for one another's chaotic past during this deep and vulnerable exploration of history. Both of them expressed surprise that they were feeling little inward push to fight right then, while the same discussion at home would have brought on a most unpleasant argument about who had had it worse. Their curiosity about this opened the door for us to explore the workings of the ANS.

Andrew: (*As we finished looking at their family history*) I'm surprised. I feel so different right now—like no part of me wants to be arguing with you. How are you feeling?

Maggie: It's weird, but I don't feel like I want to fight either. (*pause*) It's like I'm seeing you more than I'm seeing myself. (*Looking toward me*) Does that make any sense? [Curiosity is activated in both of them—door open to right-mode and left-mode learning.]

Bonnie: It makes a lot of sense. Let me ask you a question. How safe does the space between the two of you feel right now? Check with your bodies and see if you feel safe or threatened. [We'd had a short conversation about how our bodies tell us about our emotions during the history-taking process, when Andrew was having difficulty identifying what he experienced in his relationship with his father. As soon as he directed his attention to his body, he resonated with the discomfort of being in his father's presence.]

Maggie: My body feels calm all over, and my shoulders are particularly relaxed. I think I feel pretty safe. [She had reported earlier that she had to get a massage once a week to keep away headaches that came from tension in her neck, shoulders, and upper back.]

Andrew: I'm relaxed, too, and I realize now that I hardly ever feel this way. I walk around with my fists clenched and my jaw tight. I've been noticing that kind of stuff since we talked about bodies. I do it even when I'm at work, and sometimes even when I'm playing with the kids—which seems really weird since I enjoy them so much. This may be the most relaxed I've felt in months.

Bonnie: (*Smiling, enjoying their mindful discoveries*) You're both learning a lot about how your bodies reflect your internal state. My body feels relaxed and open, too. The interesting thing is that when we're in this state, we can pay attention to one another, we have room to receive one another—and that seems to feel good to both of you. (*Both nod, smiling at each other and at me.*)

Andrew: I remember feeling like this when we were first together—and we had so much fun.

Maggie: (*Leaning slightly toward Andrew*) Me, too. (*He reaches over to squeeze her hand—the first physical sign of affection since we began.*)

Bonnie: I suspect that when you were first together, you felt pretty safe with one another because you were just discovering all the ways you felt happy in each other's presence. When we feel safe, our nervous systems support connection with each other, giving us room to really pay attention to the other person and enjoy the feeling of being to-gether—just like the three of us are now. We even have hormones and neurotransmitters that get active in that state and support it continu-ing.

Andrew: But why now? Why can't we do this at home?

Me: When you think about coming home after work, what do your body and feelings tell you?

Andrew: (*He reflects for a moment, tuning into his body.*) My face imme-diately tightens and my body literally goes into fighting mode. I feel like I have to defend myself, and I haven't even walked out the door of my office. My body even begins to feel a little hot. I know I'm antici-pating that Maggie's going to be mad at me as soon as I walk in the door.

Bonnie: Maggie, what do you feel when you know that Andrew will be home soon?

Maggie: Same thing. I know he's either going to be mad about what hap-pened at work or pick a fight with me. I hate that energy, so I tense up to keep it off me. I just want him to come home with a smile so I feel like he's even glad to be here. (*Andrew starts to get defensive, but then softens when he sees she is sad rather than accusatory.*)

Bonnie: [Andrew's easy shift out of defensiveness is good evidence that they are continuing to feel safe, which lets them remain in ventral va-gal activation/interpersonal connection, so I continue.] So you both feel unsafe before you even see one another. (*Pause as all three of us feel the sadness of that situation.*) The way our nervous systems work, as soon as we feel unsafe, even if we aren't consciously aware of it and even if there's no real danger, our sympathetic nervous system acti-vates to protect us. When we really are threatened, it's very useful, but when we've gotten into a cycle of feeling unsafe all the time, regard-less of what's happening in the moment, it tragically cuts us off from one another. When our sympathetic gets active in protective mode, it narrows our focus of attention to the threat and literally shuts down the circuits that allow us to connect with one another. (*Pause to digest that information; I notice that both are alert and intent, taking in the meaning of what we're saying.*)

Andrew: (*Engaging his inner scientist in the quest for more understand-ing*) Tell me more about how that works.

Bonnie: [I am aware that Andrew's left-mode processing needs to be grounded in detail in order to support his right-mode relational advances and that Maggie operates in a more intuitive, rapid right-mode processing way, sometimes getting impatient with Andrew's slower pace.] Let me give you the short version and then you let me know what more you might need. Our nervous systems have three parts—two kinds of parasympathetic and one kind of sympathetic (*using my hands to show three strands*). In general, the parasympathetic is like the brakes in a car, and the sympathetic is like the accelerator. The one that prefers to be online is the ventral vagal parasympathetic system, the one that supports staying connected to each other. (*Staying in tune with Maggie whose alert eyes indicates that she's hanging in there so far*) It lets us stay still and engaged at the same time by quieting our heart rhythms. It also is attached to the brain circuits that animate our faces and allow us to hear tone of voice—which are main ways we share emotional connection, much more than words. (*Aware that Maggie is starting to show signs of restlessness via her body language*) Maggie, do you know that feeling of being still and safe at the same time?

Maggie: I really feel that when I'm reading with the children.

Bonnie: You feel warm and connected with them?

Maggie: Yes!

Bonnie: That's the ventral vagal. That stays activated until you feel unsafe. Sometimes that shift can happen even without us being consciously aware because our brains are always on the lookout for what they believe is dangerous. Previous experiences, like you two fighting a lot, can make us highly sensitive to certain kinds of cues, so sometimes we react quickly and powerfully to small events.

Maggie: Like when Andrew comes home with a grumpy look on his face. When I think about that, I can feel my body tense up and my heart start to race immediately (*places hand on her heart*).

Bonnie: That's the shift into sympathetic activation that shuts down your ability to connect.

Maggie: This is even making sense to me.

Andrew: I don't want you to feel unsafe with me (*looking directly at her with tenderness*).

Maggie: (*tears in her eyes*) Thank you. Maybe we can think of ways to make it safe for both of us. I like it a lot better when we're connected like this.

Bonnie: (*I say nothing; enjoying their time in ventral vagal connection, strongly sensing that they have absorbed what they needed, both viscerally and cognitively, aware that the rest of the details of the ANS are unnecessary.*)

In the wake of this session, Maggie and Andrew began to be able to sense in their bodies when they were slipping into sympathetic activation, a mindful practice that allowed them to kindly observe and thereby regulate their nervous systems. Best of all, they made an agreement that, at those times, they would stop talking about whatever was upsetting them and focus on helping whoever of them was beginning to feel unsafe, creating a coregulating partnership that began to remind them of the emotional teamwork that had been so appealing when they first met. As they felt more secure with each other, the connections between their current upsets and their childhood experiences began to flow to the surface. They told me that at times they felt like two good parents sitting with the upset children inside, listening together as the old stories surfaced. Toward the end of our time together, I asked them what they believed the turning point had been, and both pointed to the day they realized that they were creating an unsafe environment for one another. Andrew said, "When we talked about that, I pictured how Maggie became a frightened little girl because I was pissed off at work—and that is the last thing I wanted to bring home. Something shifted inside me in a big way."

Sharing information about the brain can lead to these kinds of integrative processes in which our patients expand the embrace of their own caring observers, a reflection of stronger and more enduring connections between their limbic and middle prefrontal circuits. This caring observer stance not only changes brain function in the moment, but over time builds new brain structure that supports empathy, regulation, and response flexibility. Andrew and Maggie experienced a moment-to-moment increase in *choice* about how they would relate to one another that extended beyond reducing their fighting. Based on Daniel Siegel's (2007, 2010a, 2010b) triangle of well-being, we can picture a bidirectional paths of influence in which brain, mind, and relationships continually modify one another (Figure 7.4). As Andrew and Maggie fought, the triangle held their dysregulation in place, but as we moved through the therapeutic process together, the triangle truly became one that could support their well being as a couple.

In our work, Maggie, Andrew, and I experienced the dynamic relationship of the brain-integrating empathy and connection we developed, which supported increased mindful attention to their inner worlds. This introduction of mindful attention changed their ingrained neural pathways, creating enduring changes in their brains that led to their ability to *choose* to relate to each other with greater empathy. We can begin at any point on the triangle to experience how change there then begins a cycle of integration throughout the system—a useful way to picture the therapeutic endeavor.

While we're making our way through the healing process from the initial contact, we're also developing ease in using this information during all the phases

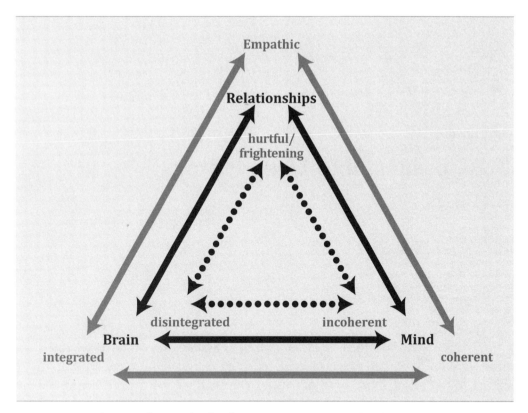

Figure 7.4. Based on Siegel's Triangle of Well-Being (2007, 2010a, 2010b). Shows the mutual influence of brain, mind, and relationships, either in the direction of regulation or dysregulation.

of relationship. Some of the practices will unfold over weeks, months, or years as we incorporate this information into our way of seeing—a true embodied paradigm modification. The image of a tapestry with new strands seems to capture the way these ideas and experiences become interwoven with our other perspectives. It may be helpful to mark the pages that call for repeat visits while we move on now to listening to the lived and spoken narratives that our patients bring to us at the beginning of the relationship.

Chapter 8

Leaning into Deep History

We may often think of history taking as asking a set of questions about our new patients' lives—an exercise in increasing explicit awareness. We gain more access to the parts of our patients' inner worlds if we think of listening for the patterns and activations of implicit history as well. This latter tale animates their bodies and mobilizes their nervous systems, guides their relational choices, speaks of their values, influences their degree of resilience, shapes the meaning they find in their lives, and so much more. When we can expand our listening to include these layers, we provide a broad space into which our patients can feel fully received. For my part, I feel like I am flying blind in regard to my patients' influential inner life until I settle into both their wordless and worded narrative. This exploration, then, is not so much a fact-finding mission as *a full-bodied entrance into the neural pathways and subjective reality of their lived experience.* It begins with the first session even before a word of early history is spoken.

Listening for Implicit History

At our first meeting, Alex alternately sat and paced for the first half, then settled into some greater degree of safety, at least enough to maintain a bit of connection as manifested through calmer, more sustained eye gaze and a sense of growing interest in our conversation. With this transition, I felt as though I was *present in his mind for the first time.* At that moment, he found a more coherent way of speaking and was able to tell me why he was here—"to figure out in my head why I cheat on every girlfriend." He explained that he didn't mean to, but it just happened, usually around the 9-month mark when things were settling into a good pattern after the initial anxiety of meeting someone new. It seemed "weird" to him that only after he was "found out" for his cheating and then "abandoned" did he give much thought to the possibility of this happening. "I'm surprised like it's never happened before. What am I—crazy?"

At this point, he was sitting on the edge of the couch, leaning toward me with wide eyes. Seeking to help him further calm his nervous system so that we could connect, I found myself breathing a little more deeply, cultivating calmness as I talked with him about how all behavior makes sense, even when we don't quite know how yet, and that we would figure it out together. As he calmed a little, I said, "When we find ourselves doing things that are in conflict with what we would consciously choose, the roots are often in our deeper mind, in patterns we learned early in life." His eyes went back to normal size, and with a deep breath, he sank into the couch for the first time.

This exchange was the beginning of his sharing his *felt/lived/embodied narrative*—and here is what I heard/saw/perceived: a body predisposed to anxiety with difficulty settling; relational behaviors with girlfriends springing from the deep well of the eternally present past, deep enough that when the urge to cheat emerged, he was so caught up in the moment that he lost even explicit awareness that these destructive actions were happening again; an attachment system eager for connection, coupled with the healthy capacity to be regulated by someone calm, warm, and with some understanding of his deeper world. It was clear from how it quieted his nervous system that the news that his behaviors and lack of awareness weren't crazy seemed profoundly reassuring. I could also feel my mind wanting to move gently toward his storehouse of memories to see and experience the inner community patterns underlying his relationship-destroying ways. As though he could feel my curiosity, he said, "Let me tell you what happened when I was only 3 years old."

Let's practice listening for the clues to implicit history. Take a few moments to sense what you know about a close friend's story. If you let go of the facts, what other ways do you have of understanding his or her implicit attachment story? His or her history after that time? Write some words about how you know as well as what you discover. Do you listen with your body, your feelings, or your intuition? What kind of knowledge arises from cultivating this kind of awareness?

_____

_____

_____

_____

_____

_____

_____

_____

_____

_____

_____

_____

_____

_____

_____

Sometimes focusing on the implicit roots is the only way to make sense of a person's self-story. Let me share a dramatic example. A brilliant and caring woman has helped thousands of young cancer patients live longer and healthier lives. From outside evidence, we know that she is loved and appreciated for her brilliance and compassion by her young patients and their parents. In therapy, she says, "I'm stupid, without a heart or head. I don't care about anyone except myself." She is rigidly glued to this experience of herself, and if encouraged to think about it differently, says, "I can say the words to you, but I know the truth." She is saying that her body and mental models know the implicit truth so deeply that her entire conscious experience takes its shape from them, no matter how different that is from how others experience her. We could say that she has poor reality testing (several therapists did—and that was the end of the relationship), or we could wonder about implicit relational learnings that happened so early they *built her brain around these felt truths*. For her, these knowings are body- and feeling-syntonic, so there is no disputing them with new thoughts. In fact, as her story emerges, it becomes clear that she is merely giving explanatory words to her experience of being utterly rejected as a baby, information that continuously pours into her left-mode, making-sense brain from her right-mode experiential circuits.

If we don't stand in her implicit shoes, her self-story makes no sense, creating such a dissonant experience in us that we may feel the need for her to reconcile her perception of herself with how the world sees her to give *us* some relief. However, if we are able to take the viewpoint of assuming that there are valid implicit influences shaping her self-knowing, the dissonance is quickly replaced by a sense of profound compassion for her suffering both as a child and as an adult, even before we know her full history.

Let's pause here to call to body and mind some times in therapy when you may have felt this painful dissonance between your patient's self-story and your perception of him or her. Notice the impact on your body, feelings, and perceptions. Sense what you want to say to this patient. See if focusing on possible implicit roots allows this dissonance to dissolve into nonjudgmental compassion, noting the shift in your embodied experience. Then write some descriptive words about the change you notice as you sample these two states of mind.

_____

_____

_____

_____

_____

_____

_____

_____

_____

_____

Often, our state of mind regarding the truth of our patients' stories or the realism of their self-assessments will have a significant influence on *their* sense of being heard and understood. Not only does our opinion in this area guide our next therapeutic moves, but the resonance between the two of us means that any doubt will stir ripples within patients even if we are verbally accepting. Nonjudgmental acceptance is rooted in our capacity to see the congruence between our patients' self-stories and the underlying implicit mental models that drive them. Once we are able to experience that perfect fit, our urge to cognitively counteract or contradict their stories will be replaced with curiosity and care concerning the roots. The shift in the room is palpable.

As we settle into our caring observer state of mind and open ourselves to receive our patients' stories, we participate in the kind of interpersonal joining that flowers in every emotionally significant relationship. We start to receive these living stories from the moment we attune with patients as our mirror neurons and resonance circuits create echoes of their internal experience within us. With Alex, his anxious movements, wide eyes, rapid breathing, and difficulty settling gave me hints about his possible early regulatory experience before I heard anything of his history. At the same time, I was internalizing his wordless experience through resonance, making room for felt attunement with his implicit story. In both these ways, my body and brain began to make a map of his inner world through both right-mode responses and a whole-brain envisioning of his story. Then, as he began to tell me about what happened to him at 3 years of age—violence between his parents that terrified him, followed by a contentious divorce—his inner presence began to take on more differentiated contours in my mind.

During our next two sessions, as he described his life, many aspects of his parents, siblings, teachers, coaches, and others began to take up residence in me as activations in my nervous system, flows of feeling, images, and increasingly complex connections between his childhood experience and his unplanned infidelities. Through both conscious attention and nonconscious attunement, my mind was building an increasingly differentiated neural "house" that we could inhabit while the healing work unfolded. Within a few weeks, a felt sense of his early history and inner community peopled my mind whenever he entered the room or came into my awareness between sessions.

The Pervasive Influence of Mirror Neurons and Resonance Circuits

What can we know about the neurobiological basis of this rich interweaving that literally embeds another human being inside us—and us in them? We are at the beginning of understanding the multiple ways in which we become part of each other. One widely acknowledged theoretical model suggests mirror neurons and resonance circuits as being likely candidates underlying this process (Iacobini, 2009; Siegel, 2006). Mirror neurons fire both when we are doing a particular action and when we observe that same action. Interestingly, another set of neurons in these regions fires for doing the action and then inhibits firing when the action is observed, solving the riddle of how we can resonate without imitating as well as differentiate between our own actions and those of other people (Mukamel et al., 2010).

So far, we might picture a one-to-one correspondence between the observed action and its echo within us, but it turns out that only about one-third of mirror neurons operate this way. These *strictly congruent* cells light up only when performing and observing the identical action. However, the other two-thirds of our mirror cells fire for observed actions that "achieve the same goal or are logically related" (Iacoboni, 2009, p. 600). These *broadly congruent* neurons seem to provide the basis for our "coordinated, cooperative, complementary actions" (p. 660), supporting our moment-to-moment dance with one another. This is true whether it is a dance of secure attachment or of abuse.

Mirror neurons are also the leading edge of a complex resonance circuit that culminates in empathy—our felt sense of oneness with another person. There may be some value in following the full path of this circuit, as best we know it, to catch all the flavors that it brings to us. When we witness a familiar intentional action, the representation of that action is sent from the *superior temporal cortex* to the *classical mirror neurons*, creating a bridge between action and *perception of intention* (Carr et al., 2003). At that moment, we are already internally participating in movement with the other person, both at the level of action and of where that action will take us together (strictly congruent and broadly congruent). This is true whether we're observing someone grasp a cup or grimace in pain. From there, the information is sent back through the *superior temporal cortex*, where we further sense the *intention of the other* and make a representation of his or her *next move* (Carr et al.). From there, the *insula* picks up the energy and information from the neocortex and passes it to the *limbic region, brain stem*, and *body*, where we nonconsciously sense the *emotional meaning for us* of the incoming message. "For us" is important. Our limbic region is also the home of prior encoding in regard to the safety or danger of particular experiences, so it will color the incoming information with our implicit perceptual bias. This sometimes results in a felt sense of the other person that reflects our own evaluation rather than a close resonance with his or her inner state. This certainly gives us every reason to be humble about what we do or don't know about another. The information is then passed, via the *insula* again, to the integrative *middle prefrontal circuits,* where the *full chord of empathy* can be completed (Goldman, 2006; Siegel, 2007). This process happens in milliseconds continually, with a few of the resulting chords resonating in consciousness, while most remain out of awareness but still influence our inner milieu and outer behaviors.

Now let's take a little time to solidify our knowledge of the resonance process in left-mode knowing. Gathering up your journal, write a paragraph or so about the neural pathways of interpersonal connection, noticing what's clear and what's cloudy, reviewing as needed until you feel a settling clarity. Transitioning from learning to speaking, spend some time with your listening partner discussing the concept of mirror neurons until you feel at ease. Notice if there are judgments about how you are learning this, and with kindness toward your judging self, release those critical or congratulatory voices into caring observation, writing a few words about the shift in your body as you move from judgment to kind acceptance.

Having practiced the intention to release any arising judgments for a while now, we may find we are doing this with greater or less ease than before. Many of us grew up in families that used judgment (good–bad, acceptable–not acceptable) as a tool for securing good behavior, probably because our parents believed that this was necessary for success in the world. If that is the case, letting go of judgments to move into curiosity about the origins of a particular behavior can be difficult because it may raise fear of failure or feel disloyal to the family. Using this small space to reflect on what flows of energy and information you internalized from your family about the importance of judgments may help ease the process of holding them less tightly.

_____

_____

_____

_____

_____

_____

_____

_____

_____

_____

_____

_____

_____

_____

We're going to return to mirror neurons and resonance circuits for a moment because they have such a strong influence on the therapeutic relationship. As Iacoboni says, their influence is "pervasive and automatic" (2009, p. 657). Let me offer one small example from the research to give a sense of how little input is required to shift our inner state without our awareness. Participants did a scrambled-sentence language task, with some exposed to sentences that contained words that might be associated with the elderly (e.g., *Florida, bingo, gray*), and others not. Then the researchers timed their walk back to the elevator. Those exposed to the "old" words moved more slowly (Bargh, Chen, & Burrows, 1996), apparently unconsciously imitating the gait of the elderly. The word given to this phenomenon is *priming*. However, as we relegate the concept to a class of experiences, we may consign it to a space in our mind that loses touch with the significance of this finding. Instead, let it point us toward the powerful, unseen influence of word choice, facial expression, posture, eye gaze, and the thousands of other small inputs we offer our patients and they bring to us. One potential effect of this awareness can be that it helps us move together in a collaborative dance that is part imitation (strictly congruent mirror neurons) and part cooperation (broadly congruent mirror neurons).

On the other hand, even our fleeting visual and auditory expressions can touch our patients' inner world in unexpected ways, influencing how they perceive us. During a week when sadness was likely somewhat visible in my eyes because of the recent death of a friend, several of my patients worried that they had displeased me in a variety ways that were consonant with their childhood experience of disappointing their parents. I am usually delighted to see my patients, so my interiority and quietness echoed in them like a loss, I suspect, and was interpreted according to their limbic perceptual bias. Of course, these same kinds of experiences unfold in us as we receive our patients' fleeting cues. Sensitivity to these kinds of shifts, whether they happen in or out of awareness, can help us be more open and curious, instead of anxious, when we feel mysterious forces moving within us or our patients. Awareness of the flood of information we are constantly sharing with one another can also protect us from leaping to judgment about what is behind our patients' behavior with us. Staying in a state of ease with *not* knowing in the moment, while remaining settled in the big picture of the unfolding healing process with our caring observers, seems to ease the process down the road.

As we said above, mirror neuron research is in its infancy, and some scientists have questioned their presence and function in humans (Lingnau, Gesierich, & Caramazza, 2009). Whatever the case, we can experientially verify that our brains contain some neural processes that weave us together. Right now, new developments are afoot in the mirror neuron world. A 2010 study has revealed additional locations of single neurons with mirroring properties in the *medial frontal cortex* and *medial temporal lobe*, including the *hippocampus*, regions implicated in encoding, retrieving, and integrating explicit memories (Mukamel et al., 2010). These new developments suggest that we may pick up more diverse flows of energy and information from others than the already rich feast of movements, intentions, and emotions proposed to be offered by classical mirror neurons and their resonance circuits (Iacoboni & Badenoch, 2010). The implications of this important research for how we internalize one another (whether in or out of the therapeutic setting) will unfold in the years ahead.

Now we're going to further ingrain this new knowledge by practicing speaking about the resonance process with particular patients and circumstances in mind. Rounding up your listening partner for some role-playing, call to body and mind a patient or two who might benefit from understanding the resonance process. Then practice talking to these people until you feel comfortable and at ease sharing in several different situations. Remembering to be daring and playful can grease the wheels nicely. After practicing, take a few moments to reflect on your developing relationship with your listening partner. In particular, what do you notice in your body, feelings, and depth of thought when you are being *listened to*? How does *attending to* your partner expand your awareness?

_____

_____

_____

_____

_____

_____

_____

_____

_____

_____

Opportunities for Sharing about Resonance Circuits

Mirror neurons and resonance circuits not only help us understand how we influence one another's brain wiring in the moment, but they also underlie the process of internalization by which we acquire a permanent inner community. Through resonance, we embed the intention and emotion of the other, then add our sensory experience of them, then weave that together with our own response to the encounter to produce the paired states of mind we experienced in Chapter 4. Many of my patients want to better understand "how these people got in there," so our conversation goes easily to resonance processes. This scientific grounding often gives them permission to recognize these states of mind as neurobiological realities rather than "some psycho-babble about inner children." With the constraint of skepticism removed, we can much more easily move into this crucial work.

Working with families offers another opportunity for fruitful sharing about resonance. One of the obstacles in doing therapy with children is that the parents understandably want quick fixes for behavioral problems. Some conversation about how their inner state echoes within their children, coupled with an understanding of their own attachment style often helps them let go of the need for an immediate change in behavior and develop a willingness to explore the roots of their own attachment. As they become more able to see how their state of mind is touching their children's state and behavior in the moment, they are often able to shift from criticism and control to calmness and understanding. This inner change then resonates within their children who feel seen, and, therefore, calmed. Parents are delighted when this change in focus from wanting acceptable behavior *fast* to an interest in creating secure attachment and learning about their youngsters' developmental needs actually leads to better-behaved kids as a natural byproduct.

Our resonance circuits certainly help us listen to the implicit story of early attachment in a way that simple left-mode awareness of the facts cannot accomplish. As we talk with patients about these particular neural processes, they are also able to understand their history in a different light. The intergenerational influences become clear, and judgment of themselves and others diminishes. This awareness helps them step into their caring observer to develop an increasingly compassionate understanding of their life experience. So even in the process of sharing their history, they are building some new neural circuitry and having initial experiences of integrative neuroplasticity.

Now we are going to shift our angle of vision a bit to see how sensitivity to attachment histories can draw us more deeply into our patients' inner worlds.

Listening for Patterns of Attachment

As we attend to the spoken part of our patient's story, we can listen for attachment themes. To whom could this person attach as a very young child? What flows of relational energy and information shaped his or her developing brain? How did these experiences implicitly define the nature of connection? How does this person respond to offers of relationship and experiences of rejection now?

We can also take in the way the tale is told. Which parts feel enlivened and which feel dead? Are some stories rich in detail and some barren and arid? Do some segments of the history agitate the body, whereas others soothe both speaker and listener? Are the past and present mixed together, or is there a smooth narrative flow in which the past is truly past? What happens in my body while the story is being told?

Neurobiological research confirms what developmental and attachment psychology has suggested: At the earliest stage of life, our mothering person/people build brain structure, laying down the pathways in which our relational energy will run most easily. The more frequent the repetition and the greater the emotional intensity when neural nets are formed, the greater the probability of them being activated again (Siegel, 1999). After initial formation, these new circuits will be myelinated, giving them additional stability and speed. Given the biological imperative of attaching, the lack of much previous wiring in our infant brains, and implicit-only memory for the first 12–18 months, we can picture a neural system that is developing lasting structure that will operate mostly out of conscious awareness and subjectively be experienced as stemming from present conditions when reawakened. For these reasons, this system is strongly constrained by these established patterns of attachment.

The Solidity of Secure Attachment

Sometimes this is a good thing. In secure attachment, the core foundation supports ongoing integration, so the neural circuits are constrained in ways that produce flexibility, coherence, and resilience, with the system primed for drawing new experience into the flow of increasing complexity—the underpinning of mental health. This may seem like an odd way to use the word *constrained*, which means limited or bound, yet that is exactly what neural structure does—it determines the content and boundaries of our brain's neural firing patterns. For example, during the earliest days, the securely attaching adult's warmth, delight, and attunement are neurobiologically grounded in the activation of his or her orbitofrontal cortex—the area most strongly associated with attachment. This, in turn, lights up the same circuits in his or her baby's brain. Then at the genetically predetermined time, around 24 months, these prewired circuits connect with the maturing limbic region, forming the beginning loop of regulation, empathy, attunement, and moral action. The

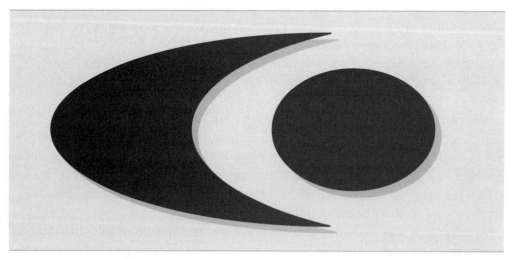

Figure 8.1. The Feeling of Secure Attachment. A sense of protection, of being known, of being delighted in, accompanied by sufficient freedom for the child to explore his or her own movement and timing. If this were animated, it would become a kind of dance of attunement in which the child feels neither squeezed nor abandoned.

The Brain-Savvy Therapist's Workbook

system is thus *constrained* in this delightful and health-producing way. Each of the diagrams in this and the following sections seeks to capture the relational essence of the particular attachment experience.

When a person with this kind of brain wiring shares his or her story, we experience a right-mode to right-mode bath in warmth, ease, and satisfaction. As the story flows, our own brain integration is supported, giving us perhaps a sense of relaxed alertness and deep seeing at the same time. Daniel Siegel's (2007) acronym FACES—flexible, adaptive, coherent, energized, and stable—as a definition of mental health, takes on living form in this embodied narrative. Sit for a moment and recall hearing that kind of narrative in therapy or from a friend. Notice the response in your body, emotions, perceptions, and overall well-being. Then write some descriptive words about what you discover.

_____

_____

_____

_____

_____

Most of the people who come to our offices aren't carrying this kind of implicit and explicit attachment story. As a way of understanding the disrupted flows of energy and information our patients bring to us, we can picture again the three distinct patterns of insecure attachment as identified by Mary Ainsworth (Ainsworth, Blehar, Waters, & Wall, 1978), Mary Main (1996), and Erik Hesse (Hesse & Main, 1999): avoidant, ambivalent, and disorganized. We discussed these previously in regard to our own histories, and are revisiting them here because it is so useful to be able to stand in our patients' attachment shoes, especially against the backdrop of our discoveries about our own attachment history. While many of us have been trained to view the people with whom we work through the lens of diagnosis, I have found the perspective of implicit attachment patterns to be a much more efficient and effective way to deeply understand the issues at hand because of how they illuminate the deep roots of the relational struggles our patients bring. Even when the occasional client comes in with a good deal of secure attachment, this awareness helps us make use of the developmentally solid ground available to us for doing whatever work does need to be addressed. On the other hand, these early-forming patterns and the neural correlates underlying them can also help us understand the developmental origins of severe symptoms. I have found that this vantage point goes a long way toward removing the stigma and fear from such diagnoses as borderline personality disorder or dissociative identity disorder.

Our greater clarity and calmness in the face of the intensity of upset become the very ground on which healing can occur.

We can begin by acknowledging what we discovered in our own attachment patterns—that, in practice, most of us develop a complex set of attachment possibilities, with perhaps one dominant style and others that manifest in different relational circumstances. As we sorted through her history, one of my patients began to clearly see that her three long-term relationships took turns echoing the pattern of attachment she'd had with her mother (chaotic), her father (distant), and her great-aunt (warm and stable). The breakdown of the first two marriages had brought her to therapy; the third relationship developed when we were near the end of our time together and culminated in a marriage that has remained satisfying for a number of years now. It seemed that as the attachment struggles with her parents took up less neural energy, there was room for the healthy pattern with her great-aunt to come to the fore.

Thanks to long experience with Mary Ainsworth's Strange Situation protocol, we know that implicit attachment patterns are neurally ingrained by the time a child is no more than 1 year old (Ainsworth et al., 1978). We also know that these pathways are held in implicit-only memory because explicit memory does not begin to be available until at least the very end of the first year. This means that our patients' explicit accounts of their earliest experiences are formed through the perceptually biased eyes of others (parents, neighbors, relatives),whereas the subjectively experienced story is held in our patients' bodies, emotions, and relational mental models. How can we catch a direct glimpse of these early days? As our calm, receptive self offers safe haven, it is likely that our patients' prewired attachment system will begin to come online, influencing how they feel in our presence and how they relate to us. As we open our minds to receiving them deeply and begin to ask questions about their early life, the emerging story will often carry the energy and information of their implicit attachment. This happens with our child patients as well, except that we will ask no questions and their attachment stories will emerge spontaneously in the sand tray, on the playroom floor, and through their interaction with us. We just need to develop the eyes to see it and the capacity to hold it.

The Arid Landscape of Avoidant Attachment

As we did with secure attachment, let's taste the flow of energy and information in the three insecure forms, beginning with the avoidant attachment ingrained by dismissing parents who implicitly teach their children to ignore or avoid connection. When parents raise their children without much emotional awareness or resonance with their inner worlds, they wire their offsprings'

Figure 8.2. The Feeling of Avoidant Attachment. Parent and child do not see or dwell in each other's faces and voices, so both are thrown back into tasks and left-mode aloneness, with competence standing in the place of connection. If this were animated, there might not be much movement.

brains to avoid contact with the enlivening information coming from right-mode processing. There is not necessarily a lack of love here, but care is demonstrated by hot meals, help with homework, and concern for success rather than interest in their children's lived experience. Because these parents can't offer attuned listening, the connections between the limbic region and middle prefrontal on the right don't develop well in the children, making for impoverished pathways between the hemispheres. At the same time, these parents are likely supporting strong development of left-mode processes in their children. Since the map of the body is located in the right mode, these children grow up with a kind of emotional blindness because they can't hear their bodies' messages. The materials for their spoken narrative are often quite sparse because the felt story takes shape in right-mode awareness before finding organization and words in the left mode. This way of knowing can hold facts and chronology, but in the telling, the story often feels lifeless. We can picture some forms of vertical integration in right-mode processing as well as the pathways between the two hemispheres being constrained in their push toward integration (Siegel, 2006). This image can perhaps give us a visceral sense of the loneliness and disconnection between parent and child whenever there is a need for emotional support.

In the playroom, we often find that avoidantly attached children tell their attachment story by jumping easily into play, working earnestly with the materials at hand, but often barely noticing that we are in the room. They are usually slow to ask for help and even slower to seek understanding. When one young boy showed frustration at not being able to get some blocks to balance well, he looked shock at his therapist's accurate reflection of his state of mind. Adults who share this narrative often tell a factual, left-mode story without a shred of life in it: for example, "We lived here, and then we moved there, and then I went to school here." Often, when asked about how these family relationships *felt*, there is only blankness or a sense of cardboard cutouts interacting with no vital energy.

To move more deeply into a felt sense of what it is like to be with someone struggling with an avoidant attachment, it is helpful to invite into awareness one of your patients who has this quality of emotional deadness. Sense the range of impacts you experience when you listen to his or her narrative, paying particular attention to any behavioral impulses that arise in response to your resonance with this person. Then write some descriptive words about this experience.

_____

_____

_____

_____

_____

_____

_____

_____

_____

_____

For now, we are becoming familiar with these implicit markers so that we can enter into our patients' inner world with greater ease and accuracy. In the coming chapters, we will explore ways to guide the brain back onto the integrative path. Since boredom, sleepiness, and anxiety are frequent responses to encountering this deadness, it is helpful to read these responses as both resonance with our patients' inner becalmed state and our normal response to lack of connection. Expanding our compassionate embrace to hold our own and our patients' minds opens the door to regulation for us as well as providing a nonjudgmental space to receive them as they are right now. One interesting aspect of avoidant attachment is that the person's limbic system does fire when there is an offer of connection (Siegel, 1999), although these activations don't rise to the level of conscious awareness because of the various blocks and undeveloped neural pathways. The ongoing inner need for attachment, however, will provide a way in, at the right time, and gives us reason to hold onto optimism even while we sample the emotional lifelessness.

The Inconsistency of Ambivalent Attachment

Ambivalent attachment, in contrast, is filled with teeming aliveness, but sometimes without much regulation. As the word indicates, parents who offer ambivalent attachment to their children alternate between attunement with their young ones and preoccupation with their own inner worlds. This means that when parents are in an integrated state, experiences of security flow easily to their children, but when unhealed childhood wounds are activated, their youngsters are caught in the distortion of the parents' altered perceptions. One moment, Mom is laughing and playing with her son on the floor; the next moment, she is sad and disappointed because the still-excruciating memory of her mother's death washes through her. Her son can make no sense of this shift in his mother because it isn't related to anything that happened between them. Feeling frightened and helpless, he may withdraw or cling in an attempt to make things right, while the chemicals of anxiety bathe his body. If this pattern continues, his nervous system will learn that this level of sympathetic arousal is normal, making it even more difficult for him to connect with his mother or anyone else for soothing regulation. During the window of time when the parents' attuned caretaking ideally is building connections between the limbic region and middle prefrontal in the child, the process is frequently disrupted by the parents' inability to maintain their own integration. Our diagram on the next page suggests the anxiety-producing inconsistency between the comfort of security and the pinch of the parents' perceptual bias shaping the child's developing sense of self and relational expectations.

Ambivalently attached children are often all over the place in the playroom, filled with energy and interest, but moving between states of connection and disconnection with us. Initially, it may not be easy to help them regulate until they get the sense that we will be able to stay in consistent attunement with them. Adults share this same attachment narrative through their heightened activation, rapid speech, difficulty organizing ideas, and often with changes between past and present tense that don't seem appropriate to the events. One moment my patient is talking about her deceased brother in the past tense, then in the present—"He is so violent with me." I can feel the dis-integrated implicit well up, bringing the experience of the old trauma into the present.

Take a few moments to allow your patients to come to mind, being receptive to those whose energy has this quality. What happens in your body, emotions, and especially in your behavioral impulses as you sit with their dysregulation? What words do you want to say to them? If you extend your compassionate attention around their experience and your own, what changes do you notice?

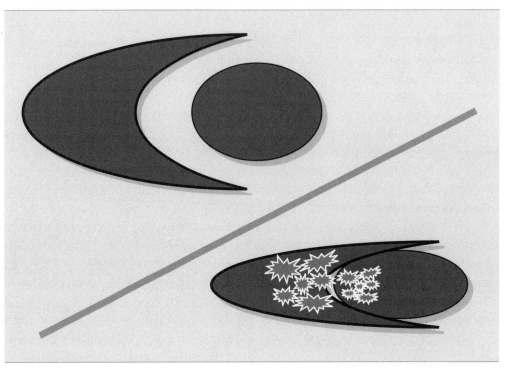

Figure 8.3. The Feeling of Ambivalent Attachment. Unpredictable alternations between the warm connection of security and the parent's engulfment in his or her own history. In this lost mode, the mothering person paints her child with the colors of her own history, losing sight of the real child who is there. The youngster experiences this as a frightening abandonment, usually ingraining a pattern of heightened anxiety. If this were animated, the dance of security would be followed by the child being squeezed into the shape of the parent's need.

_____

_____

_____

_____

_____

_____

_____

_____

As our patients' highly charged narrative unfolds, we may feel a strong need to bring order out of chaos. However, if we can hear our own anxiety or need to manage as resonant echoes of our patients' upset, we can use our own disturbance to draw more deeply into their inner worlds. Maintaining a calm, nonjudgmental space around the activation, rather than directly stopping the flow, may provide the opportunity for their first sustained experience of regulation.

The Violent Inner Landscape of Disorganized Attachment

So far, we have sampled attachment patterns that leave us with three possible coping strategies. Security offers resilience and the high likelihood of healthy relational choices. Avoidance opens the path to competence and success, while ambivalence can leave traces of connection and hope amidst the anxiety. The frightened child may find that she can soothe the parent, relieving the sense of separation, or the straight-A student may generate some delight in his otherwise emotionally invisible parents. Except with security, neither of these strategies is without cost, but they do protect us from massive fragmentation. As caring avoidance gives way to coldness or hatred, and occasional moderate chaos becomes a whirlwind of terrifying energies, our young minds can find no resting place, no means of separating from the freezing or blistering environment and no way to join it—"fright without solution" (Hesse & Main, 1999). These twin pathways lead to the same result: an inner world with no cohesion and implicit messages of ongoing relational disaster.

Our minds can easily grasp that terrifying trauma leads to fragmentation, but it may be more difficult to envision how utter rejection disorganizes the mind or how a parents' wordless inner terror produces just as much incoher-

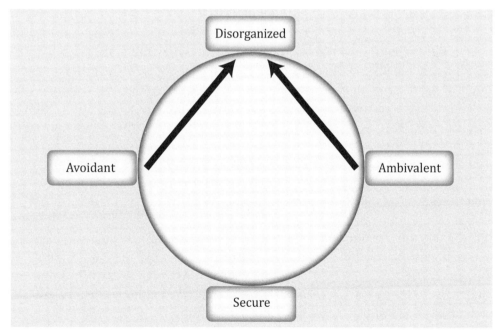

Figure 8.4. Pathways to Disorganization. If we push caring avoidance toward hatred and ambivalence in the direction of the dominance of chaos, we arrive at disorganized attachment.

ence in a child as acts of violence. If we imagine the unstructured infant limbic circuits, animated by the biological imperative to connect, seeking to meet calm, warm, brain-shaping attunement, then meeting instead the hate- or terror-filled eyes of a parent, we may be able to picture the devastating impact on the child's brain. The parents' hard rejection or terror-infused embrace pushes the child's nervous system into extreme states and begins to encode implicit memories of an impossible bind. The infant must go toward the parent, but finds only an embodied experience of annihilation or terror there. Instead of melting into continuity and regulation through their parents' eyes, these youngest ones are either cast into oblivion or caught up in the whirl of terror. In either case, there is no empathy to glue these fragments together, no alternate place to turn for comfort, and so the child's mind falls into dissociated fragments while also remaining awash in a sea of implicit mental models of utter terror, rejection, and abandonment.

Let's look at the example of a child who comes into an overtly orderly household mired in covert hatred for this particular young one. Over time, implicit mental models coalesce around repeated experiences of hatred and rejection. Some of these are then translated into verbal precepts that provide a kind of organizing receptacle to manage the child's disintegrating mind. Since our left mode must make sense of right-mode experience, completely rejected children may use the harshest self-hatred and self-blame, coupled with a conviction that they are poisonous existences who should not be part of human society, to find a way to explain the flows of energy and information in their bodies, minds, and closest relationships. This template of being a despicable creature then shapes their interactions with everyone, leading to a life that walks a tightrope of never getting close to anyone, while acting in ways that induce people to agree with their negative self-assessment, yet still doing what is necessary to survive. Interestingly, many times these deeply wounded people lead productive, helpful lives in spite of these damaging wounds, as though they have an intuitive connection that draws them to provide assistance for other people who are hurt.

To step outside of this rigidly held view of themselves exposes them to the frantic disorganization that lies just beneath the surface, so they often cling tenaciously to the life-denying self-hatred. All of this excruciating damage is implicit, which makes it impossible to challenge at the level of thought or to step outside for an alternate, current-day view of themselves. To reach the depths necessary to transform these patterns, we must first understand the implicit origins and then be able to hold the intensity with warmth, calmness, and patience long enough to wear away the implicit stronghold. We will talk more about this kind of work in the next two chapters.

A different pattern of disorganized attachment often arises from overtly abusive situations. Rather than being dominated by continual implicit distortion, much of the fragmentation may be isolated in pockets that come to life when internal or external events touch them. The rest of the time, one of the other attachment patterns governs the relational worlds of these individuals. These reawakened traumatic experiences, often held as implicit-only memory initially, generate feelings of extreme helplessness as people are pushed into highly agitated or collapsed states of mind, without their permission and often without any understanding of the reason for the disruption or clear pathway back to more organized states. Many of my patients have said, "I am insane—I should be locked up," as they deal with what seem like random shifts into states that they don't initially recognize as part of themselves.

While each person with disorganized attachment develops his or her unique set of strategies for limping through the world, the disorganization lies just beneath the surface, vulnerable to any passing internal or external experience that brings up waves on the implicit sea or touches dissociated pockets of traumatic experience. The barely concealed fragmentation creates an extreme fragility that we may experience in our bodies as great caution and hesitancy in our therapeutic movement. One patient described her situation like this. We were talking about how implicit memories of security can provide a resilient foundation. She said, "I feel like a pyramid standing on its point rather than its base." That image captures the degree of precariousness in maintaining any kind of mental coherence that is the correlate of these kinds of disastrous attachment experiences. While no symbolic image can fully capture the disintegration and pervasive terror that results from this kind of treatment, perhaps we can get a small taste from this abstract figure on the next page.

In the playroom, usually after trust has been firmly established, as children begin to touch their pockets of disorganization, they may whirl around, fall down, throw up, dissociate, become destructive, cry, scream, or become incoherent or incontinent as the waves of extreme fragmentation crash through their bodies, nervous systems, emotions, and perceptions. If, knowing their history, we can see where they have gone internally and remain calm amidst the resonance, these children are often able to respond quickly to the embrace of regulation—their systems are wide open to receive disconfirming experiences of stability, care, and compassion. With adults, one of the hallmarks of the movement into disorganized neural nets is extremely fragmented and incoherent speech, terrified eyes, sometimes interspersed with periods of collapse and dissociation.

Spend some time now reflecting on people you have seen over the years. Invite any experiences with disorganization to come to mind, noticing the effect on your body, nervous system, feelings, thoughts, and overall well-being. How did you manage your resonance with these flows of shared energy and information? Make a few descriptive notes.

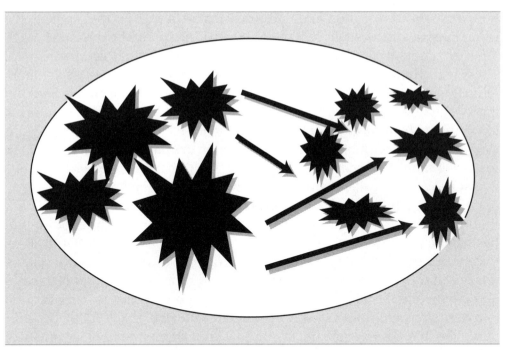

Figure 8.5. The Feeling of Disorganized Attachment. For parent and child engaged in this attachment style, there is no refuge—all roads lead to chaos. Patterned by the circuits in the parental brain, the child wires in fragmentation and terror without relief, without a continuous sense of self. Most often these fragmenting experiences are held in dissociated embers that flare up when touched by an interaction or situation that bears some resemblance to the initial experience. If this were animated, the arrows would terrify and blast parent and child into further dis-integration while the child's and parent's pieces whirl around without a sense of purpose or direction.

_____

_____

_____

_____

_____

_____

_____

_____

_____

_____

Often, our patients will initially share stories of trauma and neglect without much affect, and even without the bodily agitation that can be the leading edge of disclosure. Because of the severity of the impacts, the walls separating explicit knowledge of events from the implicit visceral upset are solid for the sake of survival. Over time, as trust builds, the full wash of disorganization will flood the room, completing the story. Words fail as terror and fragmentation disable the mind, and we may feel a similar disruption within ourselves for a moment. As we are able to contain our resonant response with clarity about what the patient is experiencing, the waves will subside within us and we will become the milieu in which the patient can also settle. In this way, history continues to unfold throughout the course of therapy, not only for those struggling with disorganization but for everyone.

Bringing It All Together

We have gone deeply into the differing attachment patterns at this point. It may be especially helpful to spend time with your listening partner, exchanging experiences you have had with your patients. This type of sharing will help you further differentiate the characteristics of the four basic patterns, while also searching out the interplay of several styles within some people. Pay particular attention to how your bodies and minds move in resonance with each person. How does your own attachment style influence how you interact with your patients? Is it different according to their pattern, with some being easier than others? Write a few notes here about that.

_____

_____

_____

_____

_____

_____

_____

_____

_____

_____

_____

_____

_____

_____

_____

_____

_____

You might also talk with one another about how and why you would share information about attachment with your patients. Would you be inclined to share it differently depending on the person's style? How would talking with a person about attachment advance the empathic connection? When would it seem unwise to have this conversation? Then select a few patients for whom this conversation would be appropriate, and practice talking with them until you and your listening partner feel a comfortable flow.

Moments arise in therapy when talking about attachment can convey both clarity and hope. If attachment status is delivered like a diagnosis, we can amplify our patients' self-rejection, hopelessness, and despair—"This is who I am, and now I understand why I can never have a relationship that will be good." However, as we weave in pictures of the brain's relational wirings at the right empathic moment, with a strong emphasis on the brain's neuroplasticity, the information can cement the partnership and define pathways for working together. After Alex told me about the violence and divorce that shattered his home when he was 3 years old, the door was open for us to begin to explore that territory.

Alex: I rarely think about those times, but it always makes me feel sick when I do.

Bonnie: (*Feeling my own stomach tighten*) What a rough time for that very young child. You were very small then.

Alex: (*Pausing, looking at his hands, connecting with something real, anxiety much less, then a deep breath as he looks up.*) I don't think they even knew I was in the room most of the time when they fought like that.

Bonnie: (*Nodding, tracking both his pain and his ability to reflect on the pain, feeling a big sigh come to the surface.*)

Alex: (*Sighing deeply at about the same time*) Do you think this has anything to do with my cheating?

Bonnie: Our brains are very vulnerable to making patterns at those young ages. How our parents relate to one another and to us makes powerful pictures that we deeply believe are how relationships must be. It's as though they etch that image onto our brains and then we find relationships that will roughly match that image, relationships that will feel the same even if the details aren't the same. Do you notice anything else in your body when you think of those times?

Alex: (*Beginning to shift and fidget, breathing escalating, eyes darting as he draws closer to the memory*) Well, I feel nervous and scared, like ants running through my whole body.

Bonnie: (*Feeling my heart rate go up a bit, too*) So this is what you

The Brain-Savvy Therapist's Workbook

learned relationships feel like. Not calm or warm or reassuring, but anxious and scary.

Alex: (*After a quiet pause, looking up sharply with strong attention*)
   THAT'S why I can't stay with my girlfriends. As soon as I feel good with them, I have to go, have to be anxious again.

Bonnie: (*Deeper breathing, nodding*)

Once he felt settled enough in our relationship to get connected to his body, Alex was always a quick study. He could make rapid comparisons between what he was feeling in the moment of memory and what he felt in the present when he was headed down a destructive track—the core of our how attachment experiences guide current relationships. Being quite a physical person, integrative pathways between his body and his limbic and middle prefrontal circuits kicked in as soon as he had some support for calmness and guidance about sticking with a particular piece of history. In this case, we didn't use any of the language of attachment categories, but we stayed centered in the relational pattern that had been encoded in his body and brain. Same information, different words. Staying with our patients' sense of direction and working with their strengths allows us to offer this information at a moment when it will nurture both empathy and awareness, leading to mindsight (Siegel, 2010a, 2010b).

What can happen when therapists come from the perspective of attachment? I once had the opportunity of working with a group of interns in Portland who had mainly been trained in cognitive–behavioral methods. We met about once a month for half a year. After beginning with some basic brain structure and function, we talked about the neurobiology of attachment and brain development in the first 2 years of life. When I returned a month later, their supervisor took me aside and said that she heard them wandering the halls talking about attachment—their own, their patients', their families'. They reported that their therapeutic work was moving more quickly, and they felt like they knew what they were doing for the first time. In what might look like a contradiction, instead of preplanning their interventions, as they had done in the cognitive–behavioral approach, they found themselves coming into sessions with a relaxed openness to what their patients were bringing. A number said that they were energized rather than tired after sessions, a sign that this work was leading to neural integration.

Although resonating with our patients' attachment stories isn't the only way to know them, it does ground us at the roots of their implicit world in a way that diagnosis doesn't. Since behaviors tend to spring from that source, it gives us a foothold at the origin of their struggles. This felt sense of their attachment patterns usually begins to unfold in the midst of their spoken family history.

The combination of our warm receptive presence, intention to see and know them deeply, and questions about early relationships begin to bring the flows of relational energy to the surface. It is helpful to approach history with a couple of basic questions: What was it like to be with your family when you were small? When did you feel safest? Least safe? When did you feel most cared for? Least cared for? When did you feel most understood? Least understood? Their answers will lead the way to the next question and the next. As we are available to walk into their inner community, they will often take us into the fully embodied experience of their early life.

Our listening minds and bodies can begin to resonate with the flow of implicit history as soon as we make first contact with our patients. Then when we move from present-day concerns to the backstory, those flows begin to differentiate into attachment patterns and inner community members. As we begin to inhabit one another's minds, we are establishing the foundation for the dance of neuroplasticity. It is as though we have joined hands and dipped our toes into the wavelets along the shore in preparation for the long team-swim through unexplored waters to the other side.

Chapter 9

Discovering the Principles of Change

Now we enter into the heart of therapy. Here we are going to focus mainly on some of the brain's *principles* of change, which can give us a framework to consider when evaluating approaches that might be the most effective. Recent research is giving us a more refined picture of how we can nurture change within the ever-present embrace of the therapeutic relationship. Moving slowly through the core concepts and the science behind them, we will pause to gain left-mode clarity, investigate our implicit and explicit responses to these paradigms, reflect on the kinds of methods we are currently using as agents of change, and practice speaking about these hopeful ideas with our listening partners. I will offer lots of examples; then you and your listening partner can add your own to settle the principles into practice. Here we go.

Revisiting Implicit Mental Models

Basically, we are asking how we can use the natural processes of our embodied brains and minds to foster *integrative neuroplasticity*—leading to brain change that manifests as increasing . . .

- Neural connectivity
- Flexibility and balance of mind
- Resilience under stress
- Capacity to experience strong feelings while remaining regulated
- Subjective sense of meaningful life
- Creativity, playfulness, and joy
- Relational goodness.

These are some of the landmarks that emerge as mental health expands. Our own experiences in Part I laid the groundwork for a paradigm that emphasizes the importance of awakening and holding right-mode experience with acceptance and kindness as an essential element in creating a neural milieu that supports change. I believe it also became apparent that the root of most of our difficulties lies in the implicit aspects of unresolved memories. We have found that these unseen mental models guide our thoughts, feelings, and behaviors in directions that continue to support and reinforce the truth of the pattern.

As we uncovered these roots in our own work, we may often have been surprised by the coherence with which our implicit model necessitates the inner or outer activities that have seemed unwanted and irrational from our left-mode viewpoint (Ecker & Hulley, 1996, 2000a, 2000b, 2008). For example, my mind tells me that getting enough sleep is a good idea, yet I continue to get up very early in the morning no matter what time I go to bed. I then feel tired and irritated at my unreasonable behavior. Moving away from the self-criticism, I ask what it would be like to sleep in a little bit on days when my schedule allows, and then I listen for my body's response to this idea. Anxiety wells up immediately, radiating from my stomach out to my chest, arms, and legs. When I sit with this bodily sensation and ask about its roots, a memory arises in which my parents are very angry, saying I am lazy because I like to sleep in on summer mornings. I see them both standing at the foot of my bed with scowls, then ripping the covers off and ordering me out to weed the garden. I can feel how I get up early now because being tired is better than facing the wrath of my inner parents. From this point of experiencing (not cognitively understanding) the connection between my implicit model and my behavior, change becomes possible.

Through our inner explorations, we have also found that these mental models are held either as the flow of relational expectations that continuously guides our perceptions and actions, or as dissociated aspects of memory that activate when prompted, steering us on courses we would not choose with our conscious minds.

• In the case of the first, we are rigidly and continuously held prisoner by unseen and unresolved relational patterns generated in the distant—and yet eternally present—past. This underground flow of anticipation influences what we expect to happen, how we behave on a moment-to-moment basis that creates what we expect, and generates perceptions that the pattern is present even when that may not be the case. In other words, we continuously, actively, and without conscious awareness construct our experience to match our implicit truth (Badenoch, 2008; Toomey & Ecker, 2007). One man's mental model of relationship is that he must be regarded as insignificant because his mothering person had no time, attention, or attunement for him. Today, he is strongly drawn to women who barely know he exists.

• With the second, we are vulnerable to the reawakening of encapsulated memories and memory fragments—with their accompanying mental models and patterns of activation. These don't have the benefit of being part of the integrating and regulating flow of the brain at large, making them the only game in town when triggered by internal or external events. Every time her teacher frowns, a 7-year-old girl becomes too anxious to sit in her seat because her implicit world tells her that hitting comes next. No matter how many times her teacher *doesn't* hit her after frowning, the child remains hypervigilant and lives on the edge of anxiety because the memory of what a frown meant in her chaotic home is still locked in a dis-integrated implicit layer of memory.

Two Paths for Changing Implicit Mental Models

We are going to explore two intertwined avenues of changing these deep patterns of implicit experience: (1) fostering *complexity in right-mode relational circuits* to increase regulation and change mental models of relationship; and (2) bringing the *implicit roots of thoughts, feelings, and behaviors into explicit awareness* as a prelude to transformation. Both of these begin with patient and therapist coming into emotionally vivid contact with the implicit experience.

Let's begin with some reflection. Thinking back through a few sessions with different patients, see if you can sense which experiences promoted contact with right-mode experience and which tended to keep the process centered in the left mode. All our sessions involve moments when we are having left-mode conversations since that is the medium of usual social discourse, and many moments have the right-mode juice of relationship. As much as possible, with curiosity rather than criticism, notice if and when there is a deliberate shift into right-mode focus to help your patient move toward implicit experience. What prompts you to do this and how do you guide this process? Then write some notes about what you discover.

_____

_____

_____

_____

_____

_____

_____

_____

_____

_____

_____

_____

_____

_____

_____

_____

After you gain some clarity, it will be helpful to spend time with your listening partner, comparing notes about right-mode and left-mode processes. The purpose here is to add a layer of awareness about where our therapeutic partnerships are headed at any moment during a session. Just changing our inner world in the direction of embracing the importance of right-mode experience begins to extend an unspoken but powerful invitation to our patients as well.

The Science of Neural Change

Let's look at some key aspects of the science of neural change. For most of the time since we humans began thinking about mental–emotional processes, people believed that once implicit memories were tucked away in long-term storage, they could never be modified. These neural pathways might be modulated by enhanced connectivity with other circuits, or an alternate set of neural nets might be put in place that would give us another possible response to similar conditions, but the implicit itself could not be changed. As with almost all new discoveries about the brain, we are finding that there is far more flexibility in implicit memory than we previously believed.

In short, studies have shown that when an implicit memory in long-term storage is actively responding to current perceptions—meaning that the neural circuit in right-mode processing holding the memory is activated and producing an emotional or behavioral response—*and* if, in addition, current perceptions clearly contradict the mental model contained in this implicit memory, then *the synapses of the memory circuit can move from a locked state into a malleable state in which new energy and information can fundamentally rewrite them, eliminating the original mental model from implicit memory* (Pedreira, Perez-Cuest, & Maldonado, 2004; Rossato, Bevilaqua, Medina, Izquierdo, & Cammarota, 2006; Winters, Tucci, & DaCosta-Furtado, 2009; for a clinically oriented review of this research, see Ecker, 2008, and Ecker & Toomey, 2008). This process of updating an implicit memory, which neuroscientsts term *reconsolidation,* may allow for a variety of opportunities for change, as we shall see. When a newly revised memory is restored, or reconsolidated, it contains a *different* implicit pattern with *modified* bodily sensations, behavioral impulses, emotions, perceptions, and global mental models, including models of relationship to self and others—the now-familiar ingredients of implicit memory. This is the clear and simple principle; application of it is a complex interpersonal process, as we shall see.

Factors Influencing the Degree of Change

It is likely that at least three factors influence the level of change: (1) the degree to which the implicit memory is *differentiated*; (2) the *emotional vividness* of the right-mode experience of that memory; and (3) the *accuracy and emotional aliveness of the new and disconfirming energy and information* added to the neural net (Badenoch, 2008; Ecker & Toomey, 2008; Fosha, Siegel, & Solomon, 2009; Schore, 2010; Toomey & Ecker, 2007, 2009). These three factors are central for understanding how we can facilitate the embodied brain's natural movement toward increasing integration. The indispensable foundation for all change processes is the resonant relationship between our patients and ourselves. This process rests on two capacities we have been developing: the conscious and nonconscious resonance between our patients and us, and the presence of mindful awareness in one or both. Often, the disconfirming experience lies in the quality of the relationship, making our capacity for attunement and stability an indispensable ingredient. In regard to mindfulness, where attention goes, so goes neural firing, so as we attend to these newly arising right-mode experiences, we will be able to hold them steadily in awareness to make room for the new energy and information.

Memory Differentiation. Let's look more deeply at the three conditions. First, memory differentiation. Many of our clients come in manifesting a state of global misery that fuels persistent relational struggles, with often-inaccurate left-mode explanations or bewilderment about why these experiences keep happening. We have found that in a trustworthy interpersonal environment—one that anticipates patients' capacities for uncovering what is needed in the moment and is open to receiving whatever arises—many times our patients' minds begin to move toward the specific blockages to integration. One person may move from overall agitation to awareness of specific body sensations, which then leads to a long-forgotten affective memory of being shamed. Another may come in feeling irritated with me, and when met with care and curiosity about the irritation, feel a rise in anxiety that is then contained and regulated within the relationship. In both cases, the general state of discomfort or defense resolved into a more differentiated experience that was connected to implicit roots and contained a manageable amount of energy and information.

Let me give a more complete example. An older man came in for a session with stomach-churning anxiety. He believed that this agitation came from financial concerns (left-mode guess/explanation). Talking about how this economy concerned him brought no relief, but as soon as we attended to one right-mode strand by directing attention to the feelings in his body when he thought about finance, the edges of his implicit terror about bodily survival came into emotionally vivid focus. Staying with this feeling, his mind further refined the experience by offering images of a hospital stay when he was 3. His parents were not there for reasons his young self could not understand, but the result was survival terror. As this memory came to conscious awareness, the rush of terror in his body intensified some, and our joined minds were able to regulate it. Then we were able to provide an experience of companionship for this child self/state of mind. During that session, we moved through these layers: first, the shift from left-mode conversation to right-mode bodily awareness, then into gradually differentiating layers to the root experience. Depending on the nature and developmental age when the implicit root was encoded, it may not connect to an explicit memory, but instead come to consciousness as a pattern of activation (sympathetic or dorsal vagal parasympathetic), a surge of emotion, intensification of bodily sensations or movements, and a shift in perception.

This process of differentiation seems to confer regulatory benefits as well in that activating smaller groups of neural nets modulates the intensity of autonomic activation. As we can see, even when language is involved, these are not primarily left-mode events. In fact, we work in a variety of ways (more below and in the next chapter) to create conditions in which left-mode inquiry is suspended or moves to the background so that the right mode can have its voice and move our patients through the process of differentiation.

Contact with Emotionally Vivid Experience. This mindful process of right-centric focus on finer and finer layers leads automatically to the second condition: coming into contact with bodily based, emotionally vivid experience. Implicit memories, whether fully dissociated by trauma or held out of conscious awareness by lack of attention, are in right-mode processing. We can't dig them out with left-mode pressure, but we can invite them into experience (sometimes initially nonconscious, then moving toward becoming conscious) by opening our attention to body sensations, behavioral impulses, and feelings, as happened with the anxiety-ridden man. As was said above, we can begin that shift by attuning our own awareness to the right mode, which then sends an unspoken resonant invitation to our patients.

Adding Disconfirming Energy. Once implicit memory is in an emotionally vivid, right-mode state, in conscious awareness for the patient–therapist joined mind, it is available for new information. The research cited above concerning unlocking synapses, coupled with decades of anecdotal clinical evidence (Badenoch, 2008; Ecker & Hulley, 1996; Schore, 2003a, 2003b, in press), suggests that in this state, various forms of energy and information that *discon-*

firm the ingrained perception of an implicit memory can be used to modify it. When terror is met by both resonance and regulating safety, or when the implicit conviction of worthlessness is met by the visceral experience of being valued, the implicit memory is transformed a little or a lot. Whether or not words are involved, the firing patterns that change involve the right-mode neural nets that hold the implicit memory. If this process is mediated by language, it seems to be most effective when the words have some of these qualities: poetic, direct, concrete, metaphorical, fresh, or descriptive—right-mode language that embodies the visceral experience (Panksepp, 2008; Schore, 2009a).

As the implicit comes into conscious awareness, new connections between the limbic and middle prefrontal regions form, increasing the strength and complexity of the regulatory circuits as well. When this newly integrated pathway is then met by an attuned other offering a disconfirming experience, or if that experience arises simultaneously in the patient's own awareness, the mind's dissonance-detecting circuits seek to resolve the conflict, often changing the implicit memory in the process (Ecker & Toomey, 2008).

There is also likely a correlation between the strength of change and the degree to which the disconfirming experience is a definite and vivid contradiction of the implicit memory (Ecker & Toomey, 2008). This is the corollary of our first proposition: Differentiation of the memory opens a clear pathway and prepares a receptive space for the just-right disconfirming experience to bring the antidote. Bruce Ecker and Laurel Hulley, the originators of coherence psychotherapy, have found that deep, lasting change appears to result most consistently when they guide the *simultaneous* experiencing of an implicit mental model brought into awareness and a new, disconfirming experience. They use the phrase *juxtaposition experience* to refer to this precise and resonant contradiction between the implicit root and the disconfirming perceptions, which they describe as a richly experiential, special form of affectively anchored cognitive dissonance (Ecker, 2008, 2010; Ecker & Hulley, 2000a, 2008). In the psychodynamic tradition, a "corrective emotional experience" (Alexander, 1946/1980) has something of the same flavor if we take this phrase to mean a conscious, felt dissonance of old and new learnings, without any invalidating or pathologizing of the old, implicit learnings as being irrational or maladaptive.

Let's spend some time reviewing these principles until there is a sense of clarity about them. In your journal, write a paragraph about each of the three, until you are satisfied with your understanding. Notice any discomfort or disagreements you have with this way of thinking, and make some notes about that, too. We are a left-centric nation, and our therapy training often emphasizes cognitive treatment options, so it wouldn't be surprising for a right-mode focus to cause some implicit and explicit concern. Write a bit in your journal about what you discover. Then see if you can call to mind and body experiences in which uncovering the implicit root and having a disconfirming experience brought change in your own or your patients' implicit mental models. When you are ready, make some notes here about that.

_____

_____

_____

_____

_____

_____

_____

_____

_____

_____

_____

_____

_____

_____

_____

As always, conversation with your listening partner will enrich the experience and settle the new discoveries more deeply in both your left- and right-mode forms of knowing.

It is vital that we distinguish this process from left-mode corrections undertaken via reframing, challenging so-called irrational thoughts and replacing them with rational ones, giving instructions for different behavior, helping our patients generate plans for new actions, and other processes that arise in the left mode. There are no direct neural connections between the amygdala on the right and verbal modules on the left, so reasoned words don't reach the source of the difficulty (Halgren, 1992). Since the implicit roots have not been addressed, these interventions can create only a new neural net that stands in opposition to the ongoing implicit knowing. The middle prefrontal cortex can quiet the amygdala, to some degree, and the person will have developed an alternative response to particular thoughts, feelings, and behaviors, but the implicit pattern has not changed. This situation leaves us vulnerable to reacti-

The Brain-Savvy Therapist's Workbook

vation of the implicit pattern under stressful conditions that take the left-mode offline (Badenoch, 2008; Ecker & Toomey, 2008; Schore, 2009a).

Instead, we garner more permanent change in right-mode processes by developing pathways up from the activated right-mode limbic region to the middle prefrontal cortex, particularly the ventromedial (orbital) cortex (Schore, 2009a). The first words that come from this experience, offered by either patient and therapist, are often spoken in language that takes shape in the right mode rather than the left (Panksepp, 2008). If this experience goes on to become part of the spoken narrative, it may take on left-mode words, but it remains tied neurobiologically to the right-mode experience so that the story keeps its coherence and aliveness. Figure 9.1 summarizes this process.

These thoughts about left-mode processing do not apply to mindful awareness as we have been practicing it here. Receptive attention is a powerful means for opening the gates so that right-mode voices can be heard. Used this way, it is a path of discovery rather than a strategy for control. Daily awareness of the body, thoughts, and feelings, as well as meditative practices dedicated to receptivity, lovingkindness, and compassion, build the brain structure of regulation and empathy (Lazar et al., 2005; Lutz et al., 2008), and broaden the scope of our caring observer so that we are able to hold our own and our patients' emotional intensity with greater steadiness and less strain.

Take a few moments to notice your explicit and implicit response to these thoughts about left-mode interventions. Notice any bodily sensations, behavioral impulses, emotions, and perceptions that arise. Then, holding them with kindness, write some notes here.

_____

_____

_____

_____

_____

_____

_____

_____

_____

_____

_____

_____

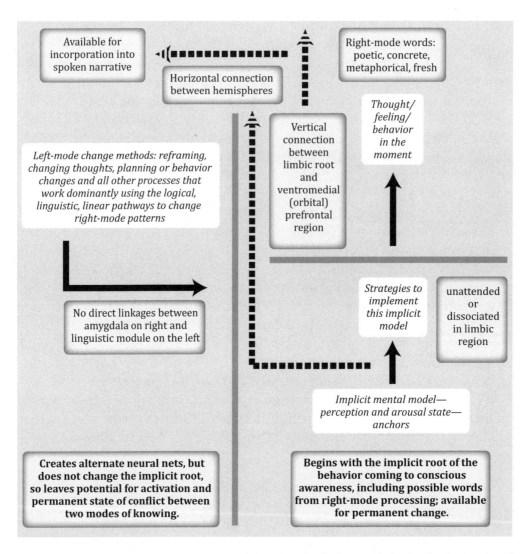

Figure 9.1. The Neurobiology of Left- and Right-Mode Neural Change Methods. The discoveries of neuroscience are allowing us to trace the pathways that are strengthened through left-centric interventions and right-centric contact with the implicit world. The former can create a new set of neural nets, but do not modify the implicit domain, while beginning with vertical integration on the right gives us the opportunity to modify the core implicit mental models that drive so much of our relationally difficult experience. Drawn from the work of Badenoch (2008), Ecker and Toomey (2008), Toomey and Ecker (2007, 2009), and Schore (2009a).

Building the Window of Tolerance

Now let's consider the factors we might bring to awareness in deciding how to implement these principles. When people sustain trauma or attachment losses early in life, before the connections between the amygdala and orbitofrontal cortex are built, their right amygdala becomes hypersensitive to stressful conditions, harbors mental models of expected danger, is encoded with terror and anguish, and lacks connection with other circuits for regulation—a truly horrendous stacking of the deck against a fulfilling life. Diagnoses such as borderline personality disorder and other Axis II conditions, dissociative identity disorder, posttraumatic stress disorder, and a whole host of somatic difficulties are often the result.

In conditions that foster secure attachment, the firing of the mothering person's orbitofrontal cortex lights up the same region in her baby even before its genetically primed time of integration with the limbic region (about 24 months). When this has occurred, linking between the limbic and orbitofrontal happens effortlessly because the circuits are prepared, and such integration continues to be supported within the relationship. Under these circumstances, interpersonal regulation gradually builds self-regulation as these links become stronger. The security of the relationship has built the foundation for right-mode complexity, which supports resilience and healthy relating.

However, in stressful early conditions, when the baby's orbitofrontal cortex isn't prewired, the linking with the limbic region is sparse and spotty when integration begins at 24 months. This makes it difficult later in life for a child or adult to regulate his or her autonomic nervous system and emotions under even moderately stressful conditions. This is sad because our capacity to regulate our bodies and emotions has everything to do with the subjective quality of our lives. If we are easily pushed into anxiety by small amounts of stress, for example, we may feel chaotic and helpless, as well as robbed of choice and well-being.

We are describing a constricted window of tolerance for right-mode processing. One aspect of the window relates to sympathetic activation and fight–flight, and the other to dorsal vagal parasympathetic activation freeze response that often manifests as collapse/dissociation. In therapy, as Allan Schore (2009a) says, we use the relationship to allow our patients "to reexperience dysregulating affects in *affectively tolerable doses in the context of a safe environment, so that overwhelming traumatic feelings can be regulated and integrated into the patient's emotional life*" (p. 130, Schore's emphasis). In other words, we are working mindfully at the edges of the window of tolerance so that together we can gradually expand our patients' ability to hold strong emotions of all kinds (see Figure 9.2). One of the sad consequences of trauma and attachment loss is the inability to tolerate both joy and fear.

We can have one potentially dysregulated edge or two. If the trauma or attachment loss led to the high sympathetic arousal of fear and anxiety, but fell short of the complete helplessness and hopelessness that leads to dissociation, then only the sympathetic system may be easily dysregulated. If, on the other hand, it became clear that fight and flight were not going to save the day, then the dorsal vagal parasympathetic freeze response, manifesting as col-

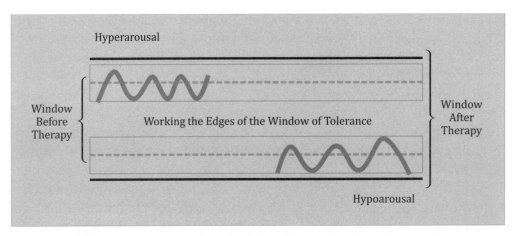

Figure 9.2. The Window of Tolerance for Right-Mode Experiencing. One of the most important aspects of therapy is to widen the affective window of tolerance to contain a greater intensity of emotion. We do the most effective work at the edges of the window of tolerance where we can hold our patients' sympathetic (hyperarousal) and dorsal vagal parasympathetic (hypoarousal) activation in our more ample window of tolerance. Based on the work of Ogden, Minton, and Pain (2006), Porges (2007), Schore (2009a), and Siegel (2006).

lapse and dissociation, and often accompanied by shame and disgust, may have been the only means of survival. In that case, it is likely that both the upper and lower affective windows of tolerance will be small.

One patient said to me, "I spent all my time imagining that it wasn't happening, and so I thought I had no imagination at all." As we work together now, she can only tolerate integrated awareness of early trauma—the confluence of body sensations/movements and autonomic arousal and emotions, accompanied by acceptance that these attacks happened—in miniscule doses. When we brush up against full awareness, it is profoundly dysregulating. In the meantime, she frequently has severe body sensations and shaking that seem unrelated to any event she remembers, so she feels as though she is lying or insane. This response alternates with periods of deadness that also make no sense to her. This dissociative splintering saved her life at the time, and now we must focus primarily on building the circuits of regulation in both windows of tolerance, bit by tiny bit, so that her widened window will be able to tolerate and hold the threads of her implicit and explicit memories as they draw together into integrated wholes. These assembled memories then become newly differentiated pieces that are ripe for linking with the flow of her larger brain processes. She is able to make use of our relationship, finding it reassuring that I understand what is happening in her body, brain, and mind when she can't. It is equally essential that my nonconscious resonance with her extreme upset is consistently held by my regulatory circuits so that we don't either escalate or dissociate together.

When the flow of our patients' inner life is disrupted because of these sparse neural connections, *right-mode to right-mode interpersonal regulation* can build the essential connections between the limbic region and the oribotfrontal cortex for the first time. This new "construction" unfolds within the therapeutic relationship as our autonomic nervous system moves in synchrony with our patients'. When the relationship is experienced as safe enough, the dissociated experiences will begin to come into conscious awareness. As we resonate together, the activation will amplify and, if our window of tolerance is broad enough to contain this energy and information, our patient will also experience a widening of his or her window. In the research of Carl Marci and colleagues (Marci & Reiss, 2005), these moments of autonomic synchrony were subjectively experienced as empathically rich interpersonal joining. This research showed that within the session, our nervous systems will flow into, out of, and back into synchrony many times. This rhythm is parallel to the dance of mother and infant as they move from attunement to rupture and back to repair over and over, laying the foundation for security, optimism, and resilience.

While these regulatory experiences take root, we are meeting our patients' emotionally vivid implicit memory of danger and absence of connection with the rich disconfirming information of safety and presence, and the mental model of attachment begins to shift. This process may unfold without words, in the millisecond interactions of warmth and containment that take place between us as the dissociated emotions are released from their limbic prison, rise into emotionally vivid awareness, and are met with resonance and containment. At other times, we may offer emotionally vivid, right-mode words that embody the specific disconfirming experience.

Let's spend some reflective time to call to body and mind some experiences in therapy (our own or with patients) when we have encountered these window-of-tolerance edges. What was the experience in body, feelings, and perceptions of both the sympathetic and dorsal vagal edges? What do you sense has happened to your affective windows of tolerance over time? Don't rush to words, but as some arise from the experience, write them here.

_____

_____

_____

_____

_____

_____

_____

_____

_____

_____

_____

Joining with your listening partner, let's switch from learning to expressive mode. Call to body and mind some patients who might benefit from understanding the principles of neural change, the circuits of regulation, what happens to those circuits in trauma or attachment stress, and how those changes create a certain kind of affective window of tolerance for them. Then talk with your listening partner about each of these topics as though he or she were these specific patients. We are covering a great deal of material here, so it will be most helpful to spend enough time working together to feel comfortable with the ideas and their translation into words in therapy.

I have found that many of my patients gain relief from shame along with some remarkable increases in commitment to our process through understanding how neural nets formed in their particular case and how these patterns can change within our relationship. The more I have been able to tailor my words to their specific situation, the better the result. *General ideas have a way of staying left-centric, whereas words drawn from my visceral awareness of their inner world seem to resonate in both hemispheres.* Spending enough time with these concepts and your listening partner to get sufficient left-mode clarity to speak with right-mode connection at moments when your patients are open to new information can fuel the change process.

Healing Through Enactments

When we are working with early trauma and attachment loss, it is particularly helpful to be aware of another process that will inevitably occur: nonconscious enactments. Allan Schore (2010, personal communication) and Efrat Ginot (2009) eloquently address this process. When our patients are unable to consciously access past experience because it was encoded before explicit memory matured or because trauma caused dissociation of at least the emotionally vivid aspects of the memory, our implicit worlds can initially only encounter each other through nonverbal processes. Whether through resonance circuits that operate with our mirror neurons or some other means, we do join and influence one another in the right mode, body to body and brain to brain. As our patients' autonomic nervous systems begin to activate, ours will as well.

Technically, an enactment is a time when, out of conscious awareness, unresolved implicit patterns in patient and therapist are activated simultaneously, leading to actions based on those patterns. If these remain out of conscious awareness, we may be drawn into experiences that reconfirm our patients' harmful early childhood encounters, or we may act in ways that provide the disconfirming experience through right-mode to right-mode communication. We will never know how many times this happens each meeting, completely out of awareness. However, sometimes both the arousal and relational behaviors do come into awareness for one or both of us, and then we can consciously participate in creating disconfirming experiences that may change a long-held implicit pattern.

Jeff and I had been working for many months with his experience of being "discarded and ruined" by his wealthy family. Both parents were involved in the development of new industry in the Northeast, so had little time or energy for the children. However, beyond this dismissing attitude lay their need to heap negative perceptions, generated solely in their own minds, on his developing sense of self. Until their deaths, they believed he was stupid (he had two advanced degrees), incapable of doing anything worthwhile (he was responsible for bridge safety in three states), and to be shunned because he had ruined the family by being born. Because of the magnitude of the disconnection between their perceptions and his actual history (coupled with my experience of him), I believed he had become the dumping ground for many of the intolerable and unacknowledged parts of themselves. I felt this was a crushing burden that he likely had carried from birth.

One day, as he was sharing his despair about ever finding a relationship in which he was seen for who he is, I felt a strong need to straighten my shoulders. In retrospect, I became aware that I had been deeply slumping in my chair as my body followed Jeff's physical–emotional collapse. As my shoulders squared, almost of their own accord, I could see him begin to brighten and recover, something that happened first in his body, followed quickly by a shift in his enlivened voice and brighter eyes. A few minutes later, I shared the experience that had come with the squared shoulders: "I feel like I want to stand strong and protect you." He paused for a while, then said, "That's really weird. When I was a kid, I used to dream that someone was pushing down on my shoulders until they were crushed and my arms were useless. The dreams were so real that even when I was awake, I constantly worried about being without working arms and completely at the mercy of my parents. In the last few years, I realized that there was never anything wrong with my shoulders. It was just that I felt crushed by them—and, as we've discovered, many times I still do." I viscerally felt the echo of *crushed*, the word that had also arisen in my mind about the quality of his attachment experience.

Ginot (2009) uses the word *entanglement* to speak about these bodily based, initially nonconscious pairings that occur continually in therapy. My body followed Jeff's experience of collapse, and upon reflection, I realized that my mind had also dulled as my chest sank into our common despair. Then I believe that my current-day attachment to him kicked in, first regulating my dorsal vagal hopelessness and then allowing me to provide the kind of experience that parents offer when they move in synchrony with their young child's inner experience. In my body's tracking of his visceral state into collapse, I believe Jeff felt seen for who he was in the moment. When that happened, our connection was strengthened, so my subsequent strong shoulders had room to become the disconfirming experience he needed. Jeff and I continued to talk about the damaging experiences of his childhood from this new, more expansive place. He could feel traces of his shoulders' former dream trauma, side by side with the possibility of developing firm, new shoulders. In keeping with the research that these freshly modified implicit circuits may stay open for several days (Suzuki et al., 2004), we agreed to keep these new shoulders experientially alive in our awareness for the next week.

It is useless to think that we can do all of this consciously because right-mode to right-mode synchrony happens in milliseconds, much too fast for conscious awareness. What we can do is prepare ourselves to be able to regulate what arises in both our patients' and our own implicit activations through our consistent efforts to increase our own neural integration. Self-nurture dovetails perfectly with care for the other.

In truth, I believe that the precursors of these potential enactments are constantly occurring because of our strong resonance with one another, and not just when we have dissociated memories in common. Sometimes this exchange of energy and information will strike a chord that stirs our unresolved implicit mental models into action; sometimes we merely experience parallel activation within our bodies, nervous systems, emotions, and perceptions— our implicit system. With practice, we will be able to better sense the difference between resonance and personal activation. For me, the calm current of awareness runs strong beneath the autonomic activation in the presence of resonance, and dims when my own dissociated experience is touched. In either case, such stirrings are calls to inner action. We have been consistently cultivating the strength of our caring observer, so there is a better chance that we will be able to listen to and then regulate these implicit surges, even the ones that reflect unresolved memories within us. Again, it is impossible to overestimate the importance of our own mental health.

Enactments can be hard to grasp intellectually, much less experientially at first. The idea seems to slip away like smoke initially, probably because it is so right-centric that it's hard for words to corral it. If it would be helpful, take a few moments to read this section again. Then, in a kind and reflective way, invite your deeper mind to show you times when this sort of experience flowered in the space between you and your patient. This, again, is a good place to write a bit and share experiences with your listening partner.

_____

_____

_____

_____

_____

_____

_____

_____

_____

_____

_____

_____

_____

_____

_____

In conclusion, we can know that until our patients' regulatory circuitry is sufficiently developed, one essential way of working is with bodily based co-regulation, as a mothering person does with her infant. As our attachment systems work together in the richness of the therapeutic relationship, we *build complexity in right-mode processes*, making room for emotional intensity without dysregulation, calming fears, developing the capacity for attuned communication and empathy, and a growing ability to make choices instead of being helplessly bound to the implicit pattern (Siegel, 2007). On this foundation, our patients will be able to bring their own caring observer into partnership with ours as we continue our work with the implicit hindrances.

About Implicit Roots

Not everyone is so internally splintered by early childhood experience to need extensive regulatory help, but everyone has an extensive array of implicit mental models that guide thoughts, feelings, and behaviors, including the unwanted ones regarded as symptoms. Ecker and Hulley (1996, 2000a, 2000b, 2008) have written extensively about their findings that the implicit learnings and memories underlying a vast range of symptoms can be brought into direct, conscious experience. This material, they further note, is always found to be coherent—a retrieval of "emotional truth" that reveals the deep sense and adaptive intent of existing symptoms while also filling in mysterious gaps and blurs in life experience. This view of symptom production is corroborated by extensive research on implicit memory by brain scientists (for a review, see Toomey & Ecker, 2007). The overall picture that emerges is the same as ours has been throughout: Symptoms make sense; there is coherence at the level of the neural nets at the roots of what we are thinking, feeling, and doing, even as our left-mode process may deem our responses irrational, sick, stupid, or broken.

We have experiences throughout life that shape our implicit perceptions for good or ill. A child who begins with good-enough attachment experiences that allow her to give expression to her outgoing and optimistic temperament through the first 5 years of life may suddenly encounter the stresses of a war or leave everything familiar to move into a threatening part of town. At the same time, these stresses also deprive her of her parents' reassuring, regulating attention, so the implicit aspects of the traumatic experiences dissociate. The resulting impact creates a new set of implicit expectations about core safety, the availability of help, and hope for good outcomes, coupled with a severely dysregulated nervous system. Although these encodings rest on the foundation of some security of attachment and established connections between the middle prefrontal cortex and limbic region, the magnitude of the disruption pulls this child into a frightened, introverted, and sometimes hopeless state of mind that is disconnected from the foundation. Now, as an adult with a more settled life, she continues to feel frightened and helpless at times that don't make sense to her left-mode awareness.

As we begin to work on these implicit roots, we won't have to focus as much on building neural structures from scratch, but instead find pathways to connect the dissociated implicit to the already-established middle prefrontal–limbic circuits. We can also anticipate greater resources for regulation and a stronger capacity for the adult self of our patient to remain present as we work. As the neural nets holding the experience of the 5-year-old open, the ingrained encodings of security will be waiting to receive them into integration.

We may also find that less severe experiences with avoidant or ambivalent attachment have connected our patients' regulatory circuits sufficiently for them to be able to come into partnership with us fairly quickly, once trust and clarity have been established. There are also genetic factors that confer greater resilience even under traumatic circumstances, so each person brings a unique situation (Kaufman et al., 2006). Only by walking through the first few sessions together will we be able to gain a sense of how much we need to focus on building the circuitry of regulation as our starting point.

Inviting the Implicit Root into Explicit Awareness

The question then arises about how we might invite either dissociated (not neurally connected) or unattended (loosely neurally connected but not usually in conscious awareness) right-mode implicit memory to come up from the limbic storehouse into explicit awareness. We have found it useful to begin with whatever experience our patients bring into the session. Within a short time after beginning therapy, I have found that people's minds begin to prepare for their sessions, often without conscious awareness, in the hours before we meet. As a result, many times they bring in an emotionally rich experience from daily life, a dream, or a relational encounter that upset them. Once we have a sense that a pattern is present—fear of criticism or abandonment anxiety, for example—there are many ways to encourage the right mode to communicate with us about the implicit roots. Here are some possibilities:

- Engaging in the symbolic and tactile experience of sand tray
- Allowing color and shape to flow onto paper through art, especially with the nondominant hand
- Exploring the physical, tangible, emergent quality of shaping and reshaping clay
- Asking what would happen if the symptom were gone and waiting for a right-mode answer to arise
- Following body sensations, behavioral impulses, and feelings to their childhood roots
- Attending to the body, particularly its movement tendencies, large and small
- Sitting in receptivity to whatever may arise in the mind and body in response to a current experience
- Attending to the relational experience unfolding between patient and therapist
- Spending time with photographs from childhood that bring up a strong resonance in the body.

In short, we can use any approach that makes the right mode more available to conscious awareness, with or without words. Creating an environment where cues for the implicit are present can be very helpful. At our place, we have paper and crayons leaning against the wall, clay in buckets, and miniatures and sand within reach. Simply having these materials in the room keeps our right mode more present as well.

Spend a few moments sorting through your own repertoire of right-mode accessing processes. With kindness, notice your belief about their usefulness compared to more left-centric methods such as reframing, guiding behavior, and such. Then write a few notes about both your right-mode ways and your beliefs about them.

_____

_____

_____

_____

_____

_____

_____

_____

_____

_____

Let me share a couple of examples of how this process may unfold. A 15-year-old young woman came in filled with anxiety for no particular reason. Sometimes it rose to the level of panic, especially in school. She speculated that she was increasingly worried about getting into college, so felt this growing pressure. Then she thought it might have to do with the illness of a dear grandparent. We talked a bit about how the left mode fishes around for an answer, but

Figure 9.3. A Teen's Sand Tray. Sense your visceral response to this sand tray picture. Such images often open the door for resonance between patient and therapist at the level of body-to-body and nervous symptom synchrony, bringing to conscious awareness the activation pattern of the implicit memory.

The Brain-Savvy Therapist's Workbook

nothing quite clicks into place as the truth of the matter. Her eyes had lingered on the sand tray shelves since she had walked into the room—often a sign that her right mode is seeking expression. After arranging the sand as it needed to be, with a fairly steep hill on one side, she focused on the anxiety in her body—in her chest, throat, and stomach. From this place, she chose three objects—a crawling baby, a prison cell on a cart, and a large snake.

At first, she worked with the sand some more, increasing the angle of the hill, then placed the cart on the hill, with the baby crawling directly in front of it. She moved the snake from one side of the cart to the other until it felt just right, like tumblers clicking into place. As we could see the snake sneaking up on the baby from behind, we both experienced a strong increase in anxiety. At this moment, there were no words for this implicit relational memory, but it was in right-mode conscious awareness, and being held by the two of us. This is the first step of the change process.

Here is another example, with words. At our agency we had stumbled across a method by accident (or inner knowing), finding that if we asked people to imagine what life would be like without a particular way of thinking, feeling, or behaving, it often produced a dramatic drop into the coherent and transparent reason for continuing the pattern. (This versatile technique is also used by Ecker & Hulley [1996, 2000a], who call it *symptom deprivation*.) I asked my patient to picture what she would feel if she stopped resisting her husband's requests for specific meals and other small gestures that were meaningful for him. After a couple of left-mode guesses—"He would like me better" and "I would feel relieved"—she drew in a sharp breath and said, "I would be terrified." Her quick breathing and wide eyes signaled her movement into sympathetic arousal. We were able to hold onto our connection as the fear escalated a bit, and then an image of her childhood compliance in the face of her father's rage flashed across her mind. Tears came quickly as she said, "If I did what he asked, I would feel just like I did with my father." Again, the first step is bringing the strands of memory together into a consciously coherent whole, rooted in an implicit knowing. In this case, her behavior came into contact with her visceral sense of consequences if the behavior were to cease. As we will see, the beginning of the change process occurs at this point of *integration between the known symptom that was in conscious awareness and the implicit reason for the symptom that was out of awareness.* As unpleasant as it was to have her husband irritated with her, that was nothing compared with the implicit terror of her father's daily rages.

Ecker and Hulley (1996, 2000a, 2000b, 2008) call this discovering the person's *pro-symptom position*—the unconscious but specific implicit knowings and feelings that view the symptom as urgent to have, despite the sufferings that come with having it. The person's conscious *anti-symptom position*, in contrast, resists the symptom, makes up stories about why it exists, thinks it is irrational and completely valueless, and wants to banish it. The pro-symptom position feels and recognizes the compelling necessity of the thought, feeling, or behavior, and can embrace that awareness.

When pro-symptom knowings from the subcortical limbic region are freshly conscious via new connective circuits to the cortex that are not solidly established, it is important to keep the new awareness alive in consciousness for the days between sessions. In this way, we are working to inhabit the new knowing consistently in order to develop a stable platform that can soon receive disconfirming experiences. As we do this, the middle prefrontal–limbic connection is also strengthened.

Without doing more than integrating the pro-symptom position, I have seen some remarkable shifts as people sit in mindful kindness with their newly discovered knowing. One young woman, searching out the roots of her obsessive need for all people to like her, got in touch with her deep experience of victimization. For the following week, she repeated "I am a victim" many times each day. The first day, she felt the powerful urge to push this away, deny it, prove it wrong—pitting her left-mode, current-day knowing against her implicit truth. Then she settled into repeating it without the resistance and soon found that she passed into a watchful, peaceful state. She described it as being at one with her victimized child in acknowledgment of the experiential truth of then, yet retaining her adult state of mind at the same time—middle prefrontal circuits and limbic interwoven in regulating harmony. By the end of the week, "I am a victim" had transformed into "I was a victim," a change of tense revealing that a piece of temporal integration had occurred, so that the eternally present past became truly past.

Through the week, she had times of quiet realization that she is no longer being victimized and times of deep grieving, leading to her release from the implicit pattern. The experience of victimization felt distant and past, as she and the child stood now in the present. She said, "I can look around me now and see and feel that I am surrounded by many people who care and some who don't, but they have no intention of harming me. They just aren't my people." Neurobiologically, we could say that integration between the middle prefrontal region and the limbic circuit appeared to be complete for this particular implicit memory. As parents, one of the most important gifts we give our children is attuning with them when they are in pain or fear (Siegel & Hartzell, 2003; Wipfler, 2006), offering them as much time and presence as they need to integrate the fractured experience. In therapy, we do that with our patients, and then they learn to do it within themselves.

Not all implicit knowings integrate this easily or with a single pass. The young woman in this example had many years of therapy under her belt and had developed familiar pathways for neural integration. Tugging at this constraint cleared the way for her to move down the path toward resolution. This experience of victimization was also the eighth implicit model we had discovered underlying her need to be liked by all, pro-symptom position after pro-symptom position, until the last was dispelled. She stayed with this resolution experience for the next few days until her original model of all others as attackers was thoroughly saturated with and revised by her new, very different perceptions. When we revisited the idea of victimization over the next few weeks, it retained the quality of past tense, of *was*.

What happened behind the scenes that allowed this process to unfold so smoothly? First, alignment with the implicit root, making the source of the symptom transparent and emotionally real; second, integration of the root into awareness; and third, a disconfirming juxtaposition (Ecker, 2008, 2010; Ecker & Hulley, 2008) of the living experience of current reality (not merely left-mode ideas *about* that) with the living experience of the embodied implicit knowing. When both are emotionally vivid and in conscious awareness concurrently, the mind seeks to resolve their mutual contradiction in favor of one of the two flows of energy and information, generally in the direction of the more adaptive and recent model of the world (Ecker & Toomey, 2008). As therapists, we can be aware of moments ripe for living disconfirmation experiences, some of them verbal, some of them relational.

If resolution does not occur soon after a juxtaposition has emerged, it is for coherent internal reasons, not because the patient or therapist has failed. It may be that the neural nets holding the implicit root and the current perception were not actually in touch with one another; or that there are other roots holding this particular tree in place. Sometimes the flood of energy and information in the old pattern simply overwhelms the disconfirmation; or the neural circuitry between the middle prefrontal and limbic regions is not developed enough yet to sustain the new connections; or the implicit pattern formed so early and is so global that the person lives within the pro-symptom position full time as the only reality, requiring many relational experiences to shift the perception even a little (Badenoch, 2008). Patience, persistence in finding implicit roots and facilitating disconfirming experiences, and vigilance against taking emotional refuge in counteractive methods will inch—or speed—the process along. As Bruce Ecker says, "Of course, [when] there is so much loss, disorientation, pain, and fear involved in letting go of a global, glorious schema organizing one's identity, moment-to-moment behavior, and view of one's future . . . it may require many 'doses' of juxtaposition delicately applied in small-enough steps for [a person] to let go of and grieve the loss" (2010, personal communication).

It is likely that we all occasionally create living disconfirmation experiences born of the resonant dance we share with our patients without thinking consciously about this process. Let's ask our deeper mind to bring us times when we have had this experience and seen the pronounced shifts that they produce. Then write a bit about them.

_____

_____

_____

_____

_____

_____

_____

_____

_____

_____

_____

_____

_____

_____

Next, spend some time reflecting on several patients to see what implicit roots you two may have unearthed at this point. How do they change the meaning of your patients' symptoms? As you become aware of how symptoms make sense in light of implicit patterns, notice how this new awareness influences your body, feelings, and particularly your perceptions. Then write some descriptive words about these new perceptions.

_____

_____

_____

_____

_____

_____

_____

_____

_____

_____

_____

_____

_____

_____

_____

Supporting Healing of Implicit Infant Wounds

I have found deep reassurance and a sense of security that settle my body as well as my mind as I come into contact with this kind of felt coherence between the thoughts, feelings, and behaviors that trouble my patients and the historical implicit roots that require them to be so. Let's conclude this chapter with a heartening example of the power of focusing on implicit change. I have had the honor of working with several people with reactive attachment disorder as adults. The quality of maternal care offered to each of these people in earliest childhood was such that their attachment system was wired backwards, so that they learned to withdraw from human contact, rely entirely on their inner perceptual world as the reality with no reference to the minds of other human beings (since their minds were not attended to even as infants), and cope with massive dysregulation through self-loathing and self-rejection of the most intense form. Most of this psychic destruction happened covertly as their mothering person's silent, cold hatred and scorn irradiated these children, in the absence of overt abuse of any kind. Under these conditions, organizing through self-hatred becomes a natural and powerful tool for controlling internal disintegration because there is no obvious perpetrator to whom one can point. What else can children implicitly conclude about their worth in the face of such hatred except that there is some core badness in them? Because surrender of the implicit position exposes these people to agonizing fragmentation, the thought of giving up this self-loathing brings on the sensation of exploding or imploding death.

   In the present moment, this implicit sea generates a multitude of body sensations, behavioral impulses, feelings, and rigidly binding perceptions: Every offer of connection is met with a movement away, and every withdrawal of connection is perceived as shaming, agonizing, and right; they must not perceive, much less acknowledge, any positive aspect of themselves; everything must go continually from bad to worse, a kind of frantic despair; deprivation is the rule in all areas—food, sleep, companionship; disorganization is proof of badness; and fragmentation is the inevitable outcome of looking away from self-hatred to focus on the relationship with a caring therapist. The list is much longer, but this gives the flavor of the ongoing double binds that appear to lock these people into their inner and outer torment forever.

None of these people struggle to find the implicit roots because they live within them every day. These compelling perceptions are so consolidated that they form a prison whose walls are covered with the graffiti of their adaptation to early childhood experience without their being able to see the origin. Everything in this jail cell "just is." As a result, these are not symptoms that are perceived as irrational, but a code of ethics and conduct, propositions for the only imaginable way of living. Given what we are learning about memory reconsolidation, where do we start when all they have is a barely habitable sea of implicit memory?

I want to preface the answer by saying that these people have given me profound respect for human resilience in emotionally disastrous conditions. All of them lead productive, helpful lives, and all have retained an underground stream of attachment energy to challenge the inner command to detach and go away. Otherwise, they would not be in my office. Because of the disparity between self-perception and what we see, we may immediately feel the need to counteract these self-images with valuing and corrective words. We may feel so much emotional conviction in this that we believe ours will become the words of disconfirmation. However, unless the sufferers are sufficiently regulated to be available to take in new information and they experience at least the possibility of a different explanation than their implicit knowing, the disconfirming words are useless. Instead, our words slam into the wall of belief that their bodily, emotionally, cognitively based view of themselves, relationships, and life's possibilities is The Only Reality (because this is what our implicit memories tell us). Attempts to offer this kind of disconfirmation immediately puts the relationship on rocky ground because the person feels unseen and unheard.

What kind of disconfirmation might reach through these rigid barriers to touch the experiential, implicit root? In the quiet cradle of safe attachment, we might find a common ground where the frantic infants can slip below their initial experiences with the mothering person to locate the glimmer of their intrinsic, genetically anchored need and wish for connection. This possibility of a safe and tranquil haven in the heart and mind of the therapist is such a good offer and the yearning has been so endlessly present that the joining begins, often in slight bodily movements in our direction—a clenched hand that relaxes and moves an inch toward us; their whole body sitting in a new location closer on the couch; eyes that glance up from their usually lap-locked gaze; a voice that begins to reveal the presence of emotion. These moments are breathtaking at a visceral level, breaking the tension of enforced separation that has inhabited the room.

Shortly after that initial connection, warmed by the light of the budding relationship, the defense of self-hatred begins to melt just a bit. While this is exactly what needs to happen, it also exposes and enlivens the massive disorganization it had been controlling by its heavy hand. The magnitude of this upwelling is potentially overwhelming for both our patients and ourselves. I find that understanding the coherence and necessity of this stage gives me a toehold in whole-brain processing that keeps me from washing down the river of disorganization and despair with my patients. We generate pictures of us going down the rapids together with me having a hand on the rudder, or me standing in the shallows fishing the patient out of the torrent with a net. Through many hours, we resonate with the frantic fragmentation, interspersed with moments of quiet connection. This capacity we are developing for co-regulation and ongoing connection is the beginning of disconfirmation. At the level of experience only, we are saying, "You are keepable. I enjoy your presence. We can find peace together. This can be good for both of us." The experience of joining cracks open the door to a new world. The consistent offer of warm, calm connection disconfirms the message that seeking attachment equals being sent away. The continual positive regard begins to offset the experience of being a bad human being. The calmness itself is an antidote to disorganization. All of this is visceral work, punctuated by right-mode words that name the experience or offer pictures and metaphors for the internal process.

Over time, a steadier quiet space emerges that is the essence of infant attachment. There is awe accompanied by an aching yearning to stay there. They say, "What is this? What is this? It is more different than a fish breathing air. Not just bigger than the universe, but different." None of them has any names for this place because it is wholly other, the place we all begin without words or even symbols—just presence. Over months of visiting this quiet place of attachment, these new neural connections begin to stabilize so that we can go there whenever we choose, and my patients can even find it on their own sometimes.

Meanwhile, life often becomes much more difficult for a period of time. The disorganization sometimes inhabits every corner of life—house, emotions, relationships, work. Yet all of these brave people cling to the necessities of life throughout the tumultuous ride. No one loses his or her job, family relationships stay intact, and long-term friendships somehow endure. Not only is the disorganization blooming, but a further implicit belief stands in the way of moving toward organization quickly: If one aspect of life gets better, something else must get worse since this was the only pattern available in early life. In childhood, if there was a moment of peace, it would be shattered by hatred in the next second. According to this implicit model, as the blissful experience of attachment grows, some other part of life must go into stress or be destroyed. One of the most challenging parts of this work is the accumulation of interlocking implicit mental models holding each other in place.

The silent devastation that underlies the suffering of these people is in many ways more damaging than prolonged abuse. The early and ongoing implicit wiring delivers only one message: You are hated, so go away; don't exist. The embodied brain becomes structured around this belief, so it cannot be challenged at any level, except by silently collaborating with the pull toward attachment against all odds. As the pool of connection grows broader and deeper, building the core brain structure of regulation and flexibility, gradual shifts in thought begin to appear. The new neural circuitry supports the possibility that there might be another viewpoint than the imprisoning implicit, making room for adding new information to the ancient neural nets. From here, progress accelerates because implicit mental models can finally be seen and experienced as emanating from early experience rather than as The Immutable Truth. This is the crucial turning point into the mainstream of therapeutic change.

Since these people can and do recover to lead integrated and fulfilling lives, they become beacons of hope for all of us. After seeing my first reactive attachment person through to a healthy conclusion, I found I had developed unshakable confidence in the embodied brain's capacity to change in the context of a stable, attuned relationship.

This is a dense chapter, challenging or reaffirming the way we have thought about the healing enterprise. Whatever our paradigm, it is becoming clear that we are in the midst of a shift in which neuroscience is guiding us toward the importance of mindful attention to right-mode processes for healing. In the embrace of a warm and kind therapeutic relationship that supports compassionate receptivity, we can become open to implicit models that underlie our thoughts, feelings, and behaviors. From there, our interpersonally integrated minds can lead us toward the disconfirming experiences that foster permanent changes in the mental models that guide our lives. In the next chapter, we are going to give these principles some additional flesh as we develop practical processes for working with memories and states of mind.

Chapter 10

Applying the Principles of Change

Reshaping Memories and Resolving
Inner Community Conflicts

Now we are going to wade more deeply into applying the principles we fleshed out in the last chapter. We could see how engaging the brain's principles of change leads us toward the implicit roots of our perceptions, feelings, and actions. What we encounter there are memories, or, we could say, the neural pathways shaped by experience. Like all paths (as compared with the forest proper), these are the routes our brains follow most easily, often without conscious awareness. When I prepare to leave the house in the morning, some of my actions require conscious attention—deciding what to wear, finding the car keys since they have many possible locations, and so on. I have to engage awareness because there are decisions to be made. Other actions happen without conscious thought—moving through the house toward the garage, unlocking the back door, opening the garage and car doors, starting the car. I can be consciously thinking of something else, while these activities are successfully guided by procedural memories and cortical invariant representations of what comes next (Hawkins & Blakeslee, 2004).

However, if I look more closely, even when I have engaged my conscious mind, implicit patterns still guide many of my responses. I am predictably irritated when I can't find my keys, uneasy about forgetting something I may need in my day, and generally enthusiastic and optimistic about the events ahead. The guiding energy and information of implicit patterns, especially in regard to our bodily and emotional responses, what motivates us, and our way of relating to self and others, are always with us. Any time we wish, we can engage our caring observer and watch the different flows of energy and information playing within us at that moment to gain a visceral sense of the pervasiveness of implicit influence.

However, as we discussed in the last chapter, these implicit pathways aren't immutable, and neuroscience is discovering more about the rules of change every day. This is hopeful information to share with our patients because, whether memories take the form of continually present implicit templates or dissociated aspects of past encounters, our people come to therapy wanting the experiences that arise from these patterns to change. James wants to find a life partner who will value him. Susan wants to be a mom who enjoys playing with her children. Charlie wants to be calm at school so he isn't always in trouble. When they arrive in our offices, their brains remember only how to find a devaluing partner, hate playing with kids, and be anxious at school. As a result, we are always doing some form of memory work with our patients to modify the paths down which they automatically walk.

Presence as Disconfirming Experience

In the last chapter, we began to explore the way that relational presence re-shapes neural circuitry. Now, we are going to deepen this awareness, reflecting on some ways that our presence alone becomes the needed disconfirmation for our patients' early implicit memories. In our therapeutic encounters, the attachment patterns and associated behaviors of earliest childhood will always be present—theirs and ours. As we continue doing our own work, we are seeking to increase the security of our own attachment (if we didn't have it before). In this way, we are preparing our embodied brains and minds to experience resonance with our patients' inner state while the underground river of consistent and compassionate care runs deep beneath the process. Disrupted attachments of all sorts leave chaotic relational patterns in their wake. Even in the case of avoidant attachment, the limbic longing for connection remains intact but out of awareness. This means that our capacity for providing moment-to-moment *calm consistency of presence and care* while resonating with the various forms of disruption is a powerful disconfirming experience all on its own. Another way of saying this is that we have widened our window of emotional tolerance so that our autonomic nervous system can move into synchrony with our patients without becoming dysregulated. These experiences of mutual resonance are powerful brain weavers. Several of our patients have described the experience of falling apart within a sea of calmness as the most significant moments in therapy.

Other disconfirming experiences are available within the relationship just by the quality of relating. For example, patients who have felt criticized throughout their young lives often behave in ways designed by their implicit model to draw disapproval or irritation from us. As we feel this resonant tension rise within us, we may be able to become aware of the river of clarity about why this is happening running at a deeper level at the same time. This clear-sightedness is often followed almost immediately by relaxation into nonjudgmental acceptance—a profoundly disconfirming juxtaposition when our patients are regulated enough to absorb it. These are always the twin questions:

- Are our patients within their window of tolerance?
- Is what we are offering an emotionally vivid disconfirming experience?

If dysregulation sets in too strongly, our patients' autonomic nervous systems shut down the ventral vagal circuit; then, because the social engagement pathways are disconnected, they are less able to take in what we are offering. Also, if our state of mind is not a precise fit for what patients are experiencing, some change may occur through their internalization of our caring presence, but a profound and permanent modification of the implicit circuits themselves will likely not occur immediately. This is not to say that there is no benefit in being simply nonjudgmentally available because that openness creates a space into which our patients' inner worlds can emerge with more clarity and depth. This is often the precursor to greater clarity for us as well—consciously and nonconsciously—leading to the emergence of the precise disconfirmations that will create permanent change. Sometimes we will be aware of our inner shifts in response to our patients' need, and other times, the millisecond interchanges will unfold out of conscious awareness.

When this increasing attunement enables us to meet our patients' despair with hope, their feeling of invisibility with being seen, or their abandonment terror with warm welcome, for example, and stay steadily in that state of mind, we are *doing* something very important even though no words may be spoken and no interventions offered. In fact, I have found that the earlier the wound and the greater the dysregulation, the more central to healing is this art of holding various flavors of this internal space.

Let's pause for a moment to invite former or present patients into mind and body, reflecting on moments in therapy of *just being*. What are these like for you? Do they increase calmness or bring unease—or some of both? Then write a few descriptive words about your experience.

_____

_____

_____

_____

_____

_____

_____

_____

_____

_____

Even if we don't experience the constant push of any early-ingrained neural nets about "early birds catching worms" and the virtue of constant progress, our minds are so conditioned by society to keep moving that entering into a state of being present without words or actions can feel stressful. It may take considerable practice to change our own implicit patterns to make this experience comfortable. As much as possible, let's receive any awareness we get of our inner impatience and restlessness with understanding and kindness. I can hear my father's stern injunction to pull myself up by my bootstraps, meaning get a move on, don't wallow. I understand now that had he wallowed, slowing down in body or mind, he would have touched his inner world and disintegrated. So his highly energized words that felt like a cattle prod to me were actually intended to protect me from what he most feared: contact with the truth his implicit mind would speak if there were any quiet moment. Developing awareness of and empathy for my inner father has helped me increase my ability to choose action or stillness.

Now let's reflect on the different flavors of wordless disconfirmation we have offered our patients. Thinking of two patients with deep, longstanding wounds, reflect on these questions and write what you discover.

- *What is their abiding mental model of how they will be treated, who they are, or what they can expect from life?*

_____

_____

_____

_____

_____

- *What words and behaviors did they use to create the expected response from you?*

_____

_____

_____

_____

_____

- *What state of mind did you consistently bring to them that they were able to take in, often below the level of conscious awareness?*

_____

_____

_____

_____

_____

- *If you were able to stay with this state (not easy when we are resonating with severely wounded people), what happened over time?*

_____

_____

_____

_____

_____

After writing here, spend some time talking about these and similar experiences with your listening partner.

Honing Our Awareness of Developmental Ages

Considering the developmental age of our patients' states of mind from moment to moment is an important guide to offering disconfirming experiences. Our inviting presence will offer safe haven to even very young states, whose experiences were so traumatic that they dissociated and stayed in this very early developmental age, with memories confined to narrow slices of historical time. They dwell in places where painful and frightening experiences were not met with integrating empathy and understanding, trapped outside of time's flow—caught in what we have called the eternally present past. Many patients have taught me to listen for and respond to clues about the age they are experiencing. I have worked with a number of people who were abused as infants, causing their brains to fragment into numerous states of mind, with some pieces never leaving the baby state. When that state of mind is dominant, even though there are remnants of an adult state that can talk, the brain seems to operate as though it were building neural connections from the ground up, the way a baby would.

Let me share a delightful example. I worked with one woman, now in her 40s, who had been physically and sexually assaulted since birth. While we did much of our work in person, we also used Skype at times. When we were in the room together, I rarely wore my glasses, and she often saw me in partial profile as we sat together on the couch. On Skype, she would see me with glasses and face-on. Initially, this difference in my appearance wasn't on her radar. Then one day she said, "I feel startled, like I don't know who you are. Could you turn your head to show me your profile?" She said she immediately relaxed when I did that. Then we experimented; I turned my head from profile to face-on to the other profile, slowly and repeatedly. This brought not only relaxation, but enormous smiles and the emergence of play—for me, a sensation like having a game of peek-a-boo with an infant. Clearly, we had connected to the right-mode limbic region where this natural capacity for interpersonally celebrated joy is rooted (Panksepp, 1998).

I also had the sense that we were helping this baby-brain state connect aspects of me into a whole person, the kind of neural differentiation process that gradually assembles pieces of a person and refines face recognition down to one or a few cells (Quiroga, Reddy, Kreiman, Koch, & Fried, 2005). While her adult state had no trouble with this task, this baby state seemed to influence her brain to function at her developmental level. The next time we saw one another in person, I put on my glasses, and she felt another part of a whole me fall into place. If this kind of early brain differentiation is truly what is being ingrained, it is a clear case of state-dependent experience in which different states of mind are associated with different neural firing patterns.

Because of the magnitude and earliness of her abuse, this woman's various states of mind were dissociated in a dramatic way even though she did not have multiple personalities. I believe that these experiences coming into conscious awareness signaled the beginning of this baby state of mind forming a relationship with me, which would lead to this young one gradually becoming integrated with the ongoing flow of her developing brain. Our capacity to see, understand, and respond to these developmental stages as real neural events creates synchronous moments that build trust, create integrative neural connections, and expand the window of tolerance for joy as well as upset. When we miss these developmental stages, feel embarrassed by them, or don't understand them, the shift in our inner state can replicate earlier times when the person was not seen, sometimes bringing on dysregulation and sometimes shutting down or re-dissociating the early process in favor of safely talking about developmentally later experiences.

As another example, some of my patients have felt a craving to hear my voice reading a story rather than talking about our process. They seem to need to hear my voice free and clear of upsetting content so that they can settle into the prosody uninterrupted. Making CDs is an effortless process these days, so this request is easy to accommodate. Soft and easy-to-pocket objects that I have had in my possession for some time also provide the tangible grounding that is meaningful for these emerging children. The psychodynamic tradition calls these transitional objects, and we now know, as a neurobiological certainty, that having such a trinket helps strengthen the neural net that holds the attachment.

Spend a few moments reflecting on your early-traumatized patients to see if you can spot moments in which different ages emerged, not because you and your patient could cognitively identify the age, but through the neural firing patterns associated with that age. Then write a bit about this mindful detective work.

_____

_____

_____

_____

_____

_____

_____

_____

_____

_____

Tracing Current-Day Experiences to Implicit Roots

Side by side with these transformative relational experiences and visits to developmentally earlier times, we can also undertake memory change through mindfully tracing current day experiences back to their implicit roots. As we move through time, we will encounter memory both as events and as inner community members who participated in these situations. We have already practiced with ourselves in Part I, and here we will be thinking about how to implement a similar process with our patients. Usually, entry into this way of working unfolds naturally. We can lay the foundation early in therapy by finding the right empathic moments in the first few sessions to talk about some or all of these, as appropriate:

- How neural nets form
- How implicit memories have a profound influence
- How every thought, feeling, and behavior has a coherent implicit reason for why it is necessary (with examples)
- How inner communities form and can be changed (with examples from patients' lives)
- How neuroplasticity is fostered in relationship—leading to hope for change.

Suzanne: Changing Implicit Memories and Reconciling the Inner Community

Disabling anxiety brought Suzanne to therapy. It welled up at about 3 months into any romantic relationship, and she was feeling "stupid, defective, and like a hopeless idiot." She said that the anxiety began each time on the day she said to herself, "I think I'm falling in love." I felt her sympathetic nervous system accelerate as she said the words, even though she wasn't currently in a relationship. We stepped into her history right away, and she shared the numerous losses she had endured at a very young age: Her mother died when she was 3, and her father left her with his warm, kind brother and sister-in-law when she was 4 because he had to travel extensively for work. She had just about settled in with them when they discovered that her uncle (and surrogate father) had advanced cancer; he passed away within 4 months. At 5, she began having severe stomachaches before school every day, and twice left her classroom to walk the five blocks home alone because she felt terrified that something had happened to her aunt.

The nightmares began shortly after that, followed by other forms of anxiety throughout her elementary school years. Then, as if by magic, the anxiety seemed to cure itself as she headed into adolescence. She got involved in a drama group, traveled with them for competitions, and threw herself into every opportunity to perform. She said that she was "fearless" on stage, and for the first time, she was happy and relaxed. She chose not to date much in high school or college, telling herself she was too busy. After graduation, she landed a delightful job with the local professional theater group and began to go out with the young men in the company. Now, 7 years later, her career was flourishing, but she was beginning to doubt she could ever marry and have children.

Even as we talked about her history, she remained baffled about why the anxiety was so overwhelming. This opened the door for us to talk about implicit memories. I explained:

> "We usually think about memory as being like 'I remember falling in love with the theater when I was 12,' but that's not the only kind of memory we have. We also have implicit memories that carry our body's responses to experiences and our emotions about them. If something happens over and over, we develop what's called a *mental model* that tells us what to anticipate in the future. The trickiest part is that when implicit memories come into play, we experience them as having to do with the present rather than the past. Even harder is that they also tell us what to expect in the future."

Her increased alertness let me know that this was reaching her as more than left-mode information.

Suzanne had shared that although her family was very loving, they also expected each other to motor on without wallowing in self-pity. As a result, Suzanne had not had sufficient opportunity to grieve all these losses. Her aunt's approach to her anxiety was always practical—rational explanations that everything was OK, coupled with distraction to get her "back on track." We talked about how these well-intended attitudes had pushed a lot of her fear of loss and abandonment deep underground, to be triggered by consciously acknowledging the growing emotional bond with her boyfriends. With just a little discussion, she could also feel how she had internalized her aunt so that she was a constant presence telling her, in a very kind way, to ignore her feelings and get on with life.

We both noticed that a strong sense of partnership had developed between us, with Suzanne saying that understanding implicit memory made her feel "less crazy and defective." She said that she really appreciated being able to "see" her brain because it meant there was something we could work with. I said, "Our brains are changing all the time, modifying old experiences so that they aren't so upsetting and making new implicit memories, too. The way you and I relate to one another is creating a memory like that." She said shyly that she really liked coming, and we both noticed that caused a little rise in anxiety. We talked about sitting with the feeling, accepting it, trusting that it made sense to her implicit world to feel tension coming with the growing attachment.

The session after that, I asked her what her deeper mind believed would happen if her anxiety wasn't there and she could stay with one of these men. Initially she said, "That would be delightful. That's just what I want." We persisted with the question a bit more, just asking if there was anything else. Suddenly, her hands flew to her stomach, doubling her over as her eyes widened in terror. In a rapid whisper, she said, "It's almost as though if I love them, they will die—like I kill them with my love." This opened the door for us to begin to do some memory and inner community work around her early losses. Because these painful deaths and her father's abandonment had happened at such an early age, I believed that we would make the most headway with disconfirming experiences if we could help the dissociated pain and fear that her younger selves carried come into conscious awareness to be met by understanding about the depth of her agony. This was one of the missing pieces that had prevented integration when the tragedies happened.

I also knew that her younger selves were bonding to me, so, as they moved into greater integration, I would be a test case for the implicit assumption that her love kills. What we didn't do was talk in rational terms about how her love hadn't killed her beloved auntie or any of the teachers who were her mentors. These experiences were not real for the dissociated children who had not been able to join the larger flow of the integrating brain, so that kind of left-mode counteractive approach not only would not touch the implicit wound, but would also make me very similar to her aunt in the ways that accidentally hurt Suzanne. Instead, we noticed the power of the implicit belief she had uncovered, and I inwardly celebrated that we had reached the point where the implicit was transparent and well differentiated. Suzanne felt relieved as she discovered that her anxiety actually made sense in light of her deeper mind's belief.

Over the course of the next few months, the memory work took several forms. Suzanne was fascinated by the miniatures on my shelves, particularly the clay parent–child pairs. Sometimes she would simply hold them; sometimes she would do a sand tray in which they would be separated, with the child buried. Without words, she was showing us how much she had died along with her loved ones. Anxiety was giving way to deep sorrow.

Sometimes the sand trays led us toward doing direct inner work with her memories and inner community pairs. After working in the sand, Suzanne often noticed intense feelings in her body, particularly an ache that extended from her belly to her throat. We followed this feeling as the thread to take us back in time to an experience when her body felt just like this. Body sensations are a component of implicit memory, and the integrated map of the body is in right-mode processing, so paying attention to sensations can lead us back to one or more emotionally vivid root experiences.

A few seconds after we asked the question, Suzanne saw her small self sitting on her bed in her aunt's house, clutching one of her stuffed animals and crying. She was seeing this memory from the viewpoint of her adult self look-

Figure 10.1. Suzanne's Mother–Daughter Pairs. All of these pairs were used in numerous sand trays. Clay figures by Debbie Berrow, http://bellpineartfarm.com.

The Brain-Savvy Therapist's Workbook

Figure 10.2. Burning and Drowning Sand Tray. The baby owl is buried near the watchful mother, who is also half buried in the sand. The dead and crooked tree had to be at just that angle to feel right. There is a sense of the world being consumed by burning and drowning at the same time, pictured both in the waves and flames and the rageful figure in the pool of water to the left. The rugged heart is a Native American spirit rattle and is there as a memorial to the buried baby. Clay figures by Debbie Berrow, http://bellpineartfarm.com and porcelain figure by Georgia Mann, http://georgiamann.com.

ing at the scene, so I asked her if we could go to the child together. I suggested that she look into her eyes or a put a hand on her back, allowing her boundaries to relax so she could experience what this child was feeling right then. As she approached, the pain in her stomach, chest, and throat increased, and she began to cry as she slipped more fully into this child's world. This was an act of neural integration as the caring adult, who is part of the flow of the larger brain, invited the circuit holding the child's dissociated experience to merge with her own current state. It was also an act of comfort, the missing experience for that little one.

After a moment, Suzanne had the sensation of the child dropping the stuffed toy to sit on her lap. The little one also took my hand. Now the three of us were emotionally and neurally linked—intrapersonal and interpersonal integration in one experience. The implicit mental model "I will be alone with my pain forever" was being replaced by "People will come to comfort me." Because I was part of the experience, she could know that both internal parts and external people would help her. Suzanne had never given voice to the implicit belief that no one helps, because she did have a loving relationship with her aunt, and emotional suppression was a familiar part of the family and community norms. After a few memory experiences, Suzanne said, "I feel like I'm being helped with this for the first time." From this, we can see that sometimes the mental model to be healed surfaces *because* the antidote arrives, rather than the other way around.

Suzanne and I settled in with the child, tracking and holding her experience. Suzanne stayed connected in a mostly visceral way, maybe one-third adult and two-thirds child, in what we could call *empathy through identification*, while I held the two of them in my mind, resonating with the deep sorrow while a river of calm warmth ran beneath the pain. There were not a lot of words—just some descriptions of what she was feeling in her body and emotions as the pain in her stomach, chest, and throat abated and her body relaxed into a sense of being safe and understood. Because the memory had moved toward resolution and the little one was feeling comfortable with us, it seemed possible to invite her into the present moment, to let her know that she didn't need to stay on that bed anymore, but could be with us instead when she was ready. Suzanne sensed that there was some hesitancy about doing that, with the child preferring us to stay with her for now on the bed in her aunt's house. Apparently, she needed us to know more about her experience before she could fully relinquish the eternally present past, enabling it to become truly past. Another way to think about this is that the energy and information in the layers of implicit memory surrounding these experiences were gradually transitioning into emotionally rich explicit awareness, and the process was not yet complete.

After awhile, the intensity of the memory began to fade, and Suzanne's adult self fully reemerged. I asked her what the experience had been like for her. She said that she understood what I meant by time travel because she had felt transported to that distant time. We talked about what this meant in terms of her brain—that she had been able to reawaken the neural nets holding this extreme loneliness and grief, and we had been able to bring a different experience into that available space. I encouraged her to revisit the memory of the three of us frequently so that we could strengthen her sense that people would be with her in her times of need. As she peeked inside again, she could see that we were still with the child who no longer felt alone—internalization of a caring other was moving forward well. We noted that the memory had not directly addressed her sense that she might kill people by loving them, but she also noticed that her anxiety was less than when we started.

Sometimes there is a one-to-one correspondence between the implicit root and the memory that arises in connection with it, but in Suzanne's case, her mind guided us to an implicit place that needed to be resolved first: her fear that no one would help her. I believe that she needed to have the experience of trustworthy companions before approaching the terror of feeling she had killed her mother and her uncle by loving them. From long experience, it seems to me that we wander in these woods with a purpose, guided by the inner logic that only our patients' minds know. I have a fairly radical trust for that process, and so feel little inclined to direct or interfere. Instead, I see myself as a Sherpa, carrying the needed supplies—consistency, curiosity, warmth, comfort, clarity, hope, willingness to resonate with whatever arises—for the trek my patients have chosen. Even with the threat of severe dysregulation established in their nervous systems and limbic brains by abuse or neglect, I have found a profound wisdom in patients' process as long as they feel anchored in steady companionship.

As the months unfolded, Suzanne and I established a rhythm in our process, making use of the sand, direct work with memories, and finally approaching her inner community members with offers of understanding and care. At one point, she discovered intense anger for her beloved aunt because she wouldn't listen to Suzanne's broken heart after her uncle died. That had felt like the last straw threatening to bring down her worn and fragile inner structure. She felt as though she might break into pieces, even physically, and her aunt seemed not to notice. We began working with this inner pair—angry, distraught child and dismissive auntie. We did some somatic work with the young girl's anger first. She could feel that her body needed movement because she had tried to be so quiet to not upset her aunt. We got up and strode around the room and nearby park with firm, purposeful strides, which soon brought her from anger to tears—and a plaintive cry from the depths of her need, "Why don't you see how bad I hurt?"

Then a remarkable thing happened—the inner aunt turned around with the kind of love in her eyes that Suzanne had often seen. Suzanne had the intuition of her saying something like "I do see you, and I will break into pieces myself if I let myself feel what you're feeling. That's why we don't talk about these things, because we will break into pieces." Suzanne described it as a wash of emotional union with her aunt, a bodily sensation of shattering, and a profound sense of understanding why the family operated as it did. Because our mirror neurons and resonance circuits internalize intentions and emotions from others, Suzanne was able to deeply sense her aunt's inner world in this way. I was able to be a comforting presence for both of these states of mind—Suzanne's and her aunt's. Suzanne emerged from this experience with a sense of peace and closeness with her aunt.

We spent a few weeks working with these two, not just in regard to her uncle's death, but also what it had been like for both of them when Suzanne's father had dropped her off and driven away. These were not so much conversations as we think of them in the world as two states of mind taking turns sampling the visceral reality of the other's experience—an inherently empathy-rich and integrative process. From the fires of conflict and fear of collapse arose strength and a sense of having endured something profound together. Thinking in neurobiological terms, we could say that the neural nets holding these terribly painful experiences had remained dissociated and in a state of permanent tension for decades. Now, as they reawakened and came to life in the present moment, both states of mind within each net felt understood by the other and by me. This new energy and information linked the conflicting parts within the net, preparing it to move into integration with the larger flow of the brain.

As we did this work, Suzanne's anxiety was steadily diminishing. One day she said, "The sum of all this work is that I know I didn't kill anyone by loving them. I mean I really *know* it, all the way through. I feel so sad—my kids inside feel so sad—that the people we loved so dearly died or went away, but that's all that's left. No guilt and no sense that I'll kill the next person I fall in love with. After all, you didn't die and we're about as close as two people can get!" Having journeyed through the underworld together, she figured that if she were poison, I would have received a lethal dose. Her words were infused with conviction, strength, and joy—not a cognitive statement, but an embodied declaration of fully embraced implicit truth. At no point had we directly tried to create a specific disconfirming experience for this core implicit belief, but we both had the sense that these layers of dissociated neural nets all contained pieces needed for resolving the root mental model. As we worked with the isolated child states of mind, a vital developmental process resumed. Connections between her amygdala and orbitofrontal cortex strengthened, forming a highway between the child's perception of the cause of her parents' disappearance and the broader view of the mature mind. From this new perspective, she could experience both the child's terror and shame and the reality of the tragic circumstances. Because of the depth of her experiencing, the child's implicit belief gradually dissolved in the light of the larger picture.

Some Guidelines for Implementation

Suzanne's story has some features in common with most memory and inner community work, and in other respects it is entirely unique. Entering the implicit world through body sensations is a pathway that can be used by many people. However, her inner aunt's spontaneous response is not typical. The same is true for us therapists—no two of us will implement these approaches to the implicit world in exactly the same way even though some basic guidelines will be helpful. With that in mind, what general principles might we develop to steer the work? Some of these have to do with the way we are present to the process, and some consider the general patterns that often emerge. As we proceed, it will be particularly enriching to recall your own experience working with memories and inner community members during Part I.

• *Impact of our explicit and implicit states of mind.* As we know by now, our state of mind will contribute to the way therapy unfolds. As J. D. Geller (2003) says, "Broadly speaking, patients have two potential sources of knowledge about their therapists: knowledge that is dependent on what the therapist chooses to verbally reveal and the knowledge that is dependent on receiving the information that is available to the senses during therapy sessions" (p. 549). Doubt, despair, pity, and anxiety find their way into our facial expressions, posture, prosody, eye gaze, intention, and emotion just as hope, stability, and warmth do. Geller continues, "Therapists have less conscious awareness of and control over the messages conveyed by their characteristic level of expressivity than over the messages conveyed by intentional self-disclosure" (p. 550). Our awareness of mirror neurons and resonance circuits has likely given us a healthy respect for how often state-of-mind exchanges occur. Geller concludes: "Analogously, patients have far less awareness of what they are learning about their therapists by receiving information during therapy sessions. In other words, the knowledge that patients acquire from encounters with the 'perceptual reality' of their therapist often remains at a tacit or subliminal level" (pp. 549–550). We might say that our perceptual reality is taken into their implicit memory, which can encode without conscious awareness. Our overall sense of hopefulness, clarity about the healing path, curiosity, warmth, and the other characteristics that are uniquely ours will embed themselves within our patients, influencing the flow of their implicit underground stream. Whether we are going to enter the world of memory via sand tray work or direct introspection, for example, our ease and confidence about a particular way of working will also impact our patients' willingness and stability within the process.

A Practice. Calling to body and mind a few of your current patients, sample your state of mind after you have been meeting with them for a few sessions. How has it changed from the initial session for each person you are recalling? Is there a pattern in your states of mind that is similar from person to person? Are there particular issues that impact your state one way or another? As best you can, undertake this investigation with curiosity and kindness, knowing that every increase in awareness has a positive influence on both people in the therapeutic relationship.

_____

_____

_____

_____

_____

_____

_____

_____

_____

_____

_____

_____

_____

_____

• *Understanding memory in a broad way.* We enter this work with a broad definition of memory, including not only explicit stories but bodily sensations, behavioral impulses, surges of emotion, perceptions, and global mental models arising from implicit memory; the pattern of particular experiences in our muscles; and our nervous system's baseline and window of tolerance, to name a few. Understanding memory in this way allows us to be more fully present as we track multiple streams of information. We can also help our clients understand the reasons why their memories won't always come back as whole stories, but may emerge as implicit fragments or simply as flows of activation within their bodies. Without this awareness, survivors of early trauma can go on doubting or dismissing their memories because they have no explicit content.

A Practice. We have been working to develop this kind of listening within ourselves throughout Part I. Bringing a few patients to mind, sense the specific streams of memory they bring into the room. Is one more prominent than another with different people? Then write a bit about what you discover.

_____

_____

_____

_____

_____

_____

_____

_____

The Brain-Savvy Therapist's Workbook

_____

_____

_____

_____

_____

_____

_____

_____

A Pathway into Memory and Inner Community Work

Now let's look at some steps in the process, allowing them to be a guide, but not holding onto them rigidly. Flexible adaptation to our patients' natural path of working, along with being at ease with variation from session to session, are keys to our patients feeling seen and trusted. Here is a list of eight steps that you can use as a quick reference. We will go into each one in more detail below.

1. Lay a foundation for understanding work with memories and inner community members.
2. Trust that whatever our patients bring into the room is a good starting place.
3. Move toward body sensation and behavioral impulses as a pathway to the right-mode implicit domain.
4. Normalize, accept without interpretation or judgment, and stay with whatever arises.
5. Enter the memory and be present with the inner community members within it.
6. Stay, track, comfort, regulate, and disconfirm.
7. Come into the present.
8. Remember the new memory.

1. *Lay a foundation for understanding work with memories and inner community members.* As with Suzanne, understanding how the brain stores implicit patterns that influence our current state of mind and behavior, as well as whatever other information fits this particular situation, can help assuage the left mode's need to know. Then the left mode can become more of an ally rather than antagonist or critic of the process. Often, this information resonates with right-mode knowing as well because we are describing processes our patients have experienced as the way things actually work. Early in the relationship, it is also helpful to talk about the inner community—how it forms, how these people/states of mind live on inside of us as part of us, and how they can

change. There is a description about the internalization process in Chapter 4 (p. 58) for your review now if any of it has gotten cloudy. This particular information usually resonates deeply with people because they have been hearing and feeling these subtle voices and nudges all their lives, so we are giving words to their already deeply known experience. As we offer these ideas, increases in trust and connection are signs that both hemispheres are listening.

2. *Trust that whatever our patients bring into the room is a good starting place.* Once we are engaged in the relationship, the brain's quest for complexity and coherence seems to guide the next steps in discovery. Whether our patients come in with stories to share, with the full flags of self-protection flying, or in a timid, quiet place, their inner world is communicating something we can discern.

3. *Move toward body sensation and behavioral impulses as a pathway to the right-mode implicit domain.* If we think in terms of neural nets, attending to any strand of energy and information will have some probability of activating the rest of the net. Since our body maps are in right-mode processing, bodily sensation and movement are natural places to start. Focusing on a tight stomach might draw in a flow of emotion, explicit images of a particular memory, a pattern of arousal, changes in muscle tension, an impulse to run, or a shift in perception as our mind begins to see through the lens of a particular mental model. *This process encourages integration of aspects of memory into a whole that we can inhabit with emotional vividness.* As we know, not all memories are encoded in explicit detail, so sometimes the visual memory may not surface. Instead, the various aspects of implicit memory will gather together into a full experience that can be held. With implicit-only memory, I have also found that the mind will sometimes create a symbolic image—a summary of the experiences that generated this particular configuration of memory: perhaps a small rabbit hiding in the bushes, or a cartoon hand coming out of the clouds to crush a tiny bug. These remind me of the way early implicit memory emerges in the sand tray as a direct expression of the central relational elements in the experience. Our vital task is to be present with whatever the mind brings, trusting that it is telling its truth.

4. *Normalize, accept without interpretation or judgment, and stay with whatever arises.* Our making-sense mind may often (and understandably) want to leap ahead to what the experience means. Instead, if we can settle into our caring observer to provide compassionate holding and witnessing support for what comes next, the process seems to find its own way. This, again, is an expression of our conviction that the mind's processes make sense and are moving in the direction of healing. Our inner attitude of support for that healing imperative marks an unseen but clear pathway for our patients' inner world.

5. *Enter the memory and be present with the inner community members within it.* When the memory first arises, our patients may experience it from

the viewpoint of observing from outside, or they may inhabit the memory from the inside. In the former case, we can imagine that focusing on the body sensation is moving the memory from the unseen implicit world toward conscious awareness, and that the middle prefrontal cortex is witnessing this, but has not yet made full contact with the visceral experience. I might say something like "We can walk into our minds just like we walk into another room. Let's see if we can go toward the child." Overtly including ourselves in the journey inward provides a sense of reassurance and support, and also awakens in the child his or her response to people from the outside world. As we moved inward toward one young man's child state of mind, he could feel the boy's wariness about my coming closer. I let him know that I understood and respected that, and would just remain in the background until he felt more comfortable. Over time, my presence seemed to become an entry point into his complex and confusing relationship with his mother. Whenever we enter the inner world, our only objective is being present, respectful, and responsive to what unfolds. Once we are present within, the work becomes entirely nondirective.

Taking us into the memory also advances the cause of internalization because where attention goes, so goes neural firing, increasing the speed with which the bonds of secure attachment can become reliable. During infant development, such intense internalization occurs as part of the critical period for the relational circuits in the brain, but as we grow older and don't have the support of those neural processes, conscious attention can significantly enhance encoding.

When our patients begin from the child's viewpoint, they may already be inhabiting the visceral reality of the experience, wide open for the addition of disconfirming energy and information. At that point, their child state of mind may be the only pattern of activation, in essence a limbic process without a connection to the middle prefrontal circuits. In those moments, the interpersonal system becomes the core of the work. Our middle prefrontal cortex witnesses the experience and provides regulation within our ample window of tolerance. The resources of two brains become one whole brain with the opportunity for wiring in new connections between the amygdala and orbitofrontal cortex—the attachment circuitry—as well as the entire middle prefrontal region.

If the memory arises as sensations, movements, emotions, and perceptions only, we can still become part of that process. I might say, "Just pull me into the ache in your chest," for example. Often, there is an immediate movement into greater intensity as the sense of resonance and calm presence widens the window of tolerance. Many of our patients have been so alone with their pain and fear that thinking of us wanting to be present, much less actually *being present*, is outside the reach of their implicit imaginings. I believe our emotionally anchored offer moves them from a mental model of having to do everything alone to the growing emotional sense that there will be help.

Sometimes memories arrive as patterns of protection that appear to bar the way to the root implicit memory from childhood. Curiosity and respect will allow us to understand their part in the inner world and their concerns about allowing the implicit to become explicit and acknowledged. One of my patients had what she described as "a nonsensical pain" in her left leg. As a precaution, she checked it out with her doctor, who found no evidence of injury. Even though we cognitively knew that it related to many instances of severe abuse, her emotional mind would not let her connect with the reality that a beloved relative had deliberately and persistently harmed her. She felt angry with herself for not being able to connect, and wanted to somehow force the issue; but I gently shared with her that I believed there was no place for coercion in the healing process, that she had been forced too much as it was. I assured her that her mind knew what it was doing and would allow those connections to be made at a time when she could endure it. After a few more weeks of dealing with other memories and further securing our bond—experiences that widened her window of tolerance for strong feelings—the physical pain and emotional knowing suddenly integrated. She was heartbroken, but together we were able to contain and comfort the younger self/state of mind who had undergone the experience.

As we discovered in Part I, we organize our memories not only by events but also by relationships—the pairs of our inner communities. At the point in memory work where we have fully entered the internal world, we will often notice that more than one person inhabits this experience—and this is an invitation to attend to each of the people/states of mind. If we have prepared our patients by helping them understand how these states formed, how much they are now us, and how each person in a pair can become active in daily life, then at the right empathic moment, we will be able to suggest and encourage contact with the non-native member of the pair. In Suzanne's case, the abundant love between her and her aunt made this process easy and natural. For people who have experienced violence or cold hatred, contact with the perpetrator almost never unfolds by itself, but it can be encouraged through gradually bringing both left-mode understanding and right-mode experiencing onboard. As early as taking history, we can begin to trace the intergenerational patterns so that our patients start to gain at least a cognitive understanding of why these heinous events occurred. Sometimes doing an inner community drawing, as we did in Chapter 4, can advance this sense of the interconnectedness of patterns across time. As blame gives way to understanding and then to a sense of the tragedy of it all, the door begins to open for both understanding that these wounded people are part of us—their intentions, their emotions, their bodily sensations and behaviors, their perceptions—and that they can be helped just as we have helped their child parts.

In my own therapy, I remember inviting my hurting and hurtful mother into our healing circle. As I asked her, "What's hurting you or scaring you?", I saw the look in her eyes shift from dark and threatening to a crumbling, decaying despair—and I understood her need to externalize a portion of her pain onto my sister and me. This was not a cognitive experience, but a tangible, visceral connection between her pain and her acts, experienced in my own body—because that's where she truly lives now. As we worked with her, I noticed moments when my hands were her hands, carrying my purse in a certain way or searching out the car keys before leaving the store, the latter being a way to assuage the anxiety of being exposed in the world when she was away from home. These movements and the motivations behind them lived in me in ways that allowed me to develop increasing compassion for her suffering. This, much more than resolving my own side of the memory, granted me a large measure of freedom from the abusive past.

6. *Stay, track, comfort, regulate, and disconfirm.* Our compassion may move us in the direction of relieving suffering as soon as our patient begins to experience pain, but the path of healing lies along a different route. As in daily life, our inner selves want to be heard and felt more than they want to be fixed and rescued. Our job is to stay empathically put, resonating with the suffering as an entry way into providing the precise shade of presence that will transform the old mental model and put down roots of a new implicit knowing. In general, the length of the stay is determined by our patients' need to emotionally connect aspects of the memory and to gain the embodied sense of being known, understood, and comforted in that place. Sometimes this occurs in a single session; more often, it extends over several visits to a particular experience.

An older woman with whom I met for an extended period did her work in a particular way. We would move into neural nets holding an experience such as isolation—something she had endured for many years—and we would settle into it sometimes for weeks or months. I could feel my impatience with the seemingly plodding pace of our progress, partly for my own inner reasons and partly because her suffering felt almost unbearable. It was as though she had to sample it from every side and be sure that I had tasted it to a similar depth. Then she would suddenly shift, taking in huge gulps of the new relational experience that seemed to completely dissolve her old mental model. By the third time of cycling through this process, we were able to talk about it, exploring the meaning. This led us to twin experiences from early in her life: a profound yearning for someone to know what was happening to her, and a mental model that suffering must be endured. Her way of doing memory work embodied both the healthy and hurtful mental models. This discovery opened the way for us to work explicitly on the new layer of implicit knowing that tied her to simply enduring.

To pull people out of the visceral experience before they are ready can be experienced as a counteractive move, and at a neurobiological level, leaves remnants of unprocessed pain and fear in the implicit domain. One exception to the guideline to stay with the pain is if our patients are moving out of their window of affective tolerance, disconnecting from us and their own regulatory resources, and moving into an escalated sympathetic or dorsal vagal state. This, too, is a memory, one of wild loss of control, so our empathic place with them is to provide resources for moving back into connection and regulation. So many strands of memory have gathered that the energy and information are overwhelming. If we can help our patients attend to the strands separately before gathering them together, it will be possible to gradually regulate the whole memory. Our first task is to be a calm presence in the room, calling our patient's name in a soft voice, encouraging eye gaze, and mentioning the present moment to help him or her come back from time travel. The experience of coregulation disconfirms the nervous system's memory of being left alone with intolerable arousal.

After we reestablish connection, working with the body's movements and sensations, separate from the emotional component, is a good starting point. The sensorimotor psychotherapy book by Pat Ogden and colleagues (Ogden, Minton, & Pain, 2006) offers excellent guidance for this kind of work. In brief, focusing attention on the body attenuates the intensity of emotion and explicit acceptance of what happened. Also, memory is an embodied process, so any release and rewiring through the body will send reshaping messages to the nervous system, brain stem, and limbic region as well. We can use any entry point to titrate the intensity, matching the pathways to our patients' natural ways of working. Sand tray, art, and clay can also be helpful embodied ways to both express and contain the flowing energies.

7. *Come into the present.* We want to encourage the past to be experienced as truly past. Part of this happens as the implicit memory becomes explicit, giving it a time stamp, and part because the old mental model meets an in-the-moment disconfirming experience. To encourage this movement, as the memory naturally comes to a close—sometimes simply shutting off when the patient has processed enough, sometimes at the end of the memory—we can invite the younger state of mind into the present, to come into the room and sense that she or he is part of the adult self now. Many patients have reported that they have a visceral and visual sensation of their physical location in the old memory (e.g., bedroom, yard, kitchen) fading into the background and dissolving. Then the next time we visit that state of mind, it feels anchored in *now* rather than *then*. The implicit lock is broken, and this state of mind is

now part of the ongoing flow of the brain. In this state, it is available to a much larger array of information, making it possible for us to foster further disconfirming experiences by holding the old knowing and new awareness together (Ecker & Toomey, 2008). If the timing for coming fully into the present isn't quite ripe, the child will either resist, asking us to stay, or we will bring layers of the child's energy and information into the present over several visits until there is the sense of being rooted here.

8. *Remember the new memory*. These tender, revised neural nets may remain open and available for strengthening for a number of days before they are reconsolidated, now carrying the new energy and information that were encoded during the work (Ecker & Toomey, 2008; Suzuki et al., 2004). Visiting the child's new state of mind frequently over the next week by calling the visceral experience to consciousness, then staying with it for a bit, will add strength to these nascent neural nets of integration that tie the limbic and middle prefrontal regions together in right-mode processing, changing the felt/lived narrative, and preparing a bridge to the left-mode spoken narrative—the subject of the next chapter.

Summing Up

In this chapter, we have focused mainly on working directly with memories, a kind of right-mode introspection that can bring implicit neural nets into emotionally vivid awareness. In my practice, this is always teamed with sand tray work, art, and, more recently, clay experiences, all unfolding within the embrace of the relationship. Moving fluidly between these experiential modes—and others that you may have developed or discovered—gives our patients the opportunity to approach the implicit from different angles and with different degrees of intensity. Once patients have experienced each of these modalities, in every session, we ask their inner world to direct us concerning what is needed for this particular experience. For almost everyone, within a few sessions, his or her inner world responds quickly and clearly. If it doesn't, there is usually an implicit mental model blocking the way. With our kind and focused attention, we can remove this hindrance to the inner world being able to express itself clearly.

We have covered a lot of ground here, although much of it is probably quite familiar from your own work. Review as much as you want from Chapters 3 and 4, especially returning to your own reflections about your personal explorations. When you feel settled in your knowledge about these processes, in your journal write a paragraph or so about how you would explain memory and inner community work to patients. Then, from your caring observer, notice with kindness if judgments arise about the work itself or about your implementation of it. I don't know anyone who doesn't struggle with self-judgment, so if you find those tendencies, surround them with as much gentleness and acceptance as you can. Then write a bit about your relationship with your judging mind.

_____

_____

_____

_____

_____

_____

_____

_____

_____

_____

_____

_____

_____

_____

Now, connect with your listening partner and share some experiences with doing memory and inner community work with your patients—what you have done so far and how you might implement it from here. Making this a regular feature of your time together will deepen these healing experiences. Some people find that this sharing also takes the sharp edges off their own self-criticism, because they feel heard and accompanied by a fellow learner.

In my travels, many therapists have told me that hearing about doing this kind of work gave them a general idea, but not the sense of exactly how to begin, how to track, and how to move into memories in a healing way once the process begins. That feeling of helplessness in the midst of a patient's memory has stopped many therapists from pursuing this path to the implicit realms. Often, our patients will begin to fall into helplessness as they descend into the experience of their child state of mind, and our resonance with that helplessness, coupled with not having a strong internal guide, can pull the process into anxiety or stop it altogether. Going through these steps until we feel a natural flow, practicing with colleagues, continuing to do our own work, and thinking about how we would move into this process with particular patients can help create enough of a framework so that the emotions that must arise for this work to be successful don't swamp us. We, too, have to build or strengthen the neural nets that support this pathway—both the circuits of regulation and the circuits of having an embodied sense of how to guide the process. Engaging in our own practice of integrative neuroplasticity with our customary kindness toward self will make these pathways even stronger.

We have focused our attention on ways to move into the deeper mind, understanding that the roots of misery lie in the dissociated and time-trapped implicit domain. However, in the course of therapy, we have many kinds of conversations, not all of which involve plumbing the depths in this way. One useful principle of practice is to provide the *most empathic response in the moment*—and that is not necessarily to move toward these deep places every time. Instead, we might picture a balance between the development of the adult self side by side with fostering healing experiences for the younger states of mind. Often after doing a powerful piece of inner work, patients need a period of consolidation in which the integrative circuits of the default network have a chance to digest what has been uncovered. These become periods in which adult-to-adult conversations may unfold. The developmental feel is different, but the patient-centric focus remains the same. We might picture this process as one of building multiple bridges so that all aspects of our patients feel valued, seen, and cherished at the appropriate developmental level.

One of my patients was working through profound despair about her parents' lack of love for her and apparent adoration of her brother. After enduring an agonizing plunge into blackness, we suddenly emerged into a sunny place, feeling as though we were holding a battered but breathing and healing baby. For the next four sessions, we discussed gardening—a passion common to the two of us. At the end of those sessions, my patient said, "I needed time to breathe, to feel the growth—literally and figuratively, to be with you and the baby and the new flowers. I hope this is all right." I responded by saying that I believed we were preparing a world in which these rescued young ones could find safety, warmth, play, and joy, so these conversations that her heart craved were just right. As our patients' windows of tolerance expand and the demands of managing so much pain and fear decrease, there is room for every delightful emotion to emerge as well. Making ample room for these in therapy, whether they come in the form of a giggling child or a profoundly celebratory adult, we have the great pleasure of sharing in the enjoyment. At the same time, we will witness our patients' lived and spoken narrative changing as well.

Chapter 11

Supporting the Emerging Narrative

At the same time we are descending into the implicit depths with our patients, we can notice that their minds are also beginning the upward climb into the daylight of a changed life. Over the course of our time together, we watch them move from having many different and often contradictory narratives that are not in contact with each other toward a single, emotionally resolved narrative that embraces a good deal of their history. As we moved through the first few weeks of therapy, Melanie said, "My father was unfailingly kind," and she went on to describe his many good deeds in the community. Later that same day, she said angrily, "My father destroyed my life," as we talked about his constantly critical ways with his two daughters. At our next visit, she said, "My father was right to be disappointed in me. I never lived up to my potential." If we look at these statements from the viewpoint of the inner community, we can begin to see the relational pairs inside—admiring daughter–civic-minded father, angry daughter–critical father (with the shamed child just beneath the surface), and self-blaming, resigned daughter–disappointed father. Because these pairs hold contradictory information about Melanie's father, they never become emotionally real at the same time. Instead, she jumps from neural net to neural net as she inhabits these various states of mind—both hers and his.

About a month after Melanie transitioned from therapy, she wrote me a note. She had worked hard on her inner community and particularly wanted me to know how she was doing with her external father.

"About my dad—I saw him last week for the first time in a decade. He looked like an old man who had been beaten down by life. I remembered how his father had made him the object of ridicule so often when he was young, so there was nothing but compassion for him even when he was critical, as always. Maybe he was kind to people in the community as a way to offer something to them that he never had—and maybe to be seen as a good person. I realize how disappointing his own life was and that nothing I did one way or the other was going to change that. I don't feel any need to try to please him, and yet as I felt less angry with him, he seemed a little softer, a little more pliable and like he might even enjoy my company a little bit. Anyway, the stuff he does doesn't make me angry anymore. I feel like things will be OK between us when he dies."

All of the aspects of her father from her former stories are present, now reconciled into a single human being with whom she is at peace.

Our patients' new narratives emerge piecemeal with each patch of completed work—much like building a patio brick by brick, a metaphor that seems to resonate well with many patients. These new stories reveal their coherence through their emotional aliveness, our patients' ability to stay with the positive and painful or frightening aspects with a good deal of regulation, and the sense of calm resolution that emanates from the storyteller. The process of neural integration underlying the creation of a coherent narrative creates a wider lens that can hold multiple aspects of our patients' lives in a single picture.

Building a Reconciled and Coherent Narrative

What can neurobiology tell us about this process of reconciling narratives? As dissociated and time-trapped neural nets open to caring and disconfirming experiences, their liberated and transformed energy and information join the larger flow of the developing brain, continually modifying the self-story that their default network is weaving without their conscious awareness. These deep changes then gradually manifest as a widening of their windows of tolerance, accompanied by shifts in feelings, behaviors, perceptions, and relational strategies. Often, but not always, they also take shape in the words of their spoken narrative. As we may recall, this process of integrating newly available information begins with a dedicated circuit, the core of the default network, that includes the medial parietal cortex (remembering events relevant to personal life), the medial prefrontal cortex (self-reflection and the creation of our experiential autobiographical memory), and the posterior cingulate cortex (an integrative region toward the back of the brain). This circuit's job is to make personal sense of the discrete flows of energy and information in our brains (Buckner et al., 2008; Raichle, 2010). Patients are often heartened to know that daydreaming (a time when the default network is especially active) as well as mindfulness can contribute to their brain's increasing complexity. As we work our way through the implicit patterns that have bound our patients, we can know that *any change of constraints means a change in their felt and lived story.*

Let me share some examples of initial constraints developed through early attachment experiences and the narrative that develops around them, followed by a change in both constraints and narrative within the embrace of the therapeutic relationship. With these kinds of stories, our minds are invited to hold the flow of therapy from beginning to transition.

Miguel: Emerging from an Implicit Prison

As an infant, Miguel's surge toward attachment was met with a wall of "no" from his mothering person. This particular experience created an implicit flow of disastrous disruption that inhabited his body and nervous system—what we call disorganized attachment. It also created the strong bodily and emotional impulse to pull away whenever he felt his own yearning for attachment come up—what we all reactive attachment disorder. By about 2 years of age, with growing neural maturity, feelings of shame (his parasympathetic response to being rejected) and disgust (internalized from his mothering person) arose and served to keep the fragmentation dissociated (Schore, 2009a). Out of these implicit flows came a story of rigid, angry self-hatred, which he unconsciously used as the organizing principle to keep the inner disarray managed.

All of these flows of energy and information resided in his earliest implicit memory, so became the permanent and compellingly true story of his life—in his body, his nervous system, his thoughts, and his feelings. Perhaps because Miguel had been emotionally disowned, his brain was wired to *disown its own knowing* about the source of his experience. When we talked about implicit memory, he could agree that everyone else had been influenced by their mothering person's treatment, but he alone brought an initial badness with him and his mother was just fine. He gave me numerous examples from later explicit memory of her verbal and emotional cruelty, but always wrote them off as justified by his being a completely defective human being. His language was laced with words such as *garbage, stupid, ugly, irredeemable, malevolent, wicked, harmful*—a lexicon of self-rejection.

This sense of himself was so deeply embedded that all evidence to the contrary had to be destroyed in some way, often by continuing to create more experiences to confirm the rigidly encoded story of badness and incompetence that defended against the implicit reality of utter disorganization. Because his perceptual glasses prevented him from seeing anything good about himself, his default network received only strands of information that had been colored by the governing implicit story of inherent badness. At the beginning of our time together, all experiences in which I perceived something contrary to his self-perception—seeing him as a likeable person doing good in the world, or in which I behaved toward him in a way that he never experienced as a child—like being treated with kindness and respect, were met with a violent recoil of his entire being. This lived narrative dominated every moment of his life. A tighter neural trap is difficult to imagine.

Let's pause for a moment to visualize the pathway from implicit torturous disorganization arising from utter rejection, to the felt story of shame and disgust, to the spoken and lived narrative of justified self-hatred, used as an organizing principle to ward off disorganization. As horrible as self-hatred and self-disgust are, they at least allow a person to function from day to day, whereas overt disorganization stops all clear thought and creates so much anxiety that the person becomes disabled. Thinking about some of your more injured patients, see if you can trace an analogous pathway. What is the implicit root that generated an experiential story, which then culminated in a spoken narrative that was completely at odds with your experience of the person? These trails are often elusive because the root is usually out of conscious awareness for both our patients and us, so it can be helpful to write down the path once you spot it.

_____

_____

_____

_____

_____

_____

_____

_____

_____

_____

Having "failed" at therapy a dozen times, Miguel made one more try, consciously hoping that he would be able to gain confirmation that the hating was correct, and possibly gain some better strategies for managing both the hating and the badness inside. Out of conscious awareness, it is likely that his unmet surge of attachment energies was actually guiding the quest. In spite of the automatic recoil from care, my consistent presence, kind regard, and clear seeing of what was happening in Miguel's adult implicit brain began to erode the held-as-truth belief that he must be discarded and destroyed. One of the greatest gifts of interpersonal neurobiology is that it allows us to truly see into the implicit world so that we are not thrown off by the spoken story. Much like water on stone, the day-to-day quietly persistent offer of ongoing presence and warm attachment often met the quiet "no" of behavioral impulses that pulled away from warmth—as well as perceptions that included things *only* going from bad to worse, the necessity of *only* badness emanating from this person, the *impossibility* of being tolerated, much less cared for, and his overwhelming fear that his presence *must* destroy me precisely because he was beginning to like me. Any counteractive move coming from the reasonable realm of my left-mode processing—"You are a valuable person"—met mounting resistance, so I needed to be very vigilant about just being with him, even when my mind so much wanted to bring him relief. Then, one day a new story began to emerge from the hours, days, weeks, and months of cultivating presence and caring. In the most quiet of quiet voices, Miguel said, "It's OK to be with you. It's OK for me to remember our time together." At first, the new narrative strand of attachment was met by a ferocious counteractive response. He immediately had to deny that this was possible, often falling into a state of terror at even having this thought. However, our times of visiting this new state gradually became more frequent. Initially, this new state of mind was as fragile as fine-spun glass, then gradually strengthened as the neural net of "together" grew thick with repetition and emotional intensity. In his body, nervous system, and feelings especially, the new narrative was taking root, while his thoughts were taking longer to shift. His fear that any sense of his goodness was a lie was one of the implicit roots that kept him from shifting more quickly, but shift he did as his attachment system responded to the consistent offer of connection.

I have returned often in these pages to some examples from the far reaches of human maltreatment, where hatred and coldness do the damage at the level of hard-to-grasp implicit encoding (rather than coming in the more obvious form of bodily harm), to help us get the feel of how these pathways both develop and resolve. The feelings that resonate in these instances are often the most difficult for us to manage within ourselves. If the symptoms on the surface and the dissonance between our patients' perceptions and our own pull us away from being able to focus on the implicit center, it becomes all too easy to escalate into activities that have no chance of altering the core experience. It is as though we begin to co-narrate the story from our patients' points of view, often with their self-hatred and despair resonating in us as "This is an impossible person and a situation that is impossible to change." With kindness toward yourself, see if there are times when you have experienced this deep resonance with patients' disruption from their persistent and implicitly driven self-stories. Sense the ways in which the shared energy and information seek to pull you into complicity with the implicit message. Then write a few gentle words.

The Brain-Savvy Therapist's Workbook

_____

_____

_____

_____

_____

_____

_____

_____

_____

_____

Our primary tool as we move into relationships like this is the strength of our caring observer, filled with wisdom about the brain and overflowing with compassion. Then we are able to meet our patients in these implicit prisons with the same tenacity that compels their minds to cling to these infant immovable truths. The brain's genetically hardwired determination to move toward integration, coupled with the strength of the attachment system, is our strong ally. In this way, we become partners in the movement toward brain-restoring connection.

Janice: A Rapidly Changing Narrative

From a different arena of early childhood experience, here is an example of a new narrative emerging quickly and with relative ease. Janice wanted to bring in her 5-year-old son, Josh, because he was showing a lot of anger toward his new sister, Sammy. During my initial meeting with Janice, she said, "His behavior is terrible. He should love her. She's just a baby." Tired new mom that she was, she had little patience for his words about wishing Sammy hadn't been born. As we talked, a narrative about the importance of respectful speech in the family of her childhood emerged. She said, "If I'd said that about my little sister, I would have been whacked." I asked her if she had been happy about her sister's birth. After a little reflection, her eyes teared. "No, but I knew better than to say anything." I asked her what she needed from her parents then. "Just to be allowed to have my feelings and know they were OK. Then I would have gotten around to loving her. As it is, I still resent her." She paused, looking intent. Then, as though a curtain had opened in her mind, allowing her to see the overall meaning, she said, "That single thing has cost me two decades of not being really with her."

For the remaining time that day, we talked about practical ways to let Josh's pain about not being in the center anymore be heard, so that together they could clear the way for him to embrace Sammy. In the first 20 minutes of our time together, Janice had gotten to the living truth of the binding implicit root that expressing true feelings meant being "whacked." Then with very minor but intentional guidance, she went to her equally vivid present-day awareness of what she had needed as a child. This juxtaposed the disconfirming experience of the power of being allowed to speak with the old model that such speech is forbidden (Ecker & Hulley, 1996, 2000a, 2000b, 2008). The old pathway instantly weakened to the point that she could viscerally feel the wisdom of doing things differently. Her narrative of what it takes to be an acceptable child had changed.

Needless to say, I never met Josh, but I did hear from Janice again when she called to say that she and her sister were seeing each other on a regular basis, talking a lot about how hard it was for both of them not to be able to express any contrary thoughts as children. Their home had been loving and stable, but a generation's-long tradition of verbal respect as the key to acceptance had kept everyone locked down. Janice also told me that she kept expecting to feel the impulse to correct Josh when he was resistant to her way of thinking, but it seemed like a distant memory. Instead, curiosity about what was behind his words stood in its place. Since her new neural net had been tested in ways likely to evoke her old pathway if it still existed, we can assume that the relationally healthy constraint had thoroughly replaced the unhealthy one.

Let's look at some times with patients when you may have observed such sudden changes in story, ones that made permanent shifts in perceptions, behaviors, and relationships. These are often easier to spot because a lot of the processing occurs in the conscious mind and takes the form of words. Even though we are approaching the implicit world, two adults with engaged middle prefrontal cortices solve it together. Write a bit about those. Take a few moments to go back to the previous practice and notice the difference in your body and feelings with the two kinds of narrative experiences.

_____

_____

_____

_____

_____

_____

_____

_____

The Brain-Savvy Therapist's Workbook

Pathways of Narrative Integration

Thinking about this transformation in neurobiological terms, we can see that Janice and her sister rested on a sufficiently firm foundation of attachment—not completely secure, but good enough—to make fairly rapid changes in the small packets of unempathic experience they carried in their implicit memory. The ties between Janice's limbic and middle prefrontal systems were firm enough to allow new upsetting information to emerge quickly and be held within an adequate window of tolerance long enough to meet the disconfirming experience and be taken into the bigger picture of healthy relating. The new felt experience also naturally and rapidly moved into left-mode processing where words helped to form and stabilize the new knowing. The journey from right-mode experience to left-mode expression was effortless. For a person like Miguel, who was hated or abused from early childhood, no such foundation exists, so the process of developing a healthier narrative rests on rebuilding the brain, beginning with the circuits of regulation.

One of the first narrative changes we see here is a widening of the window of tolerance, as limbic and middle prefrontal regions build stronger connections through their resonance with our attuning, containing brains. Instead of a nervous system story where escalation into disorganization is a constant threat, a new experiential narrative about interpersonal support and regulation for the nervous system and feelings develops very gradually. From repeated contacts that have this quality, the default network may also begin to build a new perception of believing that help is possible. None of these stories may take on words, but they do begin to influence the lived narrative, as we saw with Miguel. They produce small but very significant steps that our caring observer can see and steadily hold—sufficient regulation to stay in connection without fragmentation, greater eye contact, and changes in posture and facial expression, to name a few.

The Narrative Pathway of Posttraumatic Stress

Between these two extremes, we find many other patterns of narrative integration (Siegel, 2006). Let's look at one more. The challenge for people with histories of abuse, particularly when the abuse began early, is the massive amount of dysregulation in their nervous systems combined with tsunami-like waves of implicit energy and information that flood their embodied brains whenever those neural nets are activated. Additionally, the very structures that support integration may be injured or underdeveloped. The hypersensitive amygdala, encoded with massive fear and anticipation of more danger, is poorly connected to the regulating middle prefrontal region because the traumatic circumstances lacked sufficient empathy to create these connections (Schore, 2003a). If stress was ongoing, it is likely that the continual wash of cortisol has eaten away some tissue in the hippocampus (where explicit memories form) and prefrontal area (where the circuits of attachment and regulation reside) (Saigh & Bremner, 1999). Relationships have been the source of dysregulation rather than regulation, so feeling safe enough to move into connection so that the interpersonal system can help regulate their nervous systems is also difficult. All of these conditions are part of the initial narrative of fear and pain, coupled with the anticipation that there will be more of the same. These memories are not only established in implicit memory, but have also passed into the cortex as invariant representations that tell us what comes next (Hawkins & Blakeslee, 2004). "My life is cursed—I will never be a stable human being" was one patient's voiced core belief.

We can think about our task as opening and then integrating the encapsulated flows of energy and information left isolated by the trauma, first gathering the fragments of memories into whole memories and then helping them move into the overall flow of the brain—and doing this within the window of tolerance. This integration doesn't happen all at once. Initially, in therapy, we can often compassionately observe how these memories rush into awareness; use the relational stability we are creating together to contain them at the level of the nervous system, body sensations, and emotions; and then recede out of awareness for a while, without linking to an explicit awareness of what happened, much less to what it means to have been treated in this way. Then perhaps with the next visit to these neural nets, the memory strand may incorporate some aspects of explicit recall, and on, until the whole memory can be held in conscious awareness.

In the early stages of memories becoming more integrated, patients sometimes ask what I understand about their experience. I explain in a way that is intended to help them gain reassurance by developing a caring observer perspective on their brain's processes, but it often bounces off right-mode processing, moves briefly into left-mode cognitive understanding, only to vanish completely within moments or hours. Then the question arises again in a day or two. We could say we are making solid patio bricks (drawing strands of a particular memory together and into regulation), but not building the patio itself at this point (integrating differentiated memories with the larger brain).

At one level, the narrative is changing—there is help and there is beginning to be a new story in the nervous system about how things don't just get worse and worse with no resolution. However, at the level of integration with our patients' middle prefrontal resources, not much is happening yet. Until our patients are neurally able, our middle prefrontal region, manifesting as the caring observer state of mind, gathers these bricks and begins to assemble them internally. We are the holder of the emerging narrative for some time until our patients' regulatory circuits are built for the first time and their window of tolerance is wide enough to contain both the memory itself and the impact of knowing that it is true.

This last part is particularly important. It is one thing to viscerally embrace the details of the memory, and another to accept that a loved one, for example, harmed you in this way. One patient said, "At my most crazy-feeling moments, I know that you know something I can't know yet." That sums it up. The heart might break and the mind might fracture if the full meaning of the abuse were to come together all at once. So, bit by bit, our patients gather the strands of memory while we hold the big picture and the warm, stable, regulating space in which these fragments can coalesce. Eventually, the memory is sufficiently soothed as a whole so that the amygdalar activation that is triggered does not shut down patients' orbitofrontal and other middle prefrontal circuits. In this way, the integration of the strands of memory creates a differentiated whole that can now be linked to the ongoing flow of the larger brain—the key process in transforming patients' narratives at all levels from implicit to spoken.

Our confident state of clearly seeing how this process unfolds, which patients pick up through their resonance circuits, allows us to normalize their fragmented experiences. Then we can encourage them to focus on the healing moment rather than trying to see the big picture before it is time. Many of my patients have found reassurance in learning that they don't have to know it all at once and that someone else is minding the whole store while their brains are using their full resources to deal with a fragment. In secure attachment, we "loan" our children our middle prefrontal resources until their own can take over, using two brains to make one complete and healthy system. The brains of our abused and traumatized patients, scattered in their early days or victimized by extreme circumstances in adulthood, need the same kind of support. Over time, just as the memory fragments cohered into differentiated neural nets ripe for integration, the parts of the story gradually gather into a resolved narrative.

One sign of movement in that direction is the felt and expressed shift in the story from broken-down feelings of guilt, shame, and badness to a strong acknowledgment of having been victimized—not being a victim now, but of having been victimized then. The adult self often has a sense of straightening his or her spine to stand strong in protection of the younger selves now. When our work also includes resolution for the internalized perpetrators, a profound relaxation settles into the muscles and nervous system. Sometimes these perpetrators have melted away into rest, and sometimes they are transformed into helpful people internally. For the whole system, a compassionate narrative unfolds in which the precursors of the trauma are understood.

Many survivors of abuse take great solace in being able to give words or images to the whole story. One of my patients used about half of the miniatures on my ample sand tray shelves to build her life story along the full diagonal of my 15-foot by 10-foot office. While she also narrated in words, her body's fluid movements and her emotionally rich yet regulated presence spoke of her high degree of resolution.

If you have worked with people who were traumatized early in life, take a few moments to sense the path of their narrative resolution. What changes emerged first, and in which systems—body, nervous system, feelings, thoughts? What did you see shift in their relationships? How much verbal expression did they give to the new story? You may be able to feel the changes flowing in your body, or taking form in images or thoughts. Then write a bit about it.

_____

_____

_____

_____

_____

_____

_____

_____

_____

_____

_____

_____

_____

_____

In all these cases, even though the pathways were different, *the change in narrative arose from modifications to implicit memories, which led to a new lived and felt story before it was translated into left-mode words.* One of the beauties of our brain's natural movement toward greater coherence is that vertical integration of right-mode circuits establishes the very pathways that lead across the hemispheres to the left-mode's ability to complete a rich, embodied, whole-brain narrative (Siegel, 2006). Once dissociated experiences make their way from the amygdala, to the hippocampus, and then to the orbitofrontal and medial prefrontal cortices, they are on the neural road to the possibility of left-mode processing.

Not all parts of the narrative always make their way into words. For example, our nervous system's story may unfold in the body primarily, providing a new baseline for regulation and a larger window of tolerance. However, the act of speaking an embodied narrative gives form and stability to what has been unearthed and integrated. Our patients often deepen their sense of meaning and mastery in the telling as well. Near the end of therapy, three narratives often emerge—one holds the resolving story of this person's life, and the second the account of the therapeutic adventure. Because we have also been talking about the brain's healing process, we often find ourselves telling a parallel tale that marks the stages of brain integration as well. As we co-narrate these three passages, profound gratitude for making this journey together often emerges, a brain-integrating, mind-cohering, relationship-enhancing experience for both of us.

There has been a good deal of information that we now want to take time to digest. Let's think about the latter days of therapy with one or two patients who saw the process through to a satisfying conclusion. In your journal, write about their embodied narrative at the beginning, trace some changes through the course of therapy, and enjoy the fullness of the narrative as they transitioned out of regular meetings. Notice if the pathway of integration is different for the two patients. As always, be gentle with yourself as you are building your capacity to think in terms of embodied narratives. Kindly accepting where we are builds the circuits of compassion in our brains and opens the door to take in new information. As much work as I have done in this area, writing this chapter has opened my eyes to new areas of narrative change that can now become part of my repertoire. We are so accustomed to thinking of narrative as a spoken story that it takes time to learn to listen at many levels with different kinds of ears. Inviting your listening partner to share what he or she is discovering will help expand the bounds of narrative, since each of you will have had different experiences.

How to Support Narrative Integration

What can we do to support this integrative process? Our awareness of the many dimensions of narrative can allow us to sense subtle shifts in the way energy and information are flowing in our patients' bodies, perceptions, feelings, and relational moves—all aspects of their changing story. These right-mode changes are the precursors of a shift in the verbal manifestation. Holding the changes we observe in our kind awareness supports the continuation of that new state. We may or may not choose to mention what we are noticing, depending on whether we believe it will strengthen that state or undermine it. With one patient, I noticed that he was no longer fidgeting as much and that his speech had slowed to a more regulated rate, indicating to me a shift in the story his nervous system was telling us, and perhaps also speaking of his increasing attachment to me. I pictured saying, "Gus, I see that you are growing more calm"—and immediately saw his overwhelming and intrusive mother studying his every move. I decided to remain in resonance with the change and keep my words to myself. On the other hand, when 9-year-old Lacy, struggling to assimilate her parents' divorce, started building two houses instead of one in the playroom, I did say, "Oh! There are two houses now!" because her face radiated a sense of achievement and joy, an expansive state that I felt wanted to be met with my enthusiasm. She threw her arms around me, so that turned out to be a good choice in supporting this important resolution.

However, our empathic capacities being what they are, we won't always estimate correctly, so it's good to know that every miss brings an opportunity for repair. Angela quietly shared her first venture into having a voice with her mother—telling her mom that she wouldn't be able to pick her up at the airport because she had another commitment. Not telling her mother what that commitment was made it an even bigger deal. She shared this victory with her eyes down, peeking at me like a shy child. I felt a huge grin start to come to my face, but restrained it a bit to match her quietness. After a moment, she burst out, "Aren't you going to say something? I'm so happy! Aren't you happy?" I turned the grin loose, and we laughed together.

In addition to having our moment-to-moment attention on the unfolding narrative, we may also find times when talking about the process of narrative integration helps our patients' caring observer hold each new patch of work mindfully and with kindness. Once our patients' increased regulation shows that some connections between the limbic and middle prefrontal regions are in place, this conversation may forge a new link in the partnership between our two caring observers. Using the hand model (Siegel & Hartzell, 2003) to illustrate the pathways of vertical and horizontal integration can ground this explanation visually and tactilely. Many of my patients regularly bring their own integrating hand brain to our work, telling me what they are observing about shifts in their thoughts, feelings, perceptions, and behaviors and what these indicate about the type of neural change that has taken place. Such an increase in mindful awareness also serves to further strengthen the all-important regulatory circuits.

Along with the accumulating story, we may make the delightful discovery that curiosity, playfulness, and a greater capacity for caring blossom as well. Jaak Panksepp (2008) has identified seven motivational systems in the limbic brain: seeking, play, care, lust, rage, fear, and separation distress. When we move out of connection with others, the latter three signal our disruption and call out for containment by another. This is our emergency system responding to our intrinsic need for others. Many of our patients arrive with these emergency systems claiming much of their brain's energy, drowning out the other life-enhancing motivational flows. In the calm space that surfaces after deep, resolving work, there is room for the other motivational systems to manifest. *Accepting patients' invitation to co-celebrate the victory of deep change is as essential as the co-suffering we do when our patients are moving through the painful parts of their work.* Lingering and savoring, together we build sturdy pathways for their regular expression.

One of my patients lived in a household where such expansive states were unacceptable because both of her parents had survived the Holocaust—a tragic situation in which the suffering then dictated the suffering now. Whenever she felt a strong outward flow, whether it was curiosity, playfulness, or a romantic surge, she crushed it, feeling extreme guilt and disloyalty, as though she were denying the reality of what had happened to her parents. As we worked through all she had internalized from them, she was able to "experiment" with laughter and curiosity with me, even when she didn't dare let it out in her parents' home or in the world yet. With our practice sessions and with more resolution, it became impossible to deny these strong flows from her increasingly healthy limbic world.

We had spoken about the natural process of irrepressible delight, and she decided that she wanted to ask her parents to come in so that she could talk about the changes she was experiencing. These were loving parents who wanted their daughter to have a completely different experience from the torment they had endured, and so they were most willing to come. She was able to share her struggle with disloyalty and her fear that she would hurt her parents if she was filled with joy. All of us wept, and then her father said, "You be joyful now. We have had enough misery. Maybe your laughter can finally warm our hearts. It did when you were small, but then we all fell into the pit together. I see that now. I am so sorry." Her mother was nodding her head and reached for the hands of her husband and child. Her father continued, "It was not our intention to lock you up in our jail cell. We all escape now together." More tears—this time of joy and release. Her years of work were changing her family's tragic narrative to make room for a new intergenerational legacy. I wondered about how much gradual change had already taken place within her parents through resonating with her as she was healing, preparing a neural path for the story to shift with ease. Writing about this now, I feel such warmth and expansion in my heart.

Our awareness of narrative can also help us see when and where additional work is asking for our attention. The doldrums can encourage us to ask, "Where is that elusive implicit root?" Carin had endured wracking physical and emotional abuse as a young child. She had the most sorrowful face I had ever seen. We quickly became an earnest, solid team working on behalf of the abused children, moving through states of mind and body generated by physical and emotional cruelty as well as regular imprisonment in a closet. While she felt a growing sense of release from the memories and a good deal of compassion for her parents as a result of doing inner community work, her mind would focus on perceptions that took away any positive thought or expansive feeling almost as soon as it arose. After meeting someone who seemed like she could be a good friend, Carin told me she felt happy for the rest of the day. When she woke up the next morning, her mind said, "Think about all the years you had no friends. Is that kind of deprivation right? This is just a crumb—how can you be happy about that?" We had seen this pattern before—a burst of hope, joy, and freedom, followed by emotionally charged, compelling thoughts that plunged her into bitterness, victimization, and grief.

This time we became curious, asking her deeper mind to take us to the source of this pattern. Within moments she became viscerally aware of her role in the family: to carry the dark aspects of the family's trauma and grief as her burden so that they could enjoy one another. In her mind, she saw her mother's anguish at any joy or pleasure she experienced, and she sensed that her young self had learned before she was 5 that she was not to feel or express anything positive. This work seemed to be mostly about helping relieve her internal mother's pain, to widen her window of tolerance to make room for her daughter's joy. Because her external mother had completely dissociated her own early experience, my patient had internalized some of that avoidance, so the work took awhile. However, as the inner story gradually unfolded, mother's terror and grief surfaced around a series of losses when she was very young. These were familiar family stories that had always been told as though they had been taken in stride. Only now was Carin able to feel the significance of these tragic events.

As her internal mother softened and grieved, her daughter's caring observer and I offered comfort—and Carin began to tentatively experiment with bursts of laughter and leisurely hours of happiness. Checking on her mother's response to these overtures, Carin could see inside that her mother was at peace, not participating in the joy, but her rest not being disturbed by it either. This transformation of the implicit need held by her mother released Carin's mind from the compelling need to dispel joy. It makes neurobiological sense that if there is a consistent return to an old pattern, then there is a constraint that has yet to be modified. Because Carin and I had talked about the brain's processes throughout our time together, we could hold onto hope when we encountered the same obstacle repeatedly. We needed to move through enough of the abuse to understand that there was a deeper question that we needed to ask—and then resolution happened rather quickly.

Over time, our patients' narratives grow more comprehensive. As pain and fear are no longer the dominant internal forces, there is room for not only personal joy but also for interpersonal compassion to expand. Because understanding the mutual influence of brains, minds, and relationships has been an integral part of the therapeutic process, most patients gain the ability to deeply understand why parents and others harmed them in those particular ways. Since our work has also involved emotionally vivid contact with those we have internalized, there is a visceral knowing that supports and deepens what they have come to understand intellectually. If I haven't done so before, at this stage, I almost always offer lovingkindness and compassion meditation as a practice. Consciously radiating this goodness inward speeds integration of the now-available people into the empathic inner community. As Daniel Siegel (2010a, 2010b) would say, our patients' mindsight grows, not only for themselves but for others as well. This combination of empathy and understanding becomes the leading edge of compassionately releasing all who have hurt them. What might have seemed an outrageous suggestion at the beginning of therapy has become a natural act of forgiveness in the end.

This has been a chapter of sharing stories about stories, and so we finish by having the pleasure of reflecting once more on the unfolding narrative of someone with whom you have spent a good deal of time. Call to body and mind the feeling of satisfaction you have experienced within a rich partnership with one of your patients. From there, ask your deeper mind to bring a particular person to you. Then spend some time with your journal and with your listening partner tracing this patient's unfolding narrative. What were the key elements of the initial narrative? What were the first changes you experienced in that story? How did those changes show up—as behaviors, perceptions, words, or all of the above? When and how did the patient begin to notice the changes? How did the two of you share the final narrative—both of the patient's life story and of the healing relationship?

Near the end of our process together, most of my patients have a particular experience—as though a curtain opens in their mind, and they gain a visceral sense of the full extent of the family tragedy through the generations. JoLynn, a woman who was emerging from a lifelong depression, described it as standing on a hill to see and hold the river of pain that had engulfed everyone in her family through the generations. At this point, her neural circuitry could support the mature grief that poured through her body and mind. She wept deeply but with such self-containment, sensing the rightness of these feelings. I felt honored to accompany her in these moments. For the next few weeks, we talked about her passage out of the devastating loneliness that had destroyed so many members of her family. Then we both knew the time had come for her to transition out of this part of the work—and this brings us to the last chapter of Part II.

The Brain-Savvy Therapist's Workbook

Chapter 12

Transitioning

In the closing weeks of our work together, we listened deeply to JoLynn's inner world, hearing diverse responses to our movement toward transition. The word *transition* seems better than *ending, separation, goodbye,* and especially *termination* to embody the experience of moving from the outer support of the relationship to inner reliance on the now-established circuitry of regulation, attachment, and mindfulness, along with the internal presence of the therapist. As JoLynn and I began to speak about this change, she was aware of a subtle anxiety moving in her chest. Her caring observer circuits were so well developed that she seemed to be constantly tuned to the music of her body in a curious, respectful way. Having moved from radical distrust of her inner signals at the beginning of therapy to an appreciation for the truth of the story they tell, she felt a stream of joy beneath even painful or frightening flows of energy and information—a clear sign of advancing neural integration.

We settled into our observing minds and invited the anxious feeling to take us to its source. JoLynn saw a child of about 4, sitting alone by the well at the family farm. She was on the ground with her knees drawn up to her chest and her back against the stones. Her head was down, looking at something in her lap. Because of long practice with her inner community, JoLynn easily merged into the feelings of this child, sensing a deep sorrow beneath the anxiety. At the same time, her adult state of mind was able to surround this child with compassion. We can picture the orbitofrontal cortex reaching down to these particular neural nets in the limbic region with the synapses of attachment. Sensing that someone had come, the child raised her head to reveal what was in her lap—a small kitten who had died. Such deaths were common on the farm, but for this child, the loss was agonizing. Staying with her, JoLynn began to sense that the kitten's death resonated with the many losses this young one had already endured. In JoLynn's mind, her adult self settled next to the child who quickly crawled onto her lap. Her caring observer didn't imagine or initiate this; instead, this young state of mind—one JoLynn recognized as belonging to her mother—came out of isolation to join the empathic inner community in this form, which may have been a memory or a symbolic vessel for many moments of loss. These visual experiences seem to be the way our minds combine our intuitive knowing about our inner others with the sensory information that is common to inner community experience. In this way, memories or symbolic images arise that contain the actual energy and information of the internalized experience.

Over the next few weeks, we checked in at each visit with JoLynn's body to see what her inner world wanted to communicate. We were invited into several experiences—some with her own inner children, some with inner community members—as though they were coming forward to be seen, known, cared for, and integrated before the outer parting. It seemed as though just her intention to go out on her own prompted her mind (through attention) and brain (through its intrinsic movement toward integration) to bring forward states of mind/neural nets in need of help at this point in her therapy. Her process was so regulated and easy, I knew she would be able to work with most inner issues that might come up in the future without my outer help. As she was working inside, without any prompting from me, she indicated that she felt my presence there, so I knew that she carried me as a permanent and accessible part of herself now.

When there seemed to be nothing more arising inside as we attended to the thought of parting, we naturally moved into reflection and celebration of the path we had walked together. Over about a month's time, we revisited what she had experienced as turning points in our work. The most powerful ones included our first session when she had the visceral sensation of being understood rather than labeled as a depressed person; her first visit with her inner community, tasting the depth of depression within everyone who lived in her home when she was young; telling me of her brother's suicide and seeing the tears in my eyes that told her I was "a real person, not just a professional"; and the first day we belly-laughed together at a dumb joke we made up. When she first came for therapy, she believed that she would never laugh again. In all her reflections about our process, she said not one word about anything I had *said*, speaking only of *relational moments* that reached deep into her implicit world. She was aware that she alone in her family had broken the cycle of desolation and depression in time to influence the next generation. This, above everything else, gave her the greatest satisfaction.

JoLynn, who had used sand tray and art extensively in her process, wanted us to do a tray together for our last visit. Our first task was to arrange the sand.

After immersing ourselves in it a bit, a small azure lake emerged in the middle, seemingly by unspoken agreement. Following our bodies, we each selected about half a dozen pieces and took turns placing them. JoLynn began by making a hill to the right and placing two ostriches there to overlook the scene. I felt quite happy that she had chosen two. We paused to acknowledge our long-legged caring observers who certainly didn't have their heads in the sand. I arranged some flowers around the opposite edge, and JoLynn gently placed two glass hearts in a golden bowl and set it in the lake. Another pair. I placed the two rainbows I had selected on the right-hand shore, noticing that pair as well. Studying her remaining figures, JoLynn picked three often-used Georgia Mann porcelain figurines—one that held her rage, one that held her sorrow, and one that wore the mask of her depression. She placed them on the upper shore, and I immediately put the autumn tree nearby.

The Native American storyteller, singing the songs of attachment to her children, was JoLynn's favorite sand tray piece. With loving hands, she placed

Figure 12.1. Healing Sand Tray. JoLynn's three wounded selves, recuperating under the watchful gaze of the storytelling mother. Porcelain figures by Georgia Mann, http://georgiamann.com; Native American storyteller by Jemcz artist D. Lucero.

Figure 12.2. JoLynn's Helpers. Porcelain figures by Georgia Mann, http://georgiamann.com; clay figure by Debbie Berrow, http://bellpineartfarm.com.

this mother and her children on the hill above her wounded parts. Near the rainbow, I placed a delicate pink anemone shell and Debbie Berrow's clay figure of Release, a joyous woman holding a bird who is ready to fly. JoLynn went back to the shelves to get two more of Georgia Mann's pieces—a woman nurturing an egg and a green sprout child, ready to unfurl her fronds. These went in the tableau with the rainbows.

She rearranged the flowers a bit, picked up the two rainbows and savored the sensation of the smooth surface on her fingertips before replacing them. After running her fingers over the ridges on the shell, she experimented with helping the little bird fly from the old woman's hands. Then she said she felt finished, but brushed her fingers through the autumn leaves before really stopping. I realized she had touched every figure I had chosen. We stepped back together to see what we had created.

I felt ease and comfort flowing through my body and sensed that something similar was happening for JoLynn—a kind of amplified sense of connection, quiet joy, and rest. She spoke into our extended silence saying, "I love how the three who were wounded so badly are surrounded by the storyteller and our three helpers on the other shore. I love it!" I just smiled from the roots of my heart because that pleased me so much as well. The sense of symmetry and balance, the pairs we had both placed, and the vibrant colors of the autumn tree and yellow and purple flowers gave form to the aliveness that had now fully replaced her depression. From several angles, we took pictures that I could e-mail her later, and then found ourselves arm-in-arm walking toward

The Brain-Savvy Therapist's Workbook

Figure 12.3. A Tableau of Resolution and Comfort. Enjoying our transition tray together. Porcelain figures by Georgia Mann, http://georgiamann.com; clay figure by Debbie Berrow, http://bellpineart farm.com.

the waiting room. I felt a little wrench in my heart as I watched JoLynn depart, but I also felt the comfort of her presence lingering within me, permanently embedded as part of my inner community.

Transition in Short-Term Therapy

I chose to start with JoLynn's and my transition because it is emblematic of the closing stages when therapy is a process of thorough integrative repair, rather than a short-term directive or symptom-focused set of sessions. Some of our patients will come with a symptom that is annoying them, resting atop secure attachment, and they may not need to be with us for more than a few reparative sessions. However, I am also aware that many settings do not offer the possibility of this kind of longer-term work, even when the injuries are long-standing, and that many of you will have to build something more short-term from bits and pieces of what is offered here.

We have found that even educating people about the way their brains work can give them a solid reference point that is regulating and reassuring. Using the hand model to help them see the parts of their brains and how they work together, talking about how neural nets form and change, exploring attachment patterns, and helping them understand the connection between implicit memory and their behaviors can relieve shame and anxiety while increasing hope. In addition, we are supporting their caring observers in gaining a vantage point for having greater mindsight within themselves and with others. Our caring presence can also help settle them into a more regulated state. When beginning and transition fall so close together, we plant seeds, foster what change we can, and send them on their way filled with more hope, some skills, and perhaps some experience of how resolution is accomplished, which can act as a guide for future work.

Transition in Long-Term Work

For the remainder of the chapter, we are going to look at transition with the brain in mind as part of the longer-term process we have been cultivating. First, to settle into this theme, bring to awareness two or three recent transition processes from your own practice. Notice with kindness the response in your body, feelings, and thoughts; then write about each of these experiences with descriptive words.

_____

_____

_____

_____

_____

_____

_____

_____

_____

_____

_____

_____

To begin, we must acknowledge that there are many times when transition was not a satisfying process. Parents may pull their children from therapy because they fear the attachment they see growing between their child and the therapist, especially if the child says, "I like Julie much better than you because she's not mean!" Our patients may make the legitimate decision that they have gone as far down the path as they want or can endure, even though we can see the implicit thorn bushes waiting to pull at their clothes. Old implicit patterns about failure and unworthiness of care may gain too much momentum for the new relational experiences to offset them sufficiently for the person to stay. Money runs out, insurance stops paying, people move away. Under all those circumstances, painful and frustrating as they often are, we can know to a neurobiological certainty that these people don't depart empty-handed. They have internalized us, to some degree, and encoded something about the healing path, even if both of those are held without conscious awareness. At some implicit level, there may be a bit more hope and a bit more regulation.

The Neurobiology of Transition

When we have been able to move much further down the healing path with our patients, what does interpersonal neurobiology tell us about transition? Let's review the neuroplastic achievements we have nurtured within the embrace of our relationship. Our joined minds have built integrative pathways in the brain, wiring together the limbic and middle prefrontal regions on the right with more numerous and durable connections. This increase in complexity in the emotional, relational, and motivational circuits means that as new energy and information come in from daily life or up from our patients' implicit memory, a more generous window of tolerance allows for awareness and regulation. These particular circuits, combined with integration with left-mode processing, also support nine capacities identified by Daniel Siegel (2006, 2007, 2010a, 2010b):

- Regulation of the body, including a ventral vagal parasympathetic baseline for the autonomic nervous system
- Attuned communication, reading faces, receiving and sending signals so we and others in our lives feel felt
- Emotion regulation, a wider window of tolerance for positive and painful feelings
- Response flexibility, freedom to choose by taking the longer road from the limbic region through the middle prefrontal cortex to consider various options, rather than reacting from the speedy limbic alone.
- Empathy, co-suffering and co-celebrating, resonating with one another
- Reduction of fear through the addition of GABA-bearing synapses from the middle prefrontal cortex to the amygdala
- Insight connecting past, present, and future into a coherent whole
- Intuition, a right-mode way of knowing that reaches conscious awareness without left-mode reasoning
- Morality, because we are much less likely to harm someone when we have all of the capacities above.

This is a robust list of indicators of mental and relational health, one that we can share with our patients at any stage in therapy and celebrate as we transition. JoLynn, for example, particularly reveled in her capacity for empathy and insight, feeling how these twin modes made fulfilling relationships with her still-suffering family possible. Throughout therapy, she noticed changes in her response flexibility as old implicit templates of isolation and depression gave way to an appetite for life. For the first time in years, she could choose to accept or decline an invitation rather than feeling bound to the immobility imposed by her depression. These nine make good milestones for us as well, guiding us toward work that awaits us and revealing areas that are more whole.

Next, we will notice that over the course of our healing time together, our patients have gained a foundation for secure attachment. In addition to the developmental maturation of the right-mode circuits, we have internalized one another. This has allowed us to carry our patients with us so that they continue to exist in our minds between visits—often a delicious but unfamiliar sensation for them. When I truthfully say, "I thought about you during the week, and . . ." tears of answered need sometimes come, especially when the patient's parents lacked the capacity for inner continuity. Gradually, these newly minted implicit mental models manifest in relationships. One patient begins to find friends capable of mutuality for the first time. Another no longer needs to either idealize or denigrate me, but begins to see me as a whole person with strengths and struggles. Still another decides that being at ease with herself is more important than finding a boyfriend immediately. A momentum of healthy relating develops. In addition, our patients tell us that they are aware that we are always with them. They hear our voices, know what we might say, feel comforted in sorrow, and soothed in anxiety—like a Franklin stove installed at the heart of everyday life.

Through the consistent practice of mindful awareness of all sorts, our patients have strengthened the highway between the body, limbic, and cortical regions; perhaps thickened their middle prefrontal cortex; strengthened their anterior cingulate's attentional capacity; and created greater synchrony among brain regions. The energy in right- and left-mode processing becomes more balanced so that the capacities for introspection and reaching outward into life are both accessible and seen as valuable. Over time, we see our patients' caring observers gain strength and find that we are able to drop into the background bit by bit. As pieces of history are mindfully collected and integrated, we experience patients' comprehensive and compassionate embrace of their history.

Because we have seen these capacities increase, we can be confident that our patients have developed the structure and function that will support continued brain integration. Because these new circuits have been built and exer-

　　　　　　　　　　　　　　　　The Brain-Savvy Therapist's Workbook

cised, they are now familiar pathways in the brain and therefore much more likely to support integration in stressful times, rather than our patients falling back on old patterns such as dissociation. They have also strengthened their minds to be able to use attention as a tool of ongoing awareness and self-kindness, both of which foster further integration. Finally, new implicit mental models anticipating supportive relationships have become embedded in their limbic systems, making it much more likely that they will be able to draw healthy people to them. At the time of transition, we return to the now-familiar triangle of well-being: *integrated brain*, *coherent mind*, and *empathic relationships* as the core processes at the heart of a fulfilling life (Siegel, 2007, 2010a, 2010b). So much resonance has developed between our patients and us that our certainty about these processes radiates to them. When we couple that with shared words, we send them on their way with an ample travel kit for further growth.

A Personal Experience of Transition

When I moved from California to Washington about 2 years ago, I said farewell to many people, some of whom did not feel ready for the relationship to transition. I was leaving not only patients, but the agency I had started nearly two decades earlier, and especially the group of interns with whom I had undertaken the interpersonal neurobiology journey, so the experience had several faces for me. The process of separation from my patients began about 6 months before my departure, and an amygdalar alert about change and loss flowed through all our bodies. I felt like a parent sending her children out to find their own wings—sad and glad at the same time, with unique concerns about each child and how he or she would handle this next step. Not surprisingly, the stages of grief began to manifest—disbelief, negotiation, anger, sorrow—for about 3 months.

Then a remarkable integration process began to take place. Almost without exception, even for those who initially felt they might not survive this loss (one among so many for them), a more comprehensive view began to emerge. One woman who had imagined that I would not retire until she felt she was ready for me to go, said, "At first, I felt as though you deliberately pulled the rug out from under me, then that you didn't like me enough to stay, but then I began to think about what we have done together these last 2 years. I know that I'm not ready for you to go and it will be hard, but I also know that my mind is more stable and that I'm handling my relationships without so much conflict. So maybe that means I'll be able to begin with another therapist without making them or myself crazy."

I had seen what we might describe as borderline traits in this woman gradually diminishing during our work, and now, even with this stress, she was showing signs of neural integration, especially the links between her amygdala's abandonment alarm system and her attachment-focused orbitofrontal cortex. Our last two sessions were gentle, appropriately sad for both of us, but marked primarily by a sense of a job well begun and a future of open possibility. These transitions did a great deal to further ground my core belief in human resilience in the presence of interpersonal support. While almost all my patients had backgrounds filled with loss and grief, this parting was different because of all the warm connectedness we had nurtured together that no physical separation could take away.

Now it is time for us to transition from the process of personal development and patient support that we have cultivated with mindful awareness and kindness. As with our patients' transitions, we may step away from the words in this book, but not from the healing experiences we have woven into our brains, the strengthened attentional capacity of our minds, and our kind, empathic relationship with ourselves and our listening partners. This triangle of support, strengthened along each of its sides, will continue to develop because of the processes we have initiated. As in the therapeutic relationship, we can return to these pages as often as we want for nurturance and encouragement to continue our arc of integration. As I write these words, I have a sense of connection with you, as though time and space are irrelevant to the reality of attachment. This writing process has deepened my sense of how we are linked by the circuits of interpersonal connection, and it has granted me a fuller appreciation for the vitality of our inborn push toward greater coherence and compassion. Picturing each of you with me has helped guide my purpose of making healing the visible, tangible, delicious practice that it has been for me.

I wonder what this process has meant for you. We can think of this in right-mode and left-mode terms. As I ask this question, with great kindness and gentleness, notice your body's sensations and impulses to move. Linger with your feelings. Reflect on how your perception of yourself as a therapist and human being may have changed. Sense any shift in the quality of your relationship with yourself, those close to you in personal life, and your patients. Then taking up your journal, spend some leisurely time writing about your right-mode experience in this moment, using those now-familiar descriptive words to retain the liveliness of your visceral knowing. Next take some time to think about what you have learned, a more left-centric endeavor. Which principles are proving most valuable to you as a therapist? Which as a human being? Where do you want to go from here in terms of new learning? Now, let these two ways of knowing flow together into an embodied sense as these principles gradually permeate and shape your walk in the world. As you and your listening partner share these reflections, I trust it will also be a time of play and celebration.

Just as we might sit around the fire and share the tale of a great journey, in Part III, we are going to sum up, or we might say integrate, all that has gone before by drawing our principles together and taking a first run at developing our individual coherent narrative of therapy. We undertake this process of in-corporation—both in the sense of drawing together and taking on flesh—knowing that it is one of the truly never-ending stories.

Part III

Reinventing Our Therapeutic Paradigm in Light of Interpersonal Neurobiology

Introduction

While we have been focusing on new experiences and new learnings with the brain in mind, our default networks have been integrating the fresh information coming in as well as any changes in the implicit patterns that have emerged as the result of our work within ourselves. We have made new neural nets, expanded and strengthened those enduring ones we wish to preserve, and taken some steps toward changing those that haven't served us well. At the same time, these new ways of thinking and experiencing have encountered our established conscious and nonconscious beliefs about the therapeutic process and about ourselves as human beings. In short, we have prompted a great deal of neural change that will now integrate over time.

Although Part III lies at the end of the book, it is in many ways the beginning of a lifelong practice of bringing the support of consciousness to the process of integration. We have consistently cultivated many flavors of mindful awareness within ourselves and with our patients, and now we bring the neural nets developed by this focus to the investigation of what we believe, both implicitly and explicitly, about the therapeutic endeavor—perhaps gathering a number of disparate strands into the beginning of a coherent tapestry.

In general, with some thought, we can state our explicit beliefs as a set of propositions about how people become wounded and how they heal. These generally extend to all patients. Our implicit beliefs, on the other hand, come in two flavors: One is a blend of the core perceptions that widely influence our thoughts, feelings, and behaviors—some will support healing, others may undermine it; the second are dissociated neural nets that may be stimulated by certain experiences with patients. As always, these are not neat categories and can overlap each other. For example, I may be carrying a small, ever-present lake of despair internally as part of my legacy from a family mired in suffering through the generations. Although it is always there, a silent weight in my torso, it becomes most prominent and influential when I am in the presence of a patient who feels like giving up. If it is implicit-only, it will show itself as body sensations (heaviness), behavioral impulses (wanting to push this person away), emotions (hopelessness), and perceptions (this therapy is never going to work). It will be experienced as the truth of the present moment instead of as something I learned as a child, and so will radiate to my patient along the resonant pathways that tie the two of us. However, if I have an explicit awareness of this implicit pattern, then I will more easily identify the visceral experience as mine and be better able to contain the despair so that I can maintain support for my patient. In this way, our broad implicit patterns ebb and flow in the relationship.

We also have embodied implicit mental models that underlie our ability to hold certain states of mind on behalf of our patients: our belief in healing when we encounter our patients' conviction about the impossibility of recovery; our confidence in human resilience in the midst of their feeling irretrievably broken; our experience of tenacity in the midst of their failing strength. When these are anchored at the foundation of our being as implicit knowings, they radiate through our being to resonate with our patients and steady them at their most difficult moments. All of us carry both of these kinds of implicit models.

Dissociated neural nets, on the other hand, are apt to pop up suddenly in response to a specific experience our patient is having. One of my colleagues shared that she always felt intense anxiety whenever a patient's memory led him or her to a picnic table scene. Once she spotted the pattern, with a little reflection, she was able to explicitly recall sitting at a table in the park while her parents spoke in grief-stricken voices about Grammy's impending death. This particular grandma had been a warm source of connection for this 3-year-old girl, so the sense of loss without understanding stirred up a lot of anxiety. The more conscious we are about both kinds of implicit memories and the more we do our work to transform and integrate them, the better for our own mental health, which then becomes an asset and resource for our patients.

When we flesh out our explicit beliefs so that they become a coherent set of principles, we can then use them as a guide for the kinds of experiences we want to offer our patients. We can ask, "Which practices are most apt to foster integrative neuroplasticity for this particular person?" One person will work mostly through the relationship in the moment, whereas others may work primarily with their inner communities, inhabit the sand tray, take up crayons and paper, or find benefit from cultivating mindfulness, eye movement desensitization and reprocessing (EMDR), or psychotherapies that work directly with the body. All of these approaches, however, take the principles of neuroscience discovery into account. Here, we are going to explore our basic tenets of practice in light of the core principles of interpersonal neurobiology, and then consider the implications for our preferred ways of working with patients. There is no thought that we are doing anything definitive, but instead making a start and establishing a pattern of inquiry that we can use the rest of our lives.

On the implicit front, we will call to body and mind patients with whom we have felt significant struggle. Often, it is exactly these experiences that most illuminate our implicit flows of energy and information. At this point, we have developed a strong capacity for bringing mindful awareness to the discovery and transformation of implicit patterns, so that ability is our ally here. Our other support is our growing experience of curiosity, kindness, and gentleness toward ourselves. As we make our inner inquiry, we can also ask who in the inner community carries a particular implicit flow. At times, I am aware of my internal grandfather, a man of great learning who felt contempt for those who were not intelligent. As I worked with his inner presence in my own therapy, I discovered how his reverence for intellectual strength protected him from having to deal with the abuse he suffered at a very young age. Now, when I feel a slight stirring of superiority, a moment's focus on reassuring him quiets that old flow. Again, we will sample small experiences here as a way to create a template for ongoing work.

We might ask why this explicit and implicit investigation is an important endeavor. Many people have told me that clarification of their paradigm releases them from having to focus much on what to do next. Once the principles are embedded, presence and actions both flow easily from this inner wellspring. This makes our embodied brains and minds more fully available for the nonjudgmental and compassionate embrace of our patients' full selves. Without the clear seeing and stability offered by a settled and viscerally known paradigm, we can be swept off our inner feet by the resonance we experience with our patients, by the flow of compassion that we feel for them, or hampered in our efforts by uncertainty. However, with that support, not only do we rest in whole-brain steadiness, but compassion itself grows greatly in the light of understanding our patients' inner lives.

Chapter 13

Exploring Our Implicit and
Explicit Narratives of Practice

At every stage in our development as therapists, we have implicit and explicit streams of information that guide our practice. When I was in graduate school at Azusa Pacific University, our final project was to formulate our paradigm, based on what we had learned in class, what we had experienced in our own therapy, and what we discovered in working with one of our patients for at least a year during school. We were not to say simply that we had decided to be a cognitive–behavioral or psychodynamic therapist, but to write about our unique and emerging paradigm. It was the most clarifying experience of my long academic career.

Reconsidering the Eight Principles

We are going to undertake something similar here, beginning with our foundation in the principles of interpersonal neurobiology. The list of eight principles that grounded Part II will be our starting point, with the door open to add as many others as our experience brings to us. As many times as we read this list, we will have both implicit and explicit responses to it. Taking each principle, notice with kindness the influence it has on your *body, emotions,* and *perceptions.* Then write a few descriptive words about your implicit response in the space just beneath the concept. Over time, I have discovered that I sometimes have a subtle resistance or a particularly strong positive surge in regard to one or more of these. Sitting in curiosity with that information takes me more deeply into my relationship with these flows of energy and information as they have personal relevance for me. It has also often illuminated which inner community members may be animating the resistance or fondness.

When we sit with these principles, we are always inviting a broader integration with our implicit assumptions. After doing your first piece of descriptive writing, read the list again, attending this time to the *thoughts* that arise in connection with them. What does your left mode have to say about their validity and usefulness? As much as possible, do this with curiosity, kindness, and openness to everything your mind has to say. As we listen to our thoughts in this reflective way, there is a good chance that left mode and right mode will converge to give us a more comprehensive sense of the meaning of these principles for ourselves and our practice.

1. Our early attachment history matters.

_____

_____

_____

_____

_____

_____

_____

_____

_____

_____

_____

_____

_____

_____

2. Our bodies are part of every memory.

_____

_____

_____

_____

_____

_____

_____

_____

_____

_____

_____

_____

_____

_____

3. Our brains can and do change all the time—neuroplasticity is real.

_____

_____

_____

_____

_____

_____

_____

_____

_____

_____

_____

_____

_____

_____

_____

4. Neural integration is the foundation for our increasing well-being and can be fostered in interpersonal relationships.

_____

_____

_____

_____

_____

_____

_____

_____

_____

_____

_____

_____

_____

_____

5. Our brains are always on the path toward greater complexity and coherence, hampered in their natural course only by constraints, many of which can be changed, particularly within empathic relationships.

_____

_____

_____

_____

_____

_____

_____

_____

_____

_____

_____

_____

_____

6. Healing as well as healthy living requires the presence of both right-mode and left-mode processing.

_____

_____

_____

_____

_____

_____

_____

_____

_____

_____

_____

_____

_____

_____

7. Mindful attention is one key agent of change.

_____

_____

_____

_____

_____

_____

_____

_____

_____

_____

_____

_____

_____

8. Interpersonal oneness is real, and the therapist's mental health matters.

_____

_____

The Brain-Savvy Therapist's Workbook

_____

_____

_____

_____

_____

_____

_____

_____

_____

_____

_____

_____

_____

This list is just a beginning. Your own investigations into the meaning of neuroscience for therapy may suggest other principles of particular value to you and the way you practice. Note them here, listening for both their implicit and explicit meanings, and continuing in your journal if you need more space. As you flesh this out with several passes, you will have created your personal list of grounding principles.

_____

_____

_____

_____

_____

_____

_____

_____

_____

_____

_____

_____

_____

_____

_____

_____

_____

_____

_____

_____

After completing your individual reflections, it may be particularly helpful to compare notes with your listening partner. The unique relationship the two of you have developed with each other and with this material can support your ongoing creative explorations as perhaps no other can. In addition to looking at core principles, it would be good to take some time to talk about your ongoing experience of nonjudgment and acceptance of self. This area tends to be so challenging for most of us that the safety of an established relationship is a good place to bring our gains as well as our struggles. After your meeting, you might want to do some writing about the meaning of this relationship for you.

Reflecting on Disorder and Healing

With these principles as a reference point, let's reflect on two questions: How do we imagine that people become dis-ordered? How do they heal? I struggle with using the word _disorder_ (even with the hyphen) to describe our brain's lack of integration, our mind's incoherence, and our incapacity to either attract or offer empathic relationship. Yet I haven't been able to find a better one that doesn't also bias the conversation. Feel free to insert your own preferred word as a start on your personal understanding of the process.

If the principles we have articulated are the foundation, we could think of the answers to these two questions as framing the house of therapy. Let's start with _dis-order_: How do people become dis-ordered? Take time with this process—and get out some scratch paper. At this stage, messiness is an advantage as it will allow multiple thoughts to emerge without editing. Some quick answers may come to mind. Jot those down. Now listen for the exceptions. How do they become part of the answer? Then sit with your emerging theory and bring various patients to mind. Are they at home within this picture? What other aspects of the process of dis-ordering emerge? Are there examples of dis-ordering in your own history? Are you discovering diverse principles or a single underlying principle with many manifestations? Are particular inner community members participating in this process? If yes, what are they contributing? Visiting these questions for a while each day over the course of a week or two will give your default network an opportunity to integrate what you are discovering with what you already know, often revealing new levels of integration. When you sense that you have arrived at a satisfying place, see if you can summarize your current thoughts about the dis-ordering process in a few sentences here.

_____

_____

_____

_____

_____

_____

_____

_____

_____

_____

_____

_____

_____

_____

_____

_____

_____

_____

_____

_____

_____

_____

_____

_____

_____

_____

_____

_____

_____

_____

Now let's turn to the question of healing, using the same messy-to-coherent strategy. Beginning with the healing work you have done within these pages, what initial thoughts about the principles of your process emerge? Now explore the same question with a variety of patients in mind. What do your patients contribute to their healing process? What is your part as their therapist? Leaving aside specific healing activities, focus on the underlying principles of going from dis-ordered to coherent. Once you have a set of principles, listen for the *but* or *and* comments in your mind; then make some more notes about these additions. Listen for inner community voices as well. After spending a good deal of time over several days, begin to move toward a more coherent statement about the principles of healing and write them here.

_____

_____

_____

_____

_____

_____

_____

_____

_____

_____

_____

_____

_____

_____

_____

_____

_____

_____

_____

_____

_____

_____

_____

_____

_____

_____

_____

_____

_____

Now spend some time with your experience of this process. Was it a struggle, a playful experience, a frustrating exercise, something else? Was it accomplished with gentleness and acceptance of its emergent and never-ending quality more than with judgment—or vice versa? Was it useful? If yes, in what ways? If not, what would make it more useful? How does having these two paragraphs about dis-ordering and healing influence your body, emotions, and perceptions regarding the work you do and of yourself as a therapist?

_____

_____

_____

_____

_____

_____

_____

_____

_____

_____

_____

_____

_____

_____

_____

_____

_____

_____

_____

_____

_____

_____

_____

_____

_____

_____

_____

_____

Comparing notes with your listening partner can enrich this experience as well. As the two of you talk, notice the influence of the differences in your two viewpoints on your body, emotions, and perceptions. Does it feel like an expansive conversation that adds overtones to your own thoughts about these processes, or like a disquieting challenge to your beliefs? Is there room to accommodate differences as well as join together around similarities? Being able to talk with one another about these implicit responses can help both of you settle into your way of seeing these processes with greater security in what you have discovered. After your time together, write a bit about the meaning of this particular conversation for you.

_____

_____

_____

_____

_____

_____

_____

_____

_____

_____

_____

_____

_____

Now that the house is resting on a foundation and well framed, let's begin to add walls and rooms by reflecting on the particular methods we employ in the healing endeavor. These will include *attitudes toward out patients*, *ways of being with them*, and *concrete processes we offer* (e.g., journaling or sand tray). Various inner community members may especially impact our attitudes toward patients and our view of how it is best to be with them. Getting out the ever-helpful scratch paper, compile a list in no particular order, and without evaluation of efficacy, to encourage as much to emerge as possible. Bring many different patients to mind as well as visiting your own experience in that role. Go meticulously through a few sessions in your mind to see the different flows of experience that develop with different people. If you notice some self-criticism coming up about what you actually do in sessions, see if you can meet it with kindness and acceptance. After coming back to this discovery process a few times until you feel like your list is fairly complete, write your methods here as a reference for the next part.

_____

_____

_____

_____

_____

_____

_____

_____

_____

_____

_____

_____

_____

_____

_____

_____

_____

_____

_____

_____

_____

_____

_____

_____

_____

_____

_____

_____

_____

_____

Now we are going to spend some time shining the light of our foundational principles and our beliefs about dis-ordering and healing on our methods. By inviting this kind of integration, we are seeking to bring greater coherence to our work. Once accomplished, this can give us a powerful sense of stability that translates to our patients as a sense of hope, containment, and ease within the process. When our inner knowing about healing is aligned with what we actually do, we have greater freedom to focus in the moment on our compassionate embrace of each particular person. As difficult as this part of the process can be, the results are worth any struggle that emerges.

Let me share an example. As I was doing this comparative process myself, I became aware that I am spending more time than seems warranted by my principles in what I see as social conversation. After spending a little time gentling the burst of self-criticism, I brought in one of my central healing principles that has been with me since well before I learned about interpersonal neurobiology: Do what is most empathic in the moment, with due regard for the developmental state of the patient in that moment. Drawing several examples of these conversations to mind, I could feel how (1) sometimes these were acts of joining that served to move us into the connection that would foster our next steps, (2) sometimes I was following my patients' need to stay away from their deeper process (not always helpful), and (3) sometimes I was appropriately honoring my patients' developmental need to support their adult state of mind to balance the work we were doing with their child states. This refining process began to create a greater in-the-moment felt awareness of the meaning of seemingly social conversation that has allowed me to differentiate between when it is empathic and helpful, and when I am participating in a diversion.

All of our kind and attentive investigations here can yield such refinements, which develop into a greater natural sensitivity in the moment to the flow of the healing process. In order to maintain a gentle attitude toward ourselves, we can acknowledge that this process is endless. We might even come to delight in the unfolding experience, approaching each new investigation with curiosity.

Returning to the list of practices you created above, you may find that some are obviously in line with your principles and healing paradigm, that they foster integrative neuroplasticity and secure attachment without any doubt. Your list may also include some practices that you can imagine being helpful sometimes and not others, and another few may be clearly out of alignment. After playing around with these evaluations on scratch paper, make three rough lists in the space below.

_____

_____

_____

_____

_____

_____

_____

_____

_____

_____

_____

_____

_____

_____

_____

_____

_____

It can be helpful to call to mind the ways in which you have used these attitudes, ways of being present, and concrete practices that are clearly integrative. Sometimes this investigation will prime your mind to offer other moments when these would add integrative power to your interactions with a particular patient. Over the past 5 years, I have reflected on the silent power of having clarity about the inner world of my patients. I have seen that it opens a considerably wider door for them to walk into the areas of their mind that need healing. This awareness keeps my receptive mind sharp with each person. Pick one or two practices from your list and reflect on their healing efficacy here.

_____

_____

_____

_____

_____

_____

_____

_____

_____

_____

_____

_____

_____

_____

As with my use of social conversation, it is likely that many of our practices can either support integrative neuroplasticity, *or* reinforce patients' self-protective states of mind, *or* even further their dysregulation. In the process of exploring these possibilities, we may become more sensitive to moments when we are drifting into our patients' implicit worlds. However, we may also discover that ways of being or approaches that we think are not helpful at first glance actually have considerable healing power in certain circumstances. Grounded as I am in the belief that healing work involves contact with right-mode processes, I spent a lot of well-intentioned time trying to help an avoidantly attached older man connect with his body, but to no avail. With both of us on the verge of giving up, I felt myself pulled into my own left-mode place and began to explain the brain patterns of avoidant attachment. I felt as though I were jumping ship in some way until I noticed the spark in his eye as I talked. He felt alive to me for the first time. Later I realized that I had joined him where he lives full time, in left mode, and that had awakened his attachment system much more than my offers of right-mode empathy. This experience several years ago broadened my understanding of the innumerable ways to be empathic in the moment.

Selecting one or two of your sometimes helpful/sometimes not practices, spend time getting a sense of when they have advanced the therapy and when not. Differentiating them in this way can build neural pathways that will increase in-the-moment awareness of their likely effectiveness.

_____

_____

_____

_____

_____

_____

_____

_____

_____

_____

_____

_____

_____

_____

There may be some practices that we can humbly acknowledge have little possibility of building integrative neuroplasticity and secure attachment. They may be helpful for temporary symptom relief, but not for building overall brain structure and functioning in enduring ways. There may also be some that don't even confer that benefit. It will be helpful to understand what does not support integration or attachment in these practices. When I was working on this discovery process with a colleague, he told me that blunt confrontation was big in his arsenal. We sat with what he had come to understand about the importance of safety and attuned communication; internally revisited some sessions in which he had used his confrontational approach, watching the right-mode communication of his patients in that moment; resonated with their withdrawal; and came into contact with painful memories of his father's blunt treatment of him "for his own good." The deeper reasons for selecting a particular approach don't always emerge this easily. However, in this particular instance, my colleague's visceral experience of what establishing safety can do for the therapeutic process was a natural fit for illuminating the difficulties with his way of interacting, especially when it was done as a matter of course without regard for its empathic impact in the moment.

Most of us have picked up a variety of practices over time, often without placing them in an overall framework of the healing process. These may be inner attitudes we hold toward our patients, ways of being present with them, or external processes we offer. We talked earlier about the difference between seeing our patients as wounded and weak as a result of their injuries, or as brave and resilient by virtue of their brain's constant push toward integration and their willingness to be in therapy. Something as invisible as that can have a powerful, ongoing impact on how therapy unfolds.

Looking at those attitudes and practices that we suspect may not be helpful, let's sense how our bodies and emotions would respond to giving them up. If we have continued with them just because we learned them and haven't thought about their usefulness in terms of the big picture, we can often relinquish them with some ease. If, on the other hand, we feel upset in body and emotions at the thought of parting ways, then there is probably an implicit link maintaining their use—as there was with my colleague's continual practice of confrontation. From your list, choose one or two that seem to carry an emotional charge. Then, as we did in Part I, ask your deeper mind if there is an implicit connection that would be helpful to understand. Use the next space to write about what you discover.

_____

_____

_____

_____

_____

_____

_____

_____

_____

_____

_____

_____

_____

_____

The Brain-Savvy Therapist's Workbook

After you feel you have thoroughly contemplated these lists, it can be helpful to leave them alone for a while so that what you have learned has a chance to integrate on its own. When we have created substantial shifts, our default networks need time to rearrange and link the diverse pieces into something new. I have found that returning to all aspects of this process always yields surprising new insights into everything from core principles to my understanding of hurt and healing, which then leads to a new understanding of old practices and often suggests the addition of new ones.

To complete this part of your inquiry, spend some time again with your listening partner, reviewing the entire process so far. The act of being heard will likely bring further deepening and integration.

Discerning Our Implicit Worlds

We began this phase of our explorations in a more left-mode state of inquiry, and have been joined there by right-mode awareness of the deeper meaning of the principles, processes, and practices, as well as the pathways of disordering and healing. Now we are going to focus our mindful attention on what may lie unseen in our right-mode implicit world that is influencing the way we are with our patients. As we have been noticing, implicit patterns come in two flavors—those that flow as a constant river influencing every thought, feeling, and behavior (supportive of healing or not); and those that are more encapsulated, rising to the surface when prompted. Within this river and capsules, we will also find the interplay of inner community pairs that hold a particular flow of energy and information. We don't need to say much about the streams that support hope, resilience, patience, tenacity, and all the other implicit flavors congruent with healing.

However, when it comes to those that are potentially disruptive of the therapeutic relationship, we can notice that one capacity developing over time is our ability to distinguish between activations arising from resonance with our patients and those that, while prompted by what our patient is experiencing, belong to our implicit world. As we have developed our caring observers, we will likely find that our ability to make this distinction has increased as well. One indication is the degree to which we are swallowed up by the tide of energy and information; or, said the other way, the degree to which we can hold, consciously or unconsciously, whatever is being touched.

Already we may be able to feel that we are treading on difficult ground because we are seeking to see the unseen within a context in which we want our resonance with our patients to illuminate their inner worlds. There is no question of simply finding ways to avoid these entangling experiences because therapy must invite co-resonance of all sorts. This means we are likely to slip into and out of our own implicit wounds and activations regularly. Here, our endeavor is simply to draw into explicit awareness what may become available to our curious, kind minds at this moment, building pathways we can rely on regularly as we sense the powerful tug of these underground streams.

One place to start is bringing to body and mind patients we would say are difficult for us, asking first who in the inner community experiences the strain so that we can focus most clearly on the inner source of our discomfort. One kind of difficulty comes from the inevitable pull to move into a very injured patient's world of despair, for example, as these energies resonate within both of us. When we experience these intense flows without falling into prolonged hopelessness or protecting ourselves by moving away into disengagement, it is likely that our overall neural integration is able to hold these powerful surges. However, when we do begin to believe that healing is impossible with this person or feel a deadness in our body as soon as he or she comes into the room, we may—and I do emphasize *may*—be coming into contact with our own unhealed implicit mental models or dissociated networks. These signs at least warrant spending some reflective time with the experience.

Call to body and mind someone you would say is difficult for you. From your analytical mind, does the difficulty you experience make sense in terms of his or her history? Is this the way you would expect to resonate when he or she is in contact with this particular flow of implicit energy and information? Let me give an example. When a patient becomes overtly angry with me, it is natural for my limbic system to activate in the presence of danger. If the answer is yes, then sit with your bodily sensations, behavioral impulses, emotional surges, and perceptions to see how this resonance is playing inside you. Beneath this flow, do you sense your caring observer being able to compassionately and clearly see what is unfolding inside this person? Or is it hard to get beneath the resonant flow to find any other state of mind in yourself? In the latter case, it can be helpful to ask your deeper mind to share an earlier time when your body and emotions felt just like this, and once inside, to be open to not only the memory, but also to the inner community members who are part of this neural net. Because your brain and mind are so familiar with these pathways now, any relevant implicit experience may come easily to the explicit surface. If it is met by an emotionally alive disconfirming experience, the implicit can change immediately. Even if that juxtaposition isn't available, once the implicit comes into awareness, it often loses a good deal of its power to control the therapeutic process.

Sometimes the answer to the question about whether our inner experience makes sense in terms of our resonance with our patient's inner world is "no." In that case, we can be relatively sure that an implicit flow has been awakened within us by either an external or internal event. As above, we can attend to our body's messages and follow the trail to the implicit root. In the space below, write about your discoveries concerning the person you perceive as difficult for you, and then do the same process with one or two more patients until you begin to sense the pathway from initial disturbance to implicit resolution. If it is possible to have inner insurance against malpractice, strength in these neural circuits is it.

_____

_____

_____

_____

_____

_____

_____

_____

_____

_____

_____

_____

_____

_____

_____

_____

_____

_____

_____

_____

Another approach to understanding our implicit world's impact on therapy is to observe with kindness how our attachment style influences our therapeutic relationships. This could be the subject of an entire book, so we will just graze the surface here. It is likely that the brain structure underlying our attachment pattern has some influence on the therapeutic paradigm we choose and an ongoing effect on how we relate with our patients. It may also guide our perception of our role in therapy and our expectations of the people who come to see us. Let me offer one example. If we are currently avoidantly attached (as opposed to having an earned secure attachment after being avoidantly attached as a child), it is likely that we are most comfortable with left-mode processing. Given the opportunity to choose, we would likely resonate more with styles of therapy that are grounded in logical, language-based, linear interventions. As therapists, we might see ourselves as coaches rather than attachment figures, and we might encourage independence and competence in our patients rather than emotional processing. This is not to suggest that these are the only possible outcomes of avoidant attachment on therapeutic style, but to give an example of a line of inquiry that we can follow for ourselves.

Drawing on what you have learned of your attachment style in childhood and how it has evolved to the present day, what connections do you see among (1) your implicit mental model of relationships, (2) your choice of paradigm and practices, (3) your expectations of how your patients will participate in therapy, and (4) your role with them? These are big questions, and it may help to approach them by thinking through these connections in relation to a few patients. Jot down some initial impressions, drawing on both your right-mode and left-mode sense of this.

_____

_____

_____

_____

_____

_____

_____

_____

_____

_____

_____

_____

_____

_____

_____

_____

_____

_____

_____

To go a little deeper, you might explore any possible consistencies in the way you relate with your patients. For example, what is your bodily and emotional response when you sense a patient becoming emotionally dependent? This is often one of the most difficult experiences for us as therapists because it moves us directly into our own attachment losses and the inner community pairs that hold them. What do you viscerally believe is the overarching desired outcome of therapy that applies to all the people you see? And who holds that belief? This is not asking what you hold intellectually as the outcome, but what feels right in your being. Another way of asking this is, what kinds of gains do you see your patients making that give you ease in your body? Then take some notes about this as well. Don't worry about complete sentences, but instead give some words to what is arising fresh from your right-mode processing of these questions and moving into left-mode words.

You may have undertaken these implicit discoveries with your listening partner because that interpersonal neural pathway is now so well established. If not, you two might want to share what you are discovering in regard to your attachment and the practice of therapy now.

This kind of contact with our inner worlds, whether through being aware of which clients feel uncomfortable to us or checking in with the way our attachment pattern is currently directing our relational style, can become the beginning of a lifelong inquiry that continually shifts as we change internally. For at least a month out of every year, I keep a journal in which I record my sensations, impulses to move, emotions, perceptions, and images—in short, my implicit response, after I meet with each person. I have made some of the most helpful discoveries that led to significant transformation by letting words flow onto the page without a lot of left-mode digging or conscious organization. Even while we make our hearts and minds available to support our patients' healing, our interactions with them open inner doors to further our integration as well.

Summing Up

In this final chapter, we have consciously gathered the strands that our ever-integrating brains have been weaving beneath the surface as we moved through this workbook from topic to topic in our personal growth and professional understanding. We began by developing whole-brain pictures of principles, processes, and practices, inviting our explicit knowing and our supportive implicit flows of hope, resilience, and connection to become one model of practice. Then we encouraged implicit constraints to rise into consciousness so that we might develop the pathways for becoming aware and then resolving whatever may stand in the way of our professional efficacy and personal wholeness. We have celebrated the development of an honoring relationship with our listening partners, experiencing the power of resonance and attunement to shape the mind. This is the heart of interpersonal neurobiology—the ever-vibrating strings that connect one mind with another.

At the beginning, I said that I hoped this workbook would be so well used that, like *The Velveteen Rabbit*, it would become a living thing in your hands. Now, in addition, we can celebrate having built a house you will furnish over the years with your expanding awareness of the complex and intriguing interactions of brain, mind, and relationships. I also trust that the pathways you have established through your hard work, both individually and as a resonant pair, will mature into highways that can guide your development, ground your practice, and give your heart ease.

References

Adolphs, R. (2002). Trust in the brain. *Nature Neuroscience, 5,* 192–193.

Adolphs, R., & Tranel, D. (2004). Impaired judgment of sadness but not happiness following bilateral amygdala damage. *Journal of Cognitive Neuroscience, 16,* 453–462.

Adolphs, R., Tranel, D., & Damasio, A. R. (1998). The human amygdala in social judgment. *Nature, 393,* 470–474.

Ainsworth, M. D. S., Blehar, J. C., Waters, E., & Wall, S. (1978). *Patterns of attachment: A psychological study of the strange situation.* Hillsdale, NJ: Erlbaum.

Alexander, F., & French, T. M. (1980). *Psychoanalytic therapy: Principles and application.* New York, NY: Ronald Press. (Original work published 1946)

Allen, G., Buxton, R. B., Wong, E. C., & Courchesne, E. (1997). Attentional activation of the cerebellum independent of motor involvement. *Science, 275,* 1940–1943.

Amedi, A., Merabet, L. B., Bermpohl, F., & Pascual-Leone, A. (2005). The occipital cortex in the blind: Lessons about plasticity and vision. *Current Directions in Psychological Science, 14*(6), 306–311.

Armour, J. A., & Ardell, J. L. (2004). *Basic and clinical neurocardiology.* Cambridge, MA: Oxford University Press.

Badenoch, B. (2008). *Being a brain-wise therapist: A practical guide to interpersonal neurobiology.* New York, NY: Norton.

Bargh, J. A., Chen, M., & Burrows, L. (1996). Automaticity of social behavior: Direct effects of trait construct and stereotype-activation on action. *Journal of Personality and Social Psychology, 71,* 230–244.

Bohart, A. C. (2003). Person-centered psychotherapy and related experiential approaches. In A. S. Gurman & S. B. Messer (Eds.), *Essential psychotherapies: Theory and practice* (2nd ed., pp. 107–148). New York, NY: Guilford Press.

Bohart, A. C., Elliott, R., Greenberg, L. S., & Watson, J. C. (2002). Empathy. In J. C. Norcross (Ed.), *Psychotherapy relationships that work: Therapist contributions and responsiveness to patients* (pp. 89–108). New York, NY: Oxford University Press.

Bozarth, J. D., Zimring, F. M., & Tausch, R. (2002). Client-centered therapy: The evolution of a revolution. In D. J. Cain & J. Semman (Eds.), *Humanistic psychotherapies: Handbook of research and practice* (pp. 147–188). Washington, DC: American Psychological Association.

Brefczynski-Lewis, J. A., Lutz, A., Schaefer, H. S., Levinson, D. B., & Davidson, R. J. (2007). Neural correlates of attentional expertise in long-term meditation practitioners. *Proceedings of the National Academy of Sciences of the United States of America, 104*(27), 11483–11488. doi:10.1073/pnas.0606552104

Brown, H. (2005, August 25). A brain in the head, and one in the gut. *New York Times.* Retrieved from *http://www.nytimes.com/2005/08/24/health/24iht-snbrain.html*

Buckner, R. L., Andrews-Hanna, J. R., & Schacter, D. L. (2008). The brain's default network: Anatomy, function, and relevance to disease. *Annals of the New York Academy of Sciences, 1124,* 1–38. doi:10.1196/annals.1440.011

Carter, S. C., Harris, J., & Porges, S. W. (2009). Neural and evolutionary perspectives on empathy. In J. Decety & W. Ickes (Eds.), *The social neuroscience of empathy* (pp. 169–182). Cambridge, MA: MIT Press.

Chartrand, T. L., & Bargh, J. A. (1999). The chameleon effect: The perception–behavior link and social interaction. *Journal of Personality and Social Psychology, 76,* 893–910.

Courchesne, E., & Allen, G. (1997). Prediction and preparation: Fundamental functions of the cerebellum. *Learning and Memory, 4,* 1–35.

Cozolino, L. (2006). *The neuroscience of human relationships: Attachment and the developing social brain.* New York, NY: Norton.

Cozolino, L. (2010). *The neuroscience of psychotherapy: Healing the social brain* (2nd ed.). New York, NY: Norton.

Critchley, H. D. (2005). Neural mechanisms of autonomic, affective, and cognitive integration. *Comparative Neurology, 493,* 154–166.

Crick, F. (1994). *The astonishing hypothesis.* New York, NY: Scribners.

Dalai Lama. (2008). Seeds of compassion conference. Seattle, WA.

Damasio, A. (2000). *The feeling of what happens: Body and emotion in the making of consciousness.* New York, NY: Harvest Books.

Dobbs, D. (2006, April/May). Human see, human do. *Scientific American Mind,* 22–27.

Ecker, B. (2008). Unlocking the emotional brain: Finding the neural key to transformation. *Psychotherapy Networker, 32*(5), 42–47, 60.

Ecker, B. (2010). The brain's rules for change: Translating cutting-edge neuroscience into practice. *Psychotherapy Networker, 34*(1), 43–45, 60.

Ecker, B., & Hulley, L. (1996). *Depth oriented brief therapy: How to be brief when you were trained to be deep, and vice versa.* San Francisco, CA: Jossey-Bass.

Ecker, B., & Hulley, L. (2000a). Depth-oriented brief therapy: Accelerated accessing of the coherent unconscious. In J. Carlson & L. Sperry (Eds.), *Brief therapy with individuals and couples* (pp. 161–190). Phoenix, AZ: Zeig, Tucker & Theisen.

Ecker, B., & Hulley, L. (2000b). The order in clinical "disorder": Symptom coherence in depth-oriented brief therapy. In R. A. Neimeyer & J. Raskin (Eds.), *Constructions of disorder* (pp. 63–89). Washington, DC: American Psychological Association.

Ecker, B., & Hulley, L. (2008). Coherence therapy: Swift change at the core of symptom production. In J. D. Raskin & S. K. Bridges (Eds.), *Studies in meaning* (Vol. 3, pp. 57–84). New York, NY: Pace University Press.

Ecker, B., & Toomey, B. (2008). Depotentiation of symptom-producing implicit memory in coherence therapy. *Journal of Constructivist Psychology, 21*(2), 87–150. doi:10.1080/10720530701853685.

Einstein, A. E. (1950). Letter to Robert Marcus, February 12, 1950. *Einstein Archives.*

Fellows, L. K., & Farah, M. J. (2007). The role of the ventromedial prefrontal cortex in decision making: Judgment under uncertainty or judgment per se? *Cerebral Cortex, 17*(11), 2669–2674. doi:10.1093/cercor/bhl176

Field, T., Diego, M., & Hernandez-Reif, M. (2006). Prenatal depression effects on the fetus and newborn: A review. *Infant Behavior and Development, 29*(3), 445–455.

Fields, R. D. (2006, June/July). Beyond the neuron doctrine. *Scientific American Mind*, 21–27.

Fosha, D., Siegel, D. J., & Solomon, M. F. (Eds.). (2009). *The healing power of emotion: Affective neuroscience, development, and clinical practice*. New York, NY: Norton.

Fox, D. (2008, November 5). The secret life of the brain. *NewScientist Magazine, 2681*, 30–33.

Geller, J. D. (2003). Self-disclosure in psychoanalytic–existential therapy. *Journal of Clinical Psychology/In Session, 59*(5), 541–554.

Germer, C., & Salzberg, S. (2009). *The mindful path to self-compassion: Freeing yourself from destructive thoughts and emotions*. New York, NY: Guilford Press.

Gershon, M. D. (2009). Entering serotonergic neurons . . . finally! *Journal of Physiology, 587*(Pt 3), 507. doi:10.1113/jphysiol.2008.167676

Gershon, M. D. (1998). *The second brain*. New York, NY: HarperCollins.

Ginot, E. (2009). The empathic power of enactments: The link between neuropsychosocial processes and an expanded definition of empathy. *Psychoanalytic Psychology, 26*(3), 290–309. doi:10.3037/a0016449

Goldman, A. I. (2006). *Simulating minds: The philosophy, psychology, and neuroscience of mindreading*. New York, NY: Oxford University Press.

Greicius, M. D., Kiviniemi, V., Tervonen, O., Vainionpaa, V., Alahuhta, S., & Menon, V. (2008). Persistent default-mode network connectivity during light sedation. *Human Brain Mapping, 29*, 839–847.

Guillery, R. W., & Sherman, S. M. (2002). Thalamic relay functions and their role in corticocortical communication. *Neuron, 33*(2), 163–175.

Gusnard, D. A., Akbudak, E., Shulman, G. L., & Raichle, M. E. (2001). Medial prefrontal cortex and self-referential mental activity: Relation to a default mode of brain functioning. *Proceedings of the National Academy of Sciences, 98*(7), 4259–4264. doi:10.1073/pnas.071043098

Gusnard, D. A., & Raichle, M. E. (2001). Searching for a baseline: Functional imaging and the resting human brain. *National Review of Neurosicence, 2*, 685–694.

Halgren, E. (1992). Emotional neurophysiology of the amygdala within the context of human cognition. In J. P. Aggleton (Ed.), *The amygdala: Neurobiological aspects of emotion, memory, and mental dysfunction* (pp. 191–228). New York, NY: Wiley-Liss.

Hariri, A. R., Bookheimer, S. Y., & Maziotta, J. C. (2000). Modulating emotional responses: Effects of a neocortical network on the limbic system. *NeuroReport, 11*(1), 43–48.

Hawkins, J., & Blakeslee, S. (2004). *On intelligence: How a new understanding of the brain will lead to the creation of truly intelligent machines*. New York, NY: Times Books.

Hebb, D. O. (1949). *The organization of behavior: A neuropsychological theory*. New York, NY: Wiley.

Hesse, E., & Main, M. (1999). Unresolved/disorganized responses to trauma in non-maltreating parents: Previously unexamined risk factor for offspring. *Psychoanalytic Inquiry, 19*, 4–11.

Hill, R. (2010, Spring). Some thoughts about the genetics of being you. *Connections and Reflections: The GAINS Quarterly*, 20–27.

Holder, M. K. (2005). What does handedness have to do with brain lateralization (and who cares)?. Retrieved from http://www.indiana.edu/primate/brain.html.

Holzel, B. K., Ott, U., Hempel, H., Hackl, A., Wolf, K., Stark, R., et al. (2007). Differential engagement of anterior cingulate and adjacent medial frontal cortex in adept meditators and non-meditators. *Neuroscience Letters, 421*(1), 16–21. doi:10.1016/j.neulet. 2007.04.074

Horovitz, S. G., Fukunaga, M., de Zwart, J. A., van Gelderen, P., Fulton, S. C., & Duyn, J. H. (2008). Low frequency BOLD fluctuations during resting wakefulness and light sleep: A simultaneous EEG–fMRI study. *Human Brain Mapping, 29*, 671–682.

Iacoboni, M. (2007). Face to face: The neural basis of social mirroring and empathy. *Psychiatric Annals, 374*, 236–241.

Iacoboni, M. (2009). Imitation, empathy, and mirror neurons. *Annual Review of Psychology, 60*, 653–670.

Iacoboni, M., & Badenoch, B. (2010, Spring). Discovering our brain's many mirrors. *Connections and Reflections: The GAINS Quarterly*, 3–9.

Jackins, H. (1982). *The human side of human beings: The theory of re-evaluation counseling.* Seattle, WA: Rational Island Publishers.

Kabat-Zinn, J. (2003). *Coming to our senses: Healing ourselves and the world through mindfulness.* New York, NY: Hyperion Press.

Kabat-Zinn, J. (2005). *Wherever you go, there you are: Mindfulness meditation in everyday life.* New York, NY: Hyperion Press.

Kabat-Zinn, J., Lipworth, L., Burney, R., & Sellers, W. (1986). Four year follow-up of a meditation-based program for the self-regulation of chronic pain: Treatment outcomes and compliance. *Clinical Journal of Pain, 2*, 159–173.

Kaufman, J., Yang, B., Douglas-Palumberi, H., Grasso, D., Lipschitz, D., Houshyar, S., et al. (2006). Brain-derived neurotrophic factor. *Biological Psychiatry, 59*(8), 673–680. doi:10.1016/j.biopsych.2005.10.026

Kornfield, J. (2007, June). *The wise heart and the mindful brain.* Paper presented at the R. Cassidy Seminar, San Francisco, CA.

Lazar, S. W., Kerr, C. E., Wasserman, R. H., Gray, J. R., Greve, D. N., Treadway, M. T., et al. (2005). Meditation experience is associated with increased cortical thickness. *NeuroReport, 16*(17), 1893–1897.

LeDoux, J. E. (2002). *The synaptic self.* New York, NY: Viking.

Liu, M., Kuan, Y., Wang, J., Hen, R., & Gershon, M. D. (2009). 5-HT receptor-mediated neuroprotection and neurogenesis in the enteric nervous system of adult mice. *The Journal of Neuroscience, 29*, 9683–9699. doi:10.1523/JNEUROSCI.1145-09

Lutz, A., Brefczynski-Lewis, J., Johnstone, T., & Davidson, R. J. (2008). Regulation of the neural circuitry of emotion by compassion meditation: Effects of meditative expertise. *PLoS ONE, 3*(3), e1897. doi:10.1371/journal.pone.0001897

MacLean, P. D. (1990). *The triune brain in evolution: Role in paleocerebral functions.* New York, NY: Plenum Press.

Main, M. (1996). Introduction to the special section on attachment and psychopathology: 2. Overview of the field of attachment. *Journal of Consulting and Clinical Psychology, 64*, 237–243.

Main, M. (2000). The Adult Attachment Interview: Fear, attention, safety, and discourse processes. *Journal of the American Psychoanalytic Association, 48*, 1055–1096.

Marci, C. D., Ham, J., Moran, E. K., & Orr, S. P. (2007). Physiologic concordance, empathy, and social–emotional processing during psychotherapy. *Journal of Nervous and Mental Disease, 195*, 103–111.

Marci, C. D., & Reiss, H. (2005). The clinical relevance of psychophysiology: Support for the psychobiology of empathy and psychodynamic process. *American Journal of Psychotherapy, 259*, 213–226.

Mason, M. F., Norton, M. I., Van Horn, J. D., Wegner, D. M., Grafton, S. T., & Macrae, C. N. (2007). Wandering minds: The default network and stimulus-independent thought. *Science, 315*(5810), 393–395. doi:10.1126/science.1131295

Miller, J., Fletcher, K., & Kabat-Zinn, J. (1995). Three-year follow-up and clinical implications of a mindfulness-based stress reduction intervention in the treatment of anxiety disorders. *General Hospital Psychiatry, 17,* 192–200.

Milner, B., Squire, L. R., & Kandel, E. R. (1998). Cognitive neuroscience and the study of memory. *Neuron, 20,* 445–168.

Morgan, D. K., & Whitelaw, E. (2008). The case for transgenerational epigenetic inheritance in humans. *Mammalian Genome, 19*(6), 394–397.

Morris, J. S., Ohman, A., & Dolan, R. J. (1999). A subcortical pathway to the right amygdala mediating "unseen" fear. *Proceedings of the National Academy of Science, USA, 96,* 1680–1685.

Mukamel, R., Ekstrom, A. D., Kaplan, J., Iacoboni, M., & Fried, I. (2010). Single-neuron responses in humans during execution and observation of actions. *Current Biology, 20*(8), 750–756. doi:10.1016/j.cub.2010.02.045

Newberg, A., d'Aquili, F., & Rause, V. (2001). *Why God won't go away: Brain science and the biology of belief.* New York, NY: Ballantine Books.

Ogden, P., Minton, K., & Pain, C. (2006). *Trauma and the body: A sensorimotor approach to psychotherapy.* New York, NY: Norton.

Panksepp, J. (1998). *Affective neuroscience: The foundations of human and animal emotions.* New York, NY: Oxford University Press.

Panksepp, J. (2008). The power of the word may reside in the power of affect. *Integrative Psychological and Behavioral Science, 42*(1), 47–55.

Pedreira, M. E., Perez-Cuest, L. M., & Maldonado, H. (2004). Mismatch between what is expected and what actually occurs triggers memory reconsolidation or extinction. *Learning and Memory, 11,* 579–585.

Phelps, E. A., & LeDoux, J. E. (2005). Contributions of the amygdala to emotion processing: From animal models to human behavior. *Neuron, 48,* 175–187.

Porges, S. W. (1998). Love: An emergent property of the mammalian autonomic nervous system. *Psychoneuroendocrinology, 23*(8), 837–861. doi:10.1016/50306-4530(98)00057-2

Porges, S. W. (2003). The polyvagal theory: Phylogenetic contributions to social behavior. *Physiology and Behavior, 79*(3), 503–513. doi:10.1016/50031-9384(03)00156-2

Porges, S. W. (2004). Neuroception: A subconscious system for detecting threat and safety. *Zero to Three: Bulletin of the National Center for Clinical Infant Programs, 24*(5), 19–24.

Porges, S. W. (2007). The polyvagal perspective. *Biological Psychology, 74,* 116–143.

Porges, S. W. (2009a). Reciprocal influences between body and brain in the perception and expression of affect: A polyvagal perspective. In D. Fosha, D. J. Siegel, & M. F. Solomon (Eds.), *The healing power of emotion: Affective neuroscience, development, clinical practice* (pp. 27–54). New York, NY: Norton.

Porges, S. W. (2009b). The polyvagal theory: New insights into adaptive reactions of the autonomic nervous system. *Cleveland Clinic Journal of Medicine, 76*(2), S86–90. doi:10.3949/ccjm.67.s2.17

Post, R. M., Weiss, S. R. B., Li, H., Smith, M. A., Zhang, L. X., Xing, G., et al. (1998). Neural plasticity and emotional memory. *Development and Psychopathology, 10,* 829–856.

Quiroga, R. Q., Reddy, L., Kreiman, G., Koch, C., & Fried, I. (2005). Invariant visual representation by single neurons in the human brain. *Nature, 435,* 1102–1107.

Ray, R. A. (Ed.). (2004). *In the presence of masters: Wisdom from 30 contemporary Tibetan Buddhist teachers.* Boston, MA: Shambhala.

Raichle, M. (2010, March). The brain's dark energy. *Scientific American,* 44–49.

Rossato, J. I., Bevilaqua, L. R. M., Medina, J. H., Izquierdo, I., & Cammarota, M. (2006). Retrieval induces hippocampal-dependent reconsolidation of spatial memory. *Learning and Memory, 13,* 431–440.

Rumelhart, D. E., & McClelland, J. lo. (1986). *Parallel distributed processing: Explorations in the microstructure of cognition* (2 vols.). Cambridge, MA: MIT Press.

Saigh, P. A., & Bremner, J. D. (Eds.). (1999). *Posttraumatic stress disorder: A comprehensive text.* New York, NY: Allyn & Bacon.

Salzberg, S., & Kabat-Zinn, J. (2008). *Lovingkindness: The revolutionary art of happiness.* Boston, MA: Shambhala.

Schore, A. N. (2003a). *Affect dysregulation and disorders of the self.* New York, NY: Norton.

Schore, A. N. (2003b). *Affect regulation and the repair of the self.* New York, NY: Norton.

Schore, A. N. (2009a). Right brain affect regulation: An essential mechanism of development, trauma, dissociation, and psychotherapy. In D. Fosha, D. J. Siegel, & M. Solomon (Eds.), *The healing power of emotion: Affective neuroscience, development, and clinical practice* (pp. 112–144). New York, NY: Norton.

Schore, A. N. (2009b, August). *The paradigm shift: The right brain and the relational unconscious.* Plenary address, American Psychological Association annual convention, Toronto, Canada.

Schore, A. N. (in press). The right brain implicit self lies at the core of psychoanalysis. *Psychoanalytic Dialogues.*

Schwartz, R. C. (1997). *Internal family systems therapy.* New York: Guilford Press.

Shapiro, S. L., Walsh, R., & Britton, W. B. (2003). An analysis of recent meditation research and suggestions for future directions. *Journal for Meditation and Meditation Research, 3,* 69–90.

Siegel, D. J. (1999). *The developing mind: How relationship and the brain interact to shape who we are.* New York, NY: Guilford Press.

Siegel, D. J. (2006). An interpersonal neurobiology approach to psychotherapy: Awareness, mirror neurons, and neural plasticity in the development of well-being. *Psychiatric Annals, 36*(4), 247–258.

Siegel, D. J. (2007). *The mindful brain: Reflection and attunement in the cultivation of well-being.* New York, NY: Norton.

Siegel, D. J. (2010a). *Mindsight: The new science of personal transformation.* New York, NY: Bantam.

Siegel, D. J. (2010b). *The mindful therapist: A clinician's guide to mindsight and neural integration.* New York, NY: Norton.

Siegel, D. J., & Hartzell, M. (2003). *Parenting from the inside out: How a deeper self-understanding can help you raise children who thrive.* New York, NY: Tarcher/Putnam.

Singer, T. (2006). The neuronal basis and ontogeny of empathy and mind reading: Review of literature and implications for future research. *Neuroscience and Biobehavioral Reviews, 30*(6), 855–863. doi:10.1016/j.neubiorev.2006.06.011

Suzuki, A., Josselyn, S. A., Frankland, P. W., Masushige, S., Silva, A. J., & Kida, S. (2004). Memory reconsolidation and extinction have distinct temporal and biochemical signatures. *Journal of Neuroscience, 24,* 4787–4795.

Toomey, B., & Ecker, B. (2007). Of neurons and knowings: Constructivism, coherence psychology, and their neurodynamic substrates. *Journal of Constructivist Psychology, 20*(3), 201–245. doi:10.1080/10720530701347860

Toomey, B., & Ecker, B. (2009). Competing visions of the implications of neuroscience for psychotherapy. *Journal of Constructivist Psychology, 22*(2), 95–140. doi:10.1080/10720530802675748

Wallace, B. A. (2006). *The attention revolution: Unlocking the power of the focused mind.* Somerville, MA: Wisdom Publications.

Whitelaw, N. C., & Whitelaw, E. (2006). How lifetimes shape epigenotype within and across generations. *Human Molecular Genetics, 15*(15), R131–137.

Williams, M. (1983). *The velveteen rabbit*. New York, NY: Henry Holt. (Original work published 1922)

Winston, J. S., Strange, B. A., O'Doherty, J., & Dolan, R. J. (2002). Automatic and intentional brain responses during evaluation of trustworthiness of faces. *Nature Neuroscience, 5*, 277–283.

Winters, B. D., Tucci, M. C., & DaCosta-Furtado, M. (2009). Older and stronger object memories are selectively destabilized by reactivation in the presence of new information. *Learning and Memory, 16*(9), 545–553.

Wipfler, P. (2006). *How children's emotions work*. Palo Alto, CA: Hand in Hand.

Wipfler, P. (2009, Autumn). Helping children labeled "ADD" or "ADHD." *Connections and Reflections: The GAINS Quarterly*, 4–10.

Whyte, D. (2007). *New and selected poems: 1984–2007*. Langley, WA: Many Rivers Press.

Index

attitudes, as method/practice, 281, 286

attunement
  dance of, xvii
  integrates, 59
  narratives shaped by, 84
  power of, to shape the mind, 292
  resonance and, 151, 161; *see also* separate
    entry

autonomic nervous system (ANS)
  overview of, 114–15, 137–42
  synchrony in, 195, 212
  talking about, with patients, 152–57

awareness, mindful, 19, 187, 191, 248, 260,
  267, 268, 269; *see also* mindfulness

axon, 112

Badenoch, B., 192

Being a Brain-Wise Therapist (Badenoch), xvi,
  111

beliefs, about wounding and healing, 267–68

Berrow, D., 220, 221, 256, 257*f*

birth, shaped by in utero experiences, 41

body
  brain extends throughout, 112
  judgment affects, 36
  memory and, 130–31, 271
  reflects internal state, 153
  see also sensation

borderline personality disorder, 193

brain stem, 115–16

brain (systems)
  circuits involved in integrative process, 83
  coherence, movement toward, 131–32,
    273
  coherent narratives and, 88, 99
  complexity of, 131–32, 273
  early attachment builds, 167
  educating people about, 257–58
  extends throughout body, 112
  hemispheric divisions, 12–23
  implicit patterns, understanding how brain
    stores, 227–28
  integration, hardwired into, 51, 187, 246
  integration, patients continue to support,
    260
  left-mode processing, *see* separate entry
  meaning making hardwired into, 87
  memory in several, 42

neuronal composition, overview of, 111–12
  relational, xvii
  right-mode processing, *see* separate entry
  Siegel's hand model of, 147*f*, 148, 248, 258
  speaking/talking about, xviii, 135, 148–49,
    152–57, 217, 257–58

calm state, 138–39, 181, 209, 212; *see also* ventral vagal

case example
  of abuse, 215–16, 230, 250–51
  of autonomic nervous system, talking with
    couple, 152–56
  of brain talk with couple, 148–49
  of compassion, 103–5
  of disorganized attachment, 138–39
  of early losses and adult attachment fears,
    218–24
  of enactments, 196–97
  of expansive states as unacceptable, 249
  of implicit-to-explicit process, 202–3
  of infidelity, implicit roots of, 158–59, 161–
    62, 180–81
  of inner community, 58–60, 73–74
  of inner narrative, 82, 241–42
  of transitioning, 253–57
  of victimization, 204–5

cerebellum, 116

cerebral cortex, 120*f*

"chalkboard of the mind," 116, 121

change
  disconfirming experiences facilitate, 46,
    187, 188–89, 195, 213
  factors influencing degree of, 187–89
  in narrative by, 98–99
  neurobiology of change methods, 192*f*
  principles of change, 189
  science of neural, 186–87

choice
  complexity in right-mode process facili-
    tates, 199
  dissociation takes away, 131
  regulation allows, 156

clarity, xvii
  of brain knowledge, 128, 141
  describing experience increases, 17, 196
  relaxation and, 212–13
  talking about attachment brings, 180

clay, use of, 201, 220*f*, 232, 233
cognitive–behavioral methods
    attachment perspective vs., 181
    right-mode processes vs., 190–91
cognitive dissonance, 189
coherence
    conscious mind seeks, 54, 262
    implicit roots provide, 37, 130, 159, 160,
       184–85, 187–88, 199–200
    psychotherapy, 189
    sign of integrating brain, 4
    in therapeutic work, 282
commissures, 122
community, inner
    contradictory information held by different
       members, 236
    differentiating members, 63, 162, 182
    drawing of, 69–72, 230
    identifying layers of, 65–69
    internalized relationships/pairs as, 59, 236
    invite into present, 232–33
    meditation speeds integration of, 251
    neurobiological basis of, 58–60
    prototype of, 64*f*
    reconciling, 218–24
    responses to principles, 271
    role in therapist's reactions, 288
    talking about, 227–28
    working/being present with each member
       of, 72–81, 223, 227–33, 250–51
compassion, xvii
    case example of, 103–4
    empathy facilitated by, 191
    inner community work expands, 79
    interpretation or judgment vs., 228
    neural integration fostered by, 110, 145
    for patients, 128, 136
    patients' and therapists', mutual, 145–46
    practices that foster, 106–9
    regulation facilitated by, 40, 191
    resistance to, 104–5
    types of, 105
    understanding patients' inner lives fosters,
       269
    vulnerability and, 78
    see also kindness; lovingkindness
complexity
    of brain systems, 131–32, 273

choice facilitating by, 199
    fostering complexity in relational circuits,
       185, 193, 199, 259
    mindfulness increases, 237
confidence, 134
confusion, 130
constraints, 131–32, 168–69, 238, 215–16, 230,
    250–51, 273
continuity, 42, 96, 110
conversation, social, 282, 283
corpus callosum, 122
"corrective emotional experience," 189
cortisol, 138, 244
co–storytelling, 88
Cozolino, L., xvi
creativity, glial cells and, 112
critical voice, 4, 6
curiosity, 144, 153, 159, 164, 230, 249

Dalai Lama, 110
daydreaming, 237
"deep eyes," 24
default network
    in case example, 238
    consolidation and, 235, 267, 276
    definition of, 55, 119
    dissociated circuits and, 83
    narrative and, 83, 86, 237, 243
dendrites, 112
developmental ages, awareness of, 215–17,
    235
diagnosis, vs. implicit attachment patterns,
    169–70, 180, 181–82
differentiation/differentiating
    change facilitated by, 187–88
    inner community members, 63–81, 182
    integrative process, 14
    states of minds, 4
disclosure, 178–79
disconfirming perceptions/experiences
    anxious narrative and, 91
    in case example, 198, 205, 209
    change facilitated by, 46, 187, 188–89,
       195
    developmental ages and 215
    disorganized attachment and, 177
    implicit memories/patterns changed by,
       30, 54, 132

exercises (*continued*)
    visceral response and implicit memory, 52–56
    "we are all doing the best we can," 78–79
    what patient gains give you ease, 291
    window-of-tolerance edges, 195
    working with inner community members, 75–76
expectations
    impatience indicating, 99
    implicit, 47, 58, 104
    inner community drawing and, 70
    relational, 184–85
explicit memories
    characteristics of, 28, 53
    development of, 30–31
    implicit made explicit, 185, 201–7, 220, 222, 229, 232, 268, 288
    implicit separated from 179
eye movement desensitization and reprocessing (EMDR), 268

FACES (Siegel's), 169
failure, neural nets of, 5
family
    changing narrative of, 249
    intergenerational patterns of, 230, 251–52
    resonance circuits explained to, 166–67
    systems therapy, internal, 58
fight-flight-freeze response, 115, 140, 193; *see also* autonomic nervous system, overview of
first session, 144–50
focus, singular/sustained, 14–15, 44–45; *see also* attention
forgiveness, visceral experience of, 104–5, 251; *see also* compassion
fragmentation
    disorganized attachment leads to, 175–79
    normalizing, 245
    self-hatred and, 208–9
frontal cortex, 121
future, implicit past shapes, 45–46

gentleness, 4–6, 38; *see also* kindness; loving-kindness
Ginot, E., 196, 197
glia/glial cells, 111, 112
grace, 6, 104

grief
    in case example, 218–24
    in transitioning, 261
"gut brain," 113

hatred, effects of, 176–77, 207
healing
    beliefs about, 267–68
    memories, 234–35
    reflecting on, 276–87
    right- and left-mode processing both needed for, 132, 273
heart brain, 114–15
helplessness, 177, 234
Hesse, E., 169
hippocampus
    abuse affects, 244
    explicit memory stored in, 50, 86
    overview of, 118
history taking
    listening for implicit history, 158–62
    patients understand in different way, 167
    questions useful for eliciting, 182
hope
    genetically encoded, 64*f*
    interpersonal neurobiology and, 92
    short-term therapy builds, 258
    talking about attachment brings, 180
hopelessness, 198
Hulley, L., 189, 203
humor
    learning brain talk needs, 135
    resistance and, 38
hypothalamic–pituitary–adrenal (HPA) axis, 118
hypothalamus, 118

Iacoboni, M., 164
image, symbolic, 53, 228, 254
impatience, 13, 38, 99, 214, 231
impermanence, 109
implicit entanglements, 29–30, 127
implicit memories/world, 8
    approaches to, implementing, 224–27
    attachment patterns encoded by, 26, 35–40
    changing, 218–24, 246–47
    discerning, 287–92
    dis-integrated, 49–50, 178*f*, 185
    experiencing, 31–35, 42

explaining to patient, 218
as invariant representations, 244
made explicit, 185, 201–7, 220, 222, 229, 230–31, 232, 268, 288
parenting style affected by, 148–49
recognizing, 28–31
two kinds, 268, 287
updating, 186–87
implicit roots
coherence comes from, 37, 130, 159, 160, 184–85, 187–88, 199–200
current-day experiences traced to, 217–24
insula, 163
insular cortex, 119–20
integration/integrating
attunement integrates, 59
brain hardwired for, 51, 187, 246
coherence as sign of, 4
compassion fosters, 110, 145
differentiation as integrative process, 14
encapsulated flows of energy and information, 244
experiencing phases of, 109–10
hardwired into brain, 51, 68, 83
interpersonal, 109, 110
listening partners facilitate, 72, 75, 234
meditation speeds, 251
memory, 52–56, 57
narrative, 247–52
neural, *see* separate entry
neuroplasticity as integrative, xvi– xvii, 183–84, 235
occurs via internalization, 105
patients continue to support, 260
practicing inner community, 63–81
repair, 257
supporting or blocking, 60*f*
temporal, 45–46, 55, 109, 204
transpirational, 109, 110
intention(s)
internalizing others', 223
perception of, 163
therapist's, to know patient, 182
internalization
of caring presence, 213, 222
inner community members as, 72–73
mutual, patient and therapist, 260
neural integration occurs via, 105
resonance circuits underlying, 166

interpersonal neurobiology (IPNB)
hope and, 92
pathways to, xvi
principles of, 128–34
see also neurobiology

journal(ing)
implicit responses toward patients, 292
mindful awareness, 20–22
judgment (process)
affects body and feelings, 36
exercise eliciting, 47, 68, 141, 152, 163, 233–34
nonjudgmental/kind state of mind, 31, 38, 62, 97, 108, 161, 228
slowing, xvi
just being, 213
juxtaposition experience, 189

kindness
modifies implicit patterns, 9
observing with, 13–14
right-mode experience held with, 184
see also compassion; lovingkindness
Kornfield, J., 25

lamina 1, 115
language
left-mode words useless, 208
right-mode processes and, 189, 191, 196
left-mode processing
avoidant attachment and, 171
both modes needed, 132, 273
implicit expressed via, 30
neurobiology of change methods, 192*f*
overview of, 3, 9–10
suspending, 188
limbic system/region, 117*f*
ambivalent attachment affects, 173
amygdala, *see* separate entry
avoidant attachment affects, 171, 172
capacities of, 119
in child, 5
middle prefrontal connection with, 156, 189, 191, 200, 204, 233, 243, 248, 259
neocortex connection with, 96
orbitofrontal connection with, 145, 193, 195
prefrontal integration, 140
overview of, 117–18

mirror neurons
  internalization facilitated by, 72, 74
  narrative and, 86
  pervasive influence of, 162–66
  privacy and, xix, 123
mirroring, inaccurate or absent, 35
mortality, 109, 110
motivation, seven systems of, 249
myelin(ation), 111, 168

narrative
  anxious, 90–91
  attachment, new narrative of, 240
  changing, 97–102, 243, 246–47
  coherent, 10, 87, 88–89, 95, 105, 237–43
  cohesive, 9–10, 87, 94–95
  embodied/lived, 159, 233, 247
  emotionally resolved, 236
  exercises exploring, *see* exercises, narra-
    tive
  expanded by integration, 94
  fictional/defensive, 87, 95–97, 100
  fragmented, 92–94
  lifeless, 89–90
  neurobiology of, 83–84
  pathways of integration, 243–47
  of posttraumatic stress, 243–47
  shaped by early experience, 84–86
  supporting narrative integration, 247–52
  of therapeutic encounter, xix
  three narratives near end of therapy, 247
  whole-brain, 247
  wordless and worded, 158
neocortex, 120–22
nervous system
  autonomic nervous system, *see* separate
    entry
  enteric, 113-14
  narrative of, 92, 247, 248
  parasympathetic, 137-42, 155
  somatic, 112-13
  sympathetic nervous system, *see* separate
    entry
neural integration
  compassion fosters, 110
  internalization and, 105
  interpersonal relationships foster, 131,
    272
  time needed for, 267

neural nets
  changing ingrained, 6
  coherent, 24–25
  conscious awareness, below level of, 83
  dissociated pockets of, 8, 59; *see also* mem-
    ory
  fiction as reality, 96
  integration of, *see* neural integration
  meditation and, 24
  not all linked, 112
  repeated experiences affect, 31, 33
  science of change in, 186–87
neurobiology
  of change methods, 192*f*
  of inner community, 58–60
  of narrative, 83–84
  of transition, 259–61
  see also interpersonal neurobiology
neuroception, 58, 114, 137–38, 143
neuroplasticity
  history taking engages, 167
  integrative, xvi– xvii, 183–84, 235
  nature of, 99
  realness of, as principle, 131, 272
neurotransmitters, 111
nonjudgmental, *see* judgment
not knowing, 165
novelty, 120

observer, caring
  builds new brain structure, 156
  change in narrative facilitated by, 98–
    99
  developing patients' own, 244–45, 248,
    258, 260
  differentiation facilitated by, 75
  intense experience and, 14
  meditation/mindfulness expanding, 8, 18–
    19
  overview of, xvi, xix, 3–4
  patients' brains affected by, 133
  primary tool of, 241
occipital lobe, 121
office policies, and safety, 143
Ogden, P., 194, 232
oneness
  compassion/meditation and experiences
    of, 105, 109, 110
  interpersonal, xx, 123, 133, 274

orbitofrontal cortex, 119
    amygdalar connections with, 224
    attachment and, 168, 193, 253
    compassion and, 145
    limbic connections with, 145, 193, 195
oxytocin, 142

pace
    noticing with kindness, 13
    of work, 77
Panksepp, J., 249
paradigm shift, xvii–xviii
parasympathetic nervous system
    explaining to patients, 155
    overview of, 137–42
parent(ing)
    attunement, important gift of, 204
    brain talk used for, 148–49
    coherent narratives and style of, 88–89
    parents' relationship shapes children's
        brains, 180
    understanding own attachment style, 167
parietal lobe(s)
    medial parietal cortex, 237
    meditation quiets, 110
    overview of, 121
past, memory modifies, 42–43; *see also* eternally present past
perceptions
    core, of wounding and healing, 267–68
    disconfirming, *see* separate entry
    of intention, 163
    safety, *see also* safe
    shift in, 39–40
    therapist's, vs. patient's self–story, 160–61,
        239, 240
perpetrator
    contact with inner, 230–31
    resolution with inner, 246
playfulness, 249
polyvagal theory, 137
Porges, S., 58, 114, 137, 194
posterior cingulated cortex, 237
posttraumatic stress disorder, 193; *see also*
    trauma
practice(s)
    consistent, 19
    differentiating therapeutic, 283, 284, 285
    implicit reasons for selecting, 285–86

presence, therapist's
    disconfirming experience of, 212–15
    infant attachment, essence of, 209
    infant wound healed by, 213
    left-mode part of, 134
    persistent offering of, 240
    relational energy fostered by, 144, 182
    transformative, 230–31
    window of tolerance widened by, 229
present, invariant representations and, 43–44
priming, 164–65
principles
    of change, 189; *see also* separate entry
    of interpersonal neurobiology, 128–34
    reconsidering, 270–76
    response to, 129, 133
    of therapy, 268–69
processing, *see* left-mode processing; right-
    mode processing
protectors, 67

questions
    awareness increased by, 17, 34
    disconfirming experiences preceded by,
        213, 214–15
    disorder and healing, 276

rapport, 144
reactive attachment disorder, 207–10, 238–
    39
receptivity
    implicit models, open to, 210
    inner community members identified via,
        65
    regulation and empathy facilitated by, 191
    road to, 14–18
    sitting in, 23–24, 76
reconsolidation, of memory, 186–87, 208, 235
reframing, 190
regulation
    coregulation, 138, 156, 199, 209, 232
    differentiation facilitates, 188
    facilitated by compassion, 40
    pseudo-, 128
    quality of life experiences shaped by, 193
rejection, fragmentation results from, 175–76,
    238–39
relationship
    attuned, 19

therapeutic, influenced by attachment patterns, 26–27, 29, 134, 289–91
relaxation
    clarity brings, 212–13
    resolution with inner perpetrator brings, 246
repair(ing)
    empathic misses, 248
    integrative, 257
representations
    invariant, 43–44, 120, 211, 244
    symbolic, 53
resilience, belief/confidence in, 262, 268, 286
resistance
    compassion eliciting, 104
    gentleness eliciting, 38
    inner community members and, 65
    to principles, 270–71
    right-mode processes may evoke, 30
    validation eliciting, 240
    to wishing ourselves well, 109
resolution
    memory moving toward, 222
    requires many relational experiences, 205
resonance (circuits)
    attunement and, 151, 161; *see also* separate entry
    change rests on, 187
    compassion and lovingkindness meditation activate, 106, 107
    implicit patterns differentiated from, 287
    implicit patterns shifted via, 30
    insular cortex as crucial part of, 120
    internalization facilitated by, 72, 74
    narrative and, 86
    pervasive influence of, 162–66
    sharing about, 166–67
    as "travel kit" for future growth, 261
responsibility, of interpersonal matrix, 132
rest, 55; *see also* relaxation
right-mode processing
    accessing processes, 201–2
    both modes needed, 132, 273
    developmental maturation of, 260
    fostering complexity in relational circuits, 185, 193, 199, 259
    implicit patterns of, 8; *see also* implicit memories
    listening as, 13, 31, 33

    mindful awareness opens gates to, 191, 210
    neurobiology of change methods, 192*f*
    nonverbal messages via, 143
    overview of, 3–4, 26–28
    to right-mode, 169, 196, 198
    window of tolerance for, 194*f*
role(s)
    impact of attachment style on therapist's, 290–91
    of inner community in therapist's reactions, 288
    managing self as, 65

"sacred," 145
safe/safety
    amygdala and perception of, 114, 118
    autonomic nervous system and perception of, 137–38
    connection with others maintains, 138
    creating for patients, 142–50
    dissociated experiences emerge under safe conditions, 195
    enteric system sends information about, 114
samatha, 23
sand tray, 201, 202*f*, 203, 220, 221*f*, 228, 232, 233, 255*f*, 256*f*, 257*f*
Schore, A., xvi, 192, 193, 194, 196
Schwartz, R., 58
security, 134; *see also* safe
self
    -hatred, 207, 209, 239
    managing, 65
    -rejection, 238
    watching, 65–66
selfishness, and meditation, 108–9
sensation
    describing, 31, 32–34
    implicit memories characterized by, 28, 53, 220
    pathway to implicit domain, 228
    present moment and, 44
    separate from emotional component, 232
sensitivity
    to healing process, 282–83
    to drifting into patients' implicit worlds, 284
separateness, illusion of, xvii, xix

shame
  in case example, 238, 239
  freeze response and, 193–94
  inaccurate mirroring and, 35
  neural nets of, 5
  relief from, 196
Siegel, D., xvi, 15, 109, 119, 146, 156, 169,
    194
somatic nervous system, 112–13
somatosensory strip, 121
spinal cord, 115
splitting, *see* dissociation
states of mind
  collection of, xix, 9
  developmental ages and, 215, 235
  differentiating, 4
  empathy guiding, 24–25
  expansive, 16, 23, 24
  holding, for patients, 268
  impact of implicit and explicit, on patients,
    225
  inner community members as, *see* commu-
    nity, inner
  internalized pairs as, 57
  as traits, 38, 107, 133
stillness, 214
story/storytelling, *see* narrative
Strange Situation, 170
strategy(ies)
  coping, 92, 175
  defensive, 67
stress
  enteric system registers, 114
  posttraumatic, 193, 243–47
superior temporal cortex, 162–63
supervision, safe environment for, 143
survival
  autonomic nervous system ensures, 137
  brain stem role in, 115
sympathetic nervous system (SNS)
  ambivalent attachment affects, 173
  constricted window of tolerance activates,
    193–94
  explaining to patients, 154, 156
  overview of, 137, 139
symptom(s)
  deprivation, 203
  implicit roots of, 199–200
  pro-symptom position, 203–4

synapses, 111
synaptic clefts, 111

temporal lobes, 121
termination, *see* transitioning
thalamic–cortical sweep, 116
thalamus, 116–17
therapist
  accepting patient's invitation to co–cele-
    brate, 249
  attachment style influences therapy, 289–
    91
  holder of emerging narrative, 245
  implicit patterns of, 27
  inner community work benefits, 79
  interior conversations of, 127, 135
  mental health of, xx, 133, 198, 235, 274
  mutual influence with patient, 144, 145*f*,
    146*f*, 251
  perceptions differ from patients', 160–61,
    239, 240
  what patients bring, 150–51
therapy
  impact of implicit world on, 287–92
  principles of, 268–69
  short-term, 257–58
  systems therapy, internal, 58
  therapist's attachment style influences,
    289–91
  turning points in, 254
time/timelessness
  dissociated memory and, 8
  eternally present past, see separate entry
  implicit memory and, 29, 73
  neural integration needs, 267
  temporal integration, 45–46, 55, 109, 204
  travel, 31–32, 222
Toomey, B., 192
transitional objects, 216–17
transitioning
  case example of, 253–57
  in long-term work, 258–61
  personal experience of, 261–63
  in short-term therapy, 257–58
trauma
  dissociative identity disorder and, 50–51,
    193
  following secure attachment, conse-
    quences of, 200

neural nets and, 8

visceral memory and, 50

see also abuse; posttraumatic stress

triangle of well–being, 156, 157*f*

trust

disorganization responds to, 179

radical, 223, 228

synchronous moments build, 216

turning points, in therapy, 254

understanding

blame gives way to, 230

implicit memories don't change in response to, 30, 31

type of compassion, 105, 128

vagus nerve, 114

Velveteen Rabbit, The, xx, 292

ventral vagal

middle prefrontal region and, 144

safety, perception of, 154

secure attachment mediated by, 138

socially engaging, 114

stillness plus engagement, 138

ventromedial prefrontal cortex, 119, 191

victimization, 204–5, 245–46

visualizations (guided), 74

voice mail, 142

vulnerability, compassion and, 78, 128

waiting room, 143–44

wandering, vs. focus, 16–17

watching self (inner community member),
65–66

wheel metaphor, 15–17

Whyte, D., xvi

window of tolerance

disconfirming experiences need, 213, 216

expanding, 9, 75, 192–96, 216, 237, 243, 259

presence fosters, 229, 230

room for delightful emotion, 235

wisdom, of the brain, xviii, 134

witness(ing), middle prefrontal region, function of, 229; *see also*, separate entry

wounds

beliefs about, 267–68

implicit infant, 207–10

writing, as steppingstone to speaking, 135